One World — Past, Present and Future

Arnold Toynbee, one of the foremost historians in the world, has performed a notable service to all thinking people in this unique volume. He has surveyed the wealth of Greek historical writings, from Homer to the age of Heraclius, and from this fascinating body of literature, has chosen and translated selections which demonstrate his theory—that all civilizations pass through similar transitions and that we can better understand our own times through a study of the past.

Included in this fascinating collection are his lucid translations of Herodotus' history of Greece and Persia, Thucydides on the Trojan War, and Polybius' writings on the effects of the fall of Greece on Rome. There are also revealing selections that show the ancients' views of the techniques and function of recording history.

Professor Toynbee's sound scholarship and imaginative analysis provide an excellent introduction to Greek history for the general reader—one which will encourage him to delve further into the study of ancient history, philosophy and literature. This book is also an excellent introduction to Toynbee's master work—*The Study of History*.

"In essence, the historical experiences which wrung these thoughts out of Greek souls are akin to the experiences through which we ourselves have been passing."

—Arnold Toynbee

MENTOR Books of Related Interest

(60¢ each)

GREEK CIVILIZATION AND CHARACTER
edited by Arnold J. Toynbee

Brilliant translations of Hellenic experience and life that shed light on contemporary problems.
(#MP501)

THE GREEK WAY TO WESTERN CIVILIZATION
by Edith Hamilton

A noted scholar reveals the glorious achievements of ancient Greece in literature, art, science and democracy.
(#MP51?)

THE GREEK EXPERIENCE *by C. M. Bowra*

An extraordinary study of Greek culture, its achievements and philosophy. 48 pages of photos.
(#MP349)

THE GREEK PHILOSOPHERS *edited by Rex Warner*

Basic writings of philosophers from Thales to Plotinus, revealing the roots of Western philosophy in ancient Greece.
(#MP442)

GREEK HISTORICAL THOUGHT

From Homer to the Age of Heraclius

Introduction and Translation
by *Arnold J. Toynbee*

With two pieces newly translated
by *Gilbert Murray*

εἴπατε τῷ βασιλῆι · χαμαὶ πέσε δαίδαλος αὐλά,
οὐκέτι Φοῖβος ἔχει καλύβαν, οὐ μάντιδα δάφναν,
οὐ παγὰν λαλέουσαν, ἀπέσβετο καὶ λάλον ὕδωρ.

A MENTOR BOOK
Published by THE NEW AMERICAN LIBRARY,
NEW YORK AND TORONTO
THE NEW ENGLISH LIBRARY LIMITED, LONDON

Originally published by J. M. Dent & Sons, Ltd., London,
in the series The Library of Greek Thought.

MENTOR TRADEMARK REG. U.S. PAT. OFF. AND FOREIGN COUNTRIES
REGISTERED TRADEMARK—MARCA REGISTRADA
HECHO EN CHICAGO, U.S.A.

MENTOR BOOKS are published *in the United States* by
The New American Library, Inc.,
1301 Avenue of the Americas, New York, New York 10019,
in Canada by The New American Library of Canada Limited,
295 King Street East, Toronto 2, Ontario,
in the United Kingdom by The New English Library Limited,
Barnard's Inn, Holborn, London, E.C. 1, England

PRINTED IN THE UNITED STATES OF AMERICA

ACKNOWLEDGMENTS

I HAVE tantalized my readers by persuading Professor Gilbert Murray to do two fresh pieces of translation for me. Together with the passage which I have been allowed to reproduce from his translation of the *Agamemnon* by the kind permission of Messrs. George Allen and Co., these pieces will illuminate the art of translating from Greek into English better than I have been able to do in twenty pages of introduction and two hundred of text. I have also acknowledgments to make to Crawley's translation of Thucydides, the translation of the myth from the *Politicus* in Professor J. A. Stewart's *Myths of Plato*, and to the translation included in Professor Conway's edition of Dionysius of Halicarnassus's *Essays in Literary Criticism*. In using all these translations, my method has been to keep them at my elbow while working upon the original Greek, but not to consult them except when I found myself at a loss for phraseology or interpretation. In turning to them on these occasions, I have freely incorporated their English in my own whenever they have seemed to me to have hit upon a felicitous or an inevitable turn of expression. It would be a mistaken homage to originality to do again badly what one feels to have been done better already. Obviously the right course in such cases is to plagiarize with acknowledgments. Last but not least, I have to thank my sister, Miss Jocelyn Toynbee, for making the indexes both to this volume and to *Civilisation and Character*, and for helping me to see both volumes through the press.

CONTENTS

	PAGE
INTRODUCTION	ix
PREFACE TO THE SECOND EDITION	xxvii

PART I.—PREFACES

HERODOTUS OF HALICARNASSUS	29
THUCYDIDES OF ATHENS	31
POLYBIUS OF MEGALOPOLIS	43
DIODORUS OF AGYRIUM	48
DIONYSIUS OF HALICARNASSUS	53
THE GOSPEL ACCORDING TO ST. LUKE	59
FLAVIUS JOSEPHUS OF JERUSALEM	60
ARRIAN OF NICOMEDIA	70
APPIAN OF ALEXANDRIA	70
DIO CASSIUS COCCEIANUS OF NICAEA	76
HERODIAN THE SYRIAN	77
EUNAPIUS OF SARDIS	78
MARCUS THE DEACON	82
PROCOPIUS OF CAESAREA	84
AGATHIAS OF MYRRHINA	87
MENANDER THE GUARDSMAN	93
THEOPHYLACTUS SIMOCATTA THE EGYPTIAN	94

PART II.—THE PHILOSOPHY OF HISTORY

SECTION I.—MUTABILITY

LEAVES AND MEN	99
MORTALITY	99
THE ATHENIAN DISASTER IN SICILY	100
THE BURDEN OF MACEDON	108
THE BURDEN OF ROME	109
THE FULFILLMENT OF SCRIPTURE	110
DEATH THE LEVELER	112
A CIRCUMVENTION OF TIME	116

SECTION II.—PRIDE, DOOM AND THE ENVY OF THE GODS

	PAGE
THE AUTHORIZED VERSION	117
THE WISDOM OF SOLON	118
THE PARABLE OF POLYCRATES	119
THE REVISED VERSION	123
THE DAY OF JUDGMENT	124
THE TITAN IN HARNESS	124
RATIONALISM	125

SECTION III.—EVOLUTON

DEGENERATION	126
ACHIEVEMENT	12
THE WHEEL OF EXISTENCE	12
CYCLES OF CIVILIZATION	13
THE CONTINUITY OF HISTORY	1
THE UNIVERSALITY OF HISTORY	1
THE UNITY OF HISTORY	

SECTION IV.—LAW AND CAUSATION

DETERMINISM	13
PREMONITION	14
THE OMNIPOTENCE OF LAW	1
NATURAL LAW	1
ENVIRONMENT AND CHARACTER	143
ENVIRONMENT AND POLITICS	143
ENVIRONMENT AND RACE	144
THE DENUDATION OF ATTICA	146
CAUSATION THE ESSENCE OF HISTORY	147
ULTIMATE AND PROXIMATE CAUSES	147
THE CONSOLATIONS OF PHILOSOPHY	149

SECTION V.—ARGUMENT AND OBSERVATION

THE ORIGINS OF THE HELLENIC RACE	149
EGYPT THE CRADLE OF CIVILIZATION	150
ARE THE COLCHIANS EGYPTIANS?	154
CASTE	155

	PAGE
THE TRANSMISSION OF THE ALPHABET	156
DID THE ALCMAEONIDAE BETRAY ATHENS?	156
DID THE ARGIVES BETRAY HELLAS?	157
HOW ATHENS SAVED HELLAS	160
THE SOCIAL EFFECTS OF THE GREAT PERSIAN WAR	161
THE INFLUENCE OF SEA POWER ON HISTORY	162
THE PLAGUE AT ATHENS	165

PART III.—THE ART OF HISTORY

SECTION I.—TECHNIQUE

HERACLES AS A CHRONOLOGICAL PROBLEM	169
CHRONOLOGY EGYPTIAN AND HELLENIC	171
DOCUMENTARY EVIDENCE	173
THE PLACE OF GEOGRAPHY IN HISTORY	174
THE METHOD OF ALTERNATE CHAPTERS	177
THE FIRST PERSON IN NARRATIVE	178
SPEECHES: THEIR USE AND ABUSE	179
SPEECH AND NARRATIVE IN HISTORY	180
WHAT MAKES A GOOD HISTORICAL SUBJECT	181

SECTION II.—CRITICISM

POLYBIUS ON ZENO OF RHODES	183
DIONYSIUS OF HALICARNASSUS ON HERODOTUS,	
THUCYDIDES AND THEOPOMPUS	185
IS HERODOTUS MALICIOUS?	189
LUCIAN OF SAMOSATA ON HIS CONTEMPORARIES	195

PART IV.—EPILOGUES

XENOPHON	198
POLYBIUS	198
INDEX	203

INTRODUCTION

ANCIENT Greek or Hellenic historical thought began at the moment when the first rudiments of the poetry of Homer shaped themselves in Greek minds. It came to an end when Homer yielded precedence to the Bible as the sacred book of a Greek-speaking and Greek-writing *intelligentzia*. In the series of historical authors the latter event occurred between the dates at which Theophylactus Simocatta and George of Pisidia produced their respective works; and since they were both writing during the reign of Heraclius, that Emperor's name has been placed on the title-page of this book in order to define its horizon.[1] An historical process, however, seldom takes place abruptly, and the transition from Hellenic to Byzantine civilization (of which this literary revolution was one symptom among many) occupied from first to last a period of fully three centuries. This becomes evident as soon as we bring other aspects of life into our field of vision. Paulus, for example, an Imperial Groom of the Bedchamber and a *confrère* of his contemporary the historian Agathias, in the art of minor poetry, was still able in the sixth century after Christ to write with ease in the language and meter of Mimnermus; but the subject of his longest and most celebrated poem is the Church of Hagia Sofia—the masterpiece of an architecture antithetical in almost every feature to any Hellenic monument of Colophon or Ephesus or Athens. The change declares itself simultaneously in the field of Religion. The creed, at once primitive and profound, of Pride, Doom and the Envy of the Gods is characteristic of the Hellenic outlook upon life. It appears already articulated in the earliest strata of Homer, and it is recited with the old sardonic conviction in the last sentence of the last passage translated in

1 Heraclius reigned from A.D. 610 to 641, and he was the hero of George's historical poem, while his righthand man, the Patriarch Sergius, was the patron of Theophylactus. Any reader acquainted with Greek has only to glance at the invocation to George's poem (ed. in 1836 by I. Becker in the Bonn *Corpus Scriptorum Historiae Byzantinae*) in order to understand why I have excluded it from this book as being alien to the Hellenic tradition. On the other hand, I have included Marcus the Deacon's preface to his life of Porphyrius of Gaza as an early and interesting example of the new thought that was then already invading Hellenism from below.

the present work. The spirit of this specifically Hellenic religion is unmistakable in all the literature which it pervades; but an examination of the passage entitled "Agnosticism" which has been translated from Agathias' immediate predecessor Procopius reveals the fact that by the middle of the sixth century after Christ Hellenic religion was extinct—even in the hearts of men who had been educated in the Hellenic literary tradition and who still paid lip service to the Hellenic gods. In a rather pedantic reminiscence of a Herodotean mannerism, Procopius refrains from discussing the *arcana* of contemporary Christian controversy on the ground that the subjects professedly in dispute are by their nature incomprehensible to the human reason, and incidentally he propounds what to his mind are the bare axiomatic facts regarding the character of God. Yet anybody who has caught—from these pages or, far better, from Mr. F. M. Cornford's—the real religious outlook of Hellenism will see at once that Procopius' axioms would have appeared to Herodotus or Thucydides or Polybius to beg the fundamental questions of good and evil. Poor Procopius! How deeply he would have been mortified could he have realized that, in the estimation of his classical literary examples, his intellectual superciliousness would have stood him in no stead whatsoever, and that they would have classed him remorselessly with their reverences Hypatius and Demetrius, and with His Sacred Majesty Justinian himself, as a *type croyant* characteristic of his soft-headed age.

The Envy of the Gods was a serious matter to the Hellenes because they preferred to lay up their treasure where moth and rust doth corrupt and where thieves break through and steal. Their kingdom was emphatically a kingdom of this world. Pericles exhorted his countrymen to let the greatness of Athens "fill," not "pass," their understanding; the "salvation" debated at Melos meant bodily escape from massacre or enslavement and not the release of the soul from guilt or perdition; [1] the "Savior" *par excellence* in the Hellenic tradition was Ptolemy, son of Lagus, who successfully abstracted that title from Zeus until he forfeited it to a proletarian descendant of his Oriental subjects; and the "sin" over which Polybius declined to draw a veil was the political folly by which Diaeus and his colleagues brought the Achaean Confederacy to ruin. In other words, the world of Hellenism (and herein lies its supreme interest for us) was a world like that in which we live today, by contrast with the Christian dispensation which in the chronological sense intervenes between us,

[1] See *Civilisation and Character*, pp. 215-227.

or with that religion, yet unborn, which will undoubtedly lay up a new treasure in a new heaven as our world sinks, to founder at last like its predecessors in "the abyss where all things are incommensurable."

There is no space within the limits of this introduction to offer anything like a biographical index, however summary, of the historical authors whose works are represented in the text of the book; [1] but one or two general observations may be an aid to interpretation. In the the first place, the Hellenic historians (especially the greatest of them) were by no means purely Hellenic in race. Herodotus came from the bilingual Helleno-Carian community of Halicarnassus; Thucydides, although Athenian born and possessed (until his exile) of Athenian citizenship, had Thracian blood in his veins; [2] Josephus was a Jew, Procopius a Philistine—though, from the age of Alexander onwards, it goes without saying that Hellenic historians were drawn from all the peoples among whom the Gospel of Hellenism was successively propagated. In this phase historical writing of the Hellenic school did not even confine itself to the vehicle of the Greek language—as might have been demonstrated in this book, had space permitted, by the inclusion of translations from the Latin. [3] The unparalleled political aggrandizement of Rome enabled Roman historians to group the world's affairs round the destinies of their own city-state; and therefore, as Dionysius of Halicarnassus pointed out, they tended to cultivate a particular branch of Hellenic historical literature: the local chronicle. From this point of view the Roman historians, like the Roman adaptors of the Athenian Comedy of Manners, offered us almost our only material for reconstructing a lost branch of Hellenic literature, until the recent discovery of the Aristotelian *Constitution of Athens* restored to us, in epitome, the local chronicle of the most interesting city-state in Hellas Proper. Thus, in history

1 For this I shall refer my readers to Bury's *The Ancient Greek Historians,* and to the admirably concise but comprehensive appendices on authorities in his edition of Gibbon.

2 And also drew royalties, as he informs us himself, from the Thracian mining district of Pangaeum, whither he probably retired to write his history after the military mishap which led to his being exiled from Athens.

3 The earliest Roman historians (like their predecessor Xanthus the Lydian in the fifth century B.C.) found it most natural to practice what was a Hellenic literary art in the medium of the Greek language—though the seeds of Hellenism sometimes fell on stony ground; but they showed greater originality than the Hellenized Anatolians and Syrians, inasmuch as they evolved a version of Hellenic literature in their own vernacular language. At the same time, the literary debt is a more important fact than the linguistic originality, and Roman culture is to be regarded as a version of Hellenism, just as the Roman Empire was the last phase of Hellenic society in the political sphere. Conversely, there are historical works in the ancient Greek language (written by early Christian Fathers or by medieval Byzantines) which are products of non-Hellenic civilizations.

as in other spheres, the influence of Hellenism radiated far more widely than the Greek language or the Greek race; and that is one of the principal testimonies to its greatness. At the same time, it is equally true that some of the most profound and most illuminating creations of Hellenic historical thought were inspired by contact with non-Hellenic societies. Herodotus' eyes were opened by his study of the Syro-Iranian civilization embodied in the universal state of the Achaemenids, which in his time had attempted, and failed, to assimilate the Hellenic world. Polybius was similarly stimulated by the revelation of Roman Italy (with its broadening hinterland in the West) at a moment when Rome was achieving, in the military sense, what Persia had failed to do, while in every other department of life the victor was being carried captive by Hellenism.[1] Polybius, who came from Megalopolis in the depths of Arcadia, was the only one of the three great historical geniuses of Hellenism who was a pure Hellene in the compartively unimportant zoological sense of the word; but a civilization, at any given moment of its existence, is never a mere product of physical transmission or local environment. It is a communion of saints (and of sinners) compassed about by that great and ever-increasing cloud of witnesses that have already joined the majority of mankind; and membership in it is therefore a matter of spiritual rather than of material affiliations. It is conceivable, for instance, that the fifteenth-century Athenian historian Laonicus Chalcocondyles, who, in excellent classical Greek and in a style carefully modeled upon Herodotus and Thucydides, has recorded the rise of the Ottoman Empire, could have traced his genealogy to Erechtheus or Deucalion on both sides of the family more plausibly than Thucydides himself, or that he would have been found, if examined by a trained anthropologist, to exhibit a "more Hellenic" pigmentation, cephalic index and facial angle. Yet, for all that, Thucydides would retain his unchallenged supremacy as the greatest Hellenic historian, while Chalcocondyles would remain the ornament that he is to Byzantine—but not to Hellenic—civilization.[2] It would have been idle for Chalcocon-

[1] In everything except military conquest, the Romans surrendered to Hellenism more completely than any Oriental people east of Taurus, and they borrowed freely from the Hellenes even in military technique, as is shown by the extract from Polybius entitled "Seed on Good Ground," which is translated in *Civilisation and Character*, pp. 92-93.

[2] It may be added that, if we eventually recover, and succeed in interpreting, any historical works produced by Minoan civilization, they may conceivably be found (if they come from the continental colonies of Crete) to be written in some form of Greek. That, however, would not make them Hellenic. Indeed, it would not be surprising if they showed greater affinities to the Byzantine than to the Hellenic spirit.

dyles and his Byzantine contemporaries of the Renaissance to protest that they had Deucalion to their father, when, two thousand years before, the Heavenly Muse had already raised up children to Deucalion out of the stones of Thrace and Caria.

It is a second characteristic of Hellenic historical thought that it was by no means exclusively the creation of professional historians. The poetry of different ages, as well as the philosophy of Plato and the medical literature of the Hippocratean School, have been laid under contribution in this book because they happen to have expressed certain fundamental Hellenic historical ideas more clearly than any work of history in the technical sense. Conversely, the historians have made many contributions to Romance, Genealogy, Anthropology and Physical Science which have been excluded from this book as being alien to its subject. A more important, though equally deliberate, omission has been that of passages dealing with the history of War. Perhaps as much (to hazard a guess) as four-fifths of the total body of Hellenic historical writing that has reached us is occupied by detailed accounts of military operations—a curious fact, considering how intellectual, and speculatively intellectual, was the public for whom most works of Hellenic history were written. The limits of space, as well as the terms of reference, that have been laid down for this volume have made it necessary to renounce any attempt to illustrate this (quantitatively) great department of Hellenic history except in so far as it may happen to throw light upon other branches of Hellenic historical thought. The history of the Art of War in itself could only be treated adequately in an independent volume of the series.

The features just mentioned are possibly not peculiar to Hellenic historical writing. It is more characteristic that, even when we narrow down our range of vision to the professional historians themselves, we find that the vast majority of them were men of the world. Thucydides, Xenophon, Polybius and Josephus (four out of the five greatest figures) were all rising men of action with broken careers, who only turned their energies into a literary channel when the Envy of the Gods had deprived them of the opportunity to hold offices of state, to carry public business through political assemblies, or to command fleets or armies in the field. The private life of Herodotus, the fifth great figure is hardly known to us. His Voltairean turn of mind suggests a born observer and critic rather than an instinctive participant in affairs; yet his intellectual work was always a living and a humane activity, because he studied contemporary history and sociology, and studied them from nature, in an extensive and adventurous series of travels. In other words, he took his observations with the eyes of Odysseus and not through the lenses of Ranke, and this is a distinctive note of the Hellenic Historical School. Polybius, again, traveled as extensively in the northwestern as Herodotus had done in the southeastern hinterland of the Hellenic world of his time; and Diodorus, whose work sometimes smells pungently of the lamp, was not content (as he tells us himself) to sit in libraries at Agyrium or even at Rome. In the case of historians who were fortunate enough to live during the Time of Growth or the Time of Troubles,[1] this salutary intimacy with the active life of their society is not really surprising, unless by contrast with the phenomena of other civilizations. It is remarkable, however, to find that this feature did not disappear during the third and last phase, during which the Hellenic world lay more or less passive under the pall of the *Pax Romana*. In that age, at least, the academic historian might be expected to predominate; yet, even from the period of the Roman Empire, Dionysius and Eunapius are the only undoubted examples of the type who have found their way into the present volume. Arrian and Dio were soldiers and statesmen with as varied an experience of public life and of practical responsibilities as had ever fallen to the lot of a Xenophon or a Polybius. Herodian was probably a civil servant; Appian was either a civil servant or a member of the local aristocracy of Alexandria, which in his time still carried on the municipal administration; Marcus Diaconus was a practical (and on occasions exceedingly drastic) missionary; Priscus [2] was a lawyer, and so likewise were Procopius, Agathias and Menander, the three notable figures from the sixth century after Christ. The Bar was the last liberal profession that held out against the disintegration of Hellenic society; and, although Agathias might complain that it left him too little leisure for his historical studies, we may feel less sorry for him when we contemplate the use to which unchastened leisure was put by his successor Simocatta.

After this brief discussion of the Hellenic historians and of the world in which they lived, it may be well to close with a word upon methods of translation. In the present translator's view, the capital and almost irreparable error to be avoided by a modern Western mind in approaching any branch of Hellenic literature is to allow itself to be dominated by the thought that all this was done and felt and written between two and three thousand years ago—as though chronological antiquity implied, in this case, any corresponding

---

[1] These first two epochs of Hellenic history may be dated in round figures as running from 1125 to 431 B.C., and from 431 to 31 B.C. respectively.

[2] From whom a passage is quoted in *Civilisation and Character*, pp. 130-136.

naïveté or poverty of experience. The fact is that the relation in which we consciously stand to our own Western predecessors of three or six or twelve centuries ago has hardly any analogy to our relations with members of other civilizations, even though the life history of those civilizations may in the chronological sense be previous to ours. In spite of such chronological priority, the remote past embodied in foreign civilizations may be subjectively nearer to the life of our own day than is the recent past out of which our life has arisen. In other words, chronological priority and posteriority have little or no subjective significance except within the single span of a given civilization, while in comparing the histories of different civilizations, the direct chronological relation between them is an almost irrelevant, and therefore usually misleading, factor. In the philosophical sense, all civilizations have been and are and will continue to be contemporaneous with one another. They are all the offspring of the same family in the same generation, and the differences of age between them are infinitesimal in comparison with the immense period during which the human family had existed before any civilization was born. Therefore, in attempting to find an equation between two independent civilizations (and that is what translation from Ancient Greek into Modern English utimately means) it may be a not unprofitable exercise of the fancy to date in some approximate and conventional way their respective starting points, measure the chronological interval between these, and then subtract the amount of that interval in order to discover the century in the chronologically earlier civilization to which any given century in the later civilization corresponds from this point of view. For example, if we take 1125 B.C. as a conventional year for Hellenism, in which Hellenic civilization began to emerge out of the wreckage of the shattered Minoan world, and A.D. 675 as a conventional year of a similar kind for the West, in which Western civilization began to emerge out of the wreckage of Hellenism (in its Roman extension), we shall estimate at something like 1800 years the chronological interval between Hellenic and Western history which has always to be eliminated in order to find their correspondence, at any given stage, as measured from their respective starting points. It is hardly necessary to say that this is not intended as a historical dogma, but merely as a suggestion for arriving at a method of comparative study. By the aid of this fanciful measuring rod we can ascertain which Hellenic and which Western generations were "contemporary" with one another in the sense that they were separated from their respective starting points by an equal period of time, and therefore possessed at any rate a quantitatively (though by no means necessarily a qualitatively) equal fund of traditional experience or social heritage in the various fields of economics, politics, literature, art, religion and the rest. With this magic wand in our hands, we may amuse ourselves by translating (say) Plutarch himself, and not merely Plutarch's writings, from the Hellenic world into ours; and if we do so, we shall find that Plutarch would have been born in 1846 and would be destined to die in 1925 as a last grand survivor of the Victorians! If there is any significance at all in this, we cannot expect to appreciate Plutarch so long as we insist upon reading him in Langhorne's translation, or to reproduce him to our own satisfaction so long as we interlard our modern translation with Elizabethan tags until we have compounded a hodgepodge of "translationese" unlike any living piece of literature of our own age or any other. *A fortiori*, we cannot defend such false archaism in the case of authors who, if magically translated in person into our own world, would at this moment be either still unborn or in their early infancy. Marcus Aurelius, for example, would be not yet four years old, and would be able to look forward to living until 1980. May the Envy of the Gods spare our own children born into this Western World in 1921 from so melancholy a view of human life as their great Hellenic contemporary's!

What is the bearing of this suggested parallelism upon the translation of literature? At first sight it might appear as though we ought to translate Marcus and Plutarch into the literary English (or French or German or Italian or whatever our particular Western vernacular may be) that is being written in our own generation, and then clothe their predecessors, phase by phase, in the corresponding styles of our own literary background—maintaining the same interval of approximately eighteen centuries throughout the process. As soon, however, as we attempt to think this program out, the obstacles become apparent. In the first place, the "curves" of Western and Hellenic history do not correspond. In Hellenic the highest peak was reached (and never again equaled) during the two centuries between the years 525 and 325 B.C., which were contemporaneous (on our fanciful scheme of measurement) with the two centuries between A.D. 1275 and 1475 in the West. In our case, however, that period, though it marked a secondary peak in the life of Northern and Central Italy, was far from being the zenith in the entire life history of the whole society. The West, as a whole, rose to greater heights of self-expression (or, as Pericles might have put it, "raised more imperishable monuments of its presence for good or evil") between about the year 1775 and the European War;[1] while, in contrast, the equivalent period of Hellenic history (25 B.C.-A.D. 114) fell wholly within the latest phase of Hellenic life, during which a world stricken to death by four centuries of troubles [2] was attempting a final rally before its inevitable dissolution. We who are still young in 1924 do not yet pretend to know whether the West has just (though only just) begun to descend on its long journey *ad tartara leti,* whereas Plutarch in his old age must have known for certain, deep down in his heart (though he may never have admitted it with his intellect), that Hellas was already far advanced upon the downward road. Therefore we, with several more chapters of progress and several fewer of decline behind us than were present to Plutarch's consciousness, are bound to look back upon our predecessors with different eyes. The Hellenic medieval world of the fifth and fourth centuries B.C. was not only more mature and more triumphant in actual fact than the Western medieval world of the fourteenth and fifteenth centuries of our era, but its proportions were inevitably exaggerated in the eyes of Plutarch's generation by contrast with their own lassitude and timidity. To our modern mental vision, on the contrary, the fourteenth and fifteenth centuries (even as embodied in their Italian representatives) bear the stamp of what we either disparage as "immature" or praise as "primitive." There are elements in them, and noble elements, of which we may feel and regret the absence in ourselves; but as a whole we cannot take them quite seriously or treat their children, our predecessors, as men quite on a mental level with ourselves. We cannot even affect to do so without a certain consciousness of insincerity. Contrast with this the attitude of Plutarch [3] and Dionysius towards Herodotus and Thucydides respectively. First, they approached their medieval predecessors in an attitude of adoration, as exponents of no longer attainable and almost lost ideals; and then, in the second place, they were cruelly dazzled at close quarters by the clouds of glory with which these Titans had been transfigured by their Olympian visions. "And when he came down from the mount, Moses wist not that the skin of his face shone while he talked with him. And when Aaron and all the children of Israel saw Moses, behold, the skin of his face shone, and they were afraid to come nigh him." Did Moses' punier countrymen resent as well as fear the light which repelled them? Dionysius and Plutarch, in the same situation, were utterly unable to conceal the aversion and dis-

---

[1] World War I.

[2] 431-31 B.C.

[3] Or, at any rate, of the author, whether he be really Plutarch or not, of *Malice in Herodotus.*

may with which the "hard gemlike flame" of a Herodotus or a Thucydides inspired them. Devoted as they and all their finest contemporaries were to nursing the old age of Hellas, smoothing the ever-recurring wrinkles from her brow, stilling her fevered movements, checking her delirium and directing her thoughts (when living thoughts still flitted across her brain) away from the formidable future towards a golden or a gilded past, they could no longer bear to meet face to face the strong men armed who had loved Hellas and laughed with her and seen her as she was and beheld that she was both very good and very evil, and therefore altogether human, in the irrevocable years when Hellas and her sons were still young together. No, the Hellenes of the Empire could not face the Hellenes of the Fifty Years,[1] with their fearless intellectual curiosity, their instinctive and effortless faculty for looking truth in the face, and their consciousness of superfluous strength which gave them the heart to be humorous or sardonic in due season. That is the pathos of all archaism. It is flustered and put out of countenance whenever it ventures to look its professed models in the face.

This means that the translation of each Hellenic phase of thought and style into an equivalent Western phase would be an historical impossibility, even to a scholar endowed with a very much finer sense of language than is possessed by the present translator. Nor, if the impossible could be achieved, should we unquestionably profit by the result; for in so far as we succeeded in translating the past of Hellenic literature into the past of our own, we should be almost wantonly putting it out of focus for our modern vision. Our Western literary heritage is, in fact, the one domain of literature which is essentially "untranslatable" into the Western style of today. The moment that we attempt to modernize a sixteenth- or seventeenth-century work of English literary art, the charm of sentiment and association, and therewith most of the beauty, vanishes as if by magic;[2] while, on the other hand, when we try to yield our fancies up to the undesecrated original, we are often conscious that other elements in the essence escape us, and that the very iridescence of "Elizabethan" quaintness and age (like the colors on Roman glass) spreads a fog of obscurity between our minds and the minds by whom and for whom the

---

[1] Between the Great Persian War and the outbreak of the Peloponnesian War (480-431 B.C.).

[2] This is, of course, conspicuously the case with our Western vernacular translations of the Bible, which constitute the foundations of modern literature among the Protestant peoples. While I was translating three pieces from the New Testament, for inclusion in this book and the companion volume, out of the original Greek, the English Authorized Version again and again rose up between me and my text until I almost abandoned my task in despair.

original truth and beauty was created. It was created in a living present by living men, into whose appreciation of it no tinge of archaism entered at the creative moment; and for this reason it is virtually impossible to establish a perfect spiritual communion between us and them. It would therefore surely be mistaken from a practical point of view, even if it were possible, to translate the work of other civilizations into a form so elusive to our own powers of apprehension, while theoretically, likewise, it might well be wrong. After all, are any products of Hellenic literature immature or primitive or naïve or archaic when regarded as they really are, without the qualifying and distorting consciousness that they were brought into existence so many hundreds of years ago? The vague notion of Herodotus among modern Western readers as a simple-minded "Father of History" would have filled a Dionysius or a Plutarch with amazement. The traditional title of honor ought to be a sufficient warning in itself against the conception of its bearer with which it is usually associated among ourselves, for creation and innovation are achievements not of simple but of subtle and ruthless minds; and the subtlety and ruthlessness of Herodotus, presented in their nakedness, would undoubtedly shock many Western readers of today as deeply as they shocked the Hellenic public of the Empire. Nor, again, is *naïveté* characteristic of any stratum in Homer.[1] In fact, of all the Hellenic literature translated in this volume, the only portion that might legitimately be described, in a general way, as primitive is the poetry of Hesiod; and the passage which has been selected from the *Works and Days* shows that even this generalization has its exceptions, for there must be already a considerable fund of social experience in a mind which can feel so poignantly the horror of degeneration.[2]

[1] The sophisticated spirit of Homer (most piquantly exemplified in the treatment of the Gods) is now notorious, but it is not, of course, an exclusively Hellenic phenomenon. Comparative students of the literary genus Epic have latterly been discovering that, so far from being "primitive," the Epic, in all ages and places, has been the polished product of a cultured society—echoes of which gradually penetrate to the really primitive underworld of folklore. (See Murray's *Rise of the Greek Epic* and Chadwick's *Heroic Age*.)

[2] In its clarity, rationality and reflectiveness the medieval literature of Hellenism shows a much more striking resemblance to the pagan Scandinavian literature of the medieval West than to the contemporaneous literature of Western Christendom. Is there a historical reason for this? Professor W. P. Ker has suggested (in his *Epic and Romance*) that the Scandinavians profited through not being crushed and confused by that heritage of a Syrian and a Hellenic past which obsessed medieval Christendom, and he has shown how the Scandinavian genius became paralyzed from the moment when Western Christian romance and theology infected it. Supposing that this infection had not occured, there is no knowing to what heights medieval Scandinavian literature might not have attained in an independent development; and such an untrammeled development was precisely what the Hellenes enjoyed, because the Hellenes (unlike the Teutons) had left no remnant of the previous Minoan civilization to cross and confuse their own path towards a new light.

For these several reasons, the method of translation attempted here has been to clothe all passages from Hellenic authors of every age and every character in some form of the English which we are writing in this first half of the twentieth century after Christ; and the translator's principal effort has been concentrated upon avoiding a result which would strike the reader first and foremost as a translation, or in other words, as something unreal or secondhand. This is, as he is aware, a negative ideal, and prohibitory commandments have their recognized dangers. The danger in this case is that the result may be too topical, too colloquial, too prosaic—that it may sacrifice beauty and eternity in its effort to retrieve the realism of life. Is life wholly reconcilable with beauty and eternity, or is the relation between them always a compromise? But that is a question which would carry us far beyond our field. . . .

It only remains to touch upon a few points of detail. To begin with, Ancient Greek on the one hand and our group of modern Western vernaculars on the other are languages of a markedly different genius. In Greek the style is simple and the grammar complex, while in our languages the style is comparatively complex and the grammar simple. Reproduce any Greek passage in any modern language in its original nakedness of style, and you will have produced something that is not English or French or German or Italian. In our Western literature, as in our other forms of self-expression, there is nearly always something tortuous and complicated—a touch of the gargoyle which would have grievously offended Hellenic taste, yet which cannot be omitted in any piece of Western writing without doing violence to nature.[1] The translation is therefore often deliberately complicated in places where the original is simple. Conversely, of course (and this is a commonplace of classical scholarship), it is wholly impossible to reproduce literally in any of our languages, particularly in English, the complicated grammatical structure of so highly synthetic and syntactic a language as Ancient Greek.[2] To break the chain of a sentence without breaking the chain of the thought which it embodies is a familiar but an everlastingly fascinating problem; and in his perpetual attempt to solve it the translator has taken advantage of the technical facilities which a book printed on pages bound together offers as compared with a manuscript written on a roll. On a manuscript roll (or "volume," in the literal and original sense of the

---

[1] This gargoyle element is equally discernible in the *Divina Commedia, Hamlet, Faust* and *Les Misérables* by contrast with the greatest Hellenic works of art.

[2] Westerners of genius have attempted this in the past, under the immediate influence of the Renaissance; but neither the style of Lyly nor even the style of Milton was destined to be the formative influence in English prose.

word) it is important to avoid any break in continuity. There is no page here to offer a hospitable foot for notes, and no last sheets to give asylum to appendices. Were notes and appendices abstracted from the text to be lodged at the end of the roll, the reader's time and patience would be spent in laborious winding and unwinding, and the writing on the roll itself would rapidly be rubbed and frayed into effacement. Moreover, the next copyist would probably omit these annexes by inadvertence, and so, in the end, everybody's labor would be lost. It was therefore desirable, in any work of Hellenic literature, to incorporate the substance of notes and appendices in the text itself by way of parenthesis; and, fortunately for Hellenic authors, the grammatical complexity of the ancient Greek language gave them means of doing this which are not at our disposal. Even in Greek, however, the effort was often a *tour de force,* and again and again the translator has found not only his own overtaxed ingenuity, but his original's over-involved thought, relieved beyond measure by the employment of our modern contrivance.[1]

The translator has had another problem to face in determining his policy towards certain crucial names and words. Should the Greek words "Hellas" and "Hellenes," for example, be retained or converted into "Greece" and "Greeks"? After much consideration, the alternative of conversion into the more familiar names has been rejected because, in modern English, the latter have a double association. Primarily, to many people, they suggest an existing state and an existing nation rather than a vanished world, and the implications of the stronger suggestion may have a distorting effect upon the fainter. Ancient Hellas was not a state but a universe containing hundreds of states which were chronically at war with one another until the last phase in their history; and the ancient Hellenes were not a nation but a society of nations, some of whom spoke non-Greek vernacular tongues. The names "Hellas" and "Hellene" have therefore been left as they stand, and they are to be read with all (and more than all) the imaginative and emotional connotations that are conveyed to us by the names "Europe" and "European."[2] On the other hand,

[1] Author's and translator's notes are carefully distinguished from one another throughout.

[2] It is a curious point that the name which has become canonized has in neither case been scientifically accurate. In the east and southeast of the continent of Europe there are many peoples still alien or only recently converted to "European" civilization, while, conversely, in speaking of "European" civilization we do not intend to exclude from its pale the peoples of West European origin in America. "The West" and "Western" are more accurate terms, but they do not possess the sanction of custom. Similarly, there were Greek-speaking peoples in the northwestern parts of continental Greece who were expressly referred to as "non-Hellenes" by

the name of the language has always been translated "Greek," since "Hellenic" in this connection would be puzzling, while a Western analogy ought to save us from misunderstanding. Just as "Europeans" speak and write in English, French, German, Italian and so on, without for that reason being any the less members one of another in their possession of a common civilization, so, while the majority of Hellenes always spoke and wrote in Greek, there came in course of time to be other Hellenes (with as good a title to the name from the spiritual point of view) who expressed their Hellenic culture in Etruscan, Latin, Lydian, Phrygian, Lycian or Aramaic.

A complementary problem arose over the Greek word "barbarian." Should it be left as it stood or be paraphrased? And in this case the translator has chosen the second alternative, because (as it appears to him) the original word hardly ever possesses the same connotation in Greek as the borrowed word possesses in English. In Greek its meaning is very much more extensive and more varied. In cases in which the root idea is negative, the right translation is surely "non-Hellenic" or "non-Hellenes." It often, however, refers to members of rival and in some respects superior civilizations, in reference to which the use of the English word "barbarian" would be wholly misleading when it can be bettered by "Oriental." Lastly, there are a few cases in which "tribesman" seems the natural equivalent, but these are rare.[1]

"Polis," again, has seldom been translated "city," because that word suggests to our minds an urban agglomeration upon a scale unknown to the Hellenic world except at a very few spots during a comparatively short period of its history,[2] whereas it emphatically does not suggest a sovereign state. By contrast, the Hellenic "Polis," while generally inferior to an English country town in its material proportions, enjoyed a political life and individuality on an entirely different plane from the glorified vestry which is the highest political organization of a "mammoth" Western city. The "Polis" was juridically a "state" and emotionally a "country," while its people were a

Thucydides, in whose time the non-Greek-speaking peoples of Lycia, Caria, Etruria, and even of Latium and Carthage, had a better claim than the Eurytanes, the Thesproti or the Chaones to be regarded as members of Hellenic society.

1 The fact that the Hellenes employed an identical word to express this diversity of meanings is of some historical interest, because it brings out their self-absorption and their tendency to ignore what other societies had achieved. This was a serious weakness which largely contributed to the eventual victory of Syria in the long and dramatic contest waged by the two civilizations in the diverse fields of war, politics, economics and religion.

2 Hellenic observers did come across urban agglomerations of our Western type and scale, but they found them beyond their own borders in the homes of the (in their time petrified) civilizations of Egypt and Mesopotamia.

"nation," whether they turned out a thousand strong or in rather larger or smaller numbers in order to cross swords with the armies of some less corporate and less self-conscious, and therefore to their minds politically inferior, leviathan like the Persian Empire. All these English words have consequently been employed according to occasion, while in the less frequent cases in which the original Greek text intended the word "Polis" in the topographical and material sense, it has almost always been translated "town."

Where "write" and "writer" or "read" and "reader" occur in the English, the English reader must not forget that "recite" and "composer," or "hear" and "hearer," are generally the equivalents in the Greek. Oral transmission was a more natural method of communicating the contents of a literary work in a society in which the reproduction of copies was a slower and more costly business than it has latterly been in the West since the comparatively recent introduction of printing. From Herodotus' day to Simocatta's, a public recital to a select audience by the author himself was the ordinary method of publication. It follows that "Logos," in that one of its many meanings which implies the spoken word, should be translated "narrative" [1] or "work" or "writing"; that the address delivered by a diplomatic mission should be described as a *note verbale;* and that "rhetoric" (an art which has little place in our life) should occasionally be rendered "journalism." Finally, the reader will notice that Greek names, both of persons and of places, have been reproduced in the English text in their traditional Latin form.[2] This has been done with the purely negative object of saving the reader from a perpetual series of slight ocular shocks which might needlessly distract his mind from the thought and the language by making him too conscious of the spelling. A glance at the orthography employed by Browning in *Balaustion's Adventure* or in his translation of the *Trilogy of Aeschylus* will explain the ocular effect which the present translator has sought to avoid. The Latin orthography is familiar to our eye because we use it for transliterating the compound words borrowed or newly coined from the Greek in our ever-growing scientific vocabulary. Therefore words in this orthography do not stand out from the page or interrupt the passage of our eye as it travels along the lines. This may, perhaps, be a sacrifice of

[1] A word which itself implies oral transmission in the original Latin.
[2] I have not gone the length of disguising Hellenic Gods under the names of the rudimentary Latin deities which were conventionally equated with them; and in the case of some localities which are familiar or even celebrated among ourselves, I have employed our own name for them, *e.g.* "Dardanelles" instead of "Hellespont."

accuracy to ease in a non-essential matter; but we shall have to discover more than we yet know regarding the pronunciation of Ancient Greek before we can seriously maintain that the preservation of the exact Greek orthography is any appreciable assistance towards the reconstruction of the spoken word, as it first issued from the author's mouth to fall upon the ears of his contemporaries.

These, however, are trivialities upon which the success or failure of this book will not depend. The book will stand or fall by the view of history upon which it is based, and of which some indication has been given already in this introduction. The essential postulate is that in the successive or simultaneous careers of the various known civilizations—Egyptian and Mesopotamian and Minoan, Indian and Far Eastern, Hellenic and Syro-Iranian, Byzantine and Western and Middle Eastern —the historical vision reveals to us a profoundly significant and profoundly moving repetition of human experience on the heroic scale. When formulated in terms, this postulate may present the appearance of a somewhat formidable dogma; and yet, implicitly, it has surely always been the creed of every classical scholar. Were we not convinced that the Hellenic consciousness, even in the fragmentary expressions of it that have reached us, was in some inward sense at least as full of vitality and as richly stored with experience, or in other words was as "modern," as our own, we should not have been drawn towards it as irresistibly as we have been drawn, and should not have given all the mental labor which we have given to the then impossible enterprise of entering into communion with our Hellenic contemporaries. The readers of this book, however, will probably be, for the most part, English-speaking people who have been educated in other than classical studies, and who therefore do not possess this vivid personal experience, dating from childhood, of what the classics in the original may mean to a modern Western mind. The impression made upon such readers will be a truer test of whether the book has failed or succeeded, and every historian knows that success in his superhuman endeavor is only granted to him by a miracle.

"The hand of the Lord was upon me and carried me out in the Spirit of the Lord, and set me down in the midst of the valley which was full of bones, and caused me to pass by them round about; and, behold, there were very many in the open valley, and, lo, they were very dry. And he said unto me: 'Son of man, can these bones live?' And I answered: 'O Lord God, thou knowest.' Again he said unto me: 'Prophesy upon these bones and say unto them: *O ye dry bones, hear the Word of the Lord. Thus saith the Lord God unto these bones: Behold, I will cause breath to enter into you and ye shall live; and I will lay sinews upon you and will bring up flesh upon you and cover you with skin and put breath in you, and ye shall live; and ye shall know that I am the Lord.'* So I prophesied as I was commanded; and, as I prophesied, there was a noise, and behold a shaking, and the bones came together, bone to his bone; and when I beheld, lo, the sinews and the flesh came up upon them, and the skin covered them above, but there was no breath in them. Then said he unto me: 'Prophesy unto the wind, prophesy, son of man, and say to the wind: *Thus saith the Lord God: Come from the four winds, O breath, and breathe upon these slain, that they may live.'* So I prophesied as he commanded me, and the breath came into them, and they lived and stood up upon their feet—an exceeding great army."

ARNOLD J. TOYNBEE.

LONDON.

PREFACE TO THE SECOND EDITION

THINKING is as unnatural and arduous an activity for human beings as walking on two legs is for monkeys. We seldom do more of it than we have to; and our disinclination to think is generally greatest at the times when we are feeling the most comfortable. Since this human antipathy to the labor of thought is no less manifest in public life than it is in private affairs, Mankind does not do very much of its historical thinking in easy and prosperous times. In such times we are mostly content just to live through history without realizing that we are traveling down its stream; and, though in the past the spells of anything like general well-being in human affairs have usually been short, they have also usually been long enough to lull people into the delusion that history is something disagreeable that is never going to overtake their own generation, though they know quite well that, in other times and places, other people have sometimes met with historic disasters.

When history duly overtakes us in our turn, as is bound to happen sooner or later, our own disagreeable experiences then goad us into beginning to think again about human history and human destiny, and in our modern Western world our own minds have been turning back in this direction since 1914; but twentieth-century Western man, with a most exceptionally comfortable quarter of a millennium behind him, is not very well equipped for this necessary but difficult intellectual task. In our own experience, we have so far no more than thirty-six years of flagrant sin and suffering behind us to illuminate our understandings; and, though we have managed to crowd a great deal of both kinds of experience into this brief span of time, the span is nevertheless still too short to allow us to see human history in perspective in the light of what we have been doing and been suffering ourselves.

This is where Greek historical thought may help us; for in Greek and Roman history the corresponding time of tribulation lasted, not just for thirty-six years, but for as many as eleven hundred, if we are to date the breakdown of the Hellenic civilization from the outbreak of the Atheno-Peloponnesian War in 431 B.C., and are to see its final dissolution in the last phase of the break-up of the Roman Empire in the seventh century of the Christian era. From beginning to end of that span of no less than eleven centuries, Greek thinkers were reflecting on the mystery of human life in the light of experiences of kinds that have recently become familiar to us; and passages from the surviving works of Greek literature in which this long debate was carried on have been translated in the present volume in the belief that they have a topical interest for contemporary Western readers.

In essence, the historical experiences which wrung these thoughts out of Greek souls are akin to the experiences through which we ourselves have been passing. The Greek thoughts here reproduced in English are reflections, in human minds, of world wars and class wars, cultural encounters at close quarters between peoples with sharply different social heritages, atrocities and acts of heroism, and all the other enigmatic patterns, woven in the parti-colored web of Good and Evil, that stimulate human minds to wrestle with the paradoxes of Human Nature.

In A.D. 1950 we have even more to learn from Greek historical thought than we had in A.D. 1924.

A. J. T.

1950.

PART ONE
Prefaces

HERODOTUS OF HALICARNASSUS
(*ca.* 495–425 B.C.)
HISTORY OF EAST AND WEST
(Oxford text, ed. by C. Hude: Book I. chapters 1–5)

HERODOTUS of Halicarnassus presents the results of his researches in the following work, with the twofold object of saving the past of mankind from oblivion and ensuring that the extraordinary achievements of the Hellenic and the Oriental worlds shall enjoy their just renown—particularly the transactions which brought them into conflict with one another.

The Persian historians lay the responsibility for the quarrel upon the Phoenicians. According to them the Phoenicians, who had lived on the shores of the Red Sea before they migrated to the Mediterranean, had no sooner settled in their present home than they embarked on distant voyages. They carried Egyptian and Assyrian freights, and one of the markets that they visited was Argos—at that time the leading country in the region now called Hellas. The Phoenicians accordingly visited Argos (so the story goes) in order to dispose of their wares, and within five or six days of their arrival they had almost sold them out, when a number of women, including the king's daughter,[1] came down to the shore. The women had stopped at the ship's stern and were bidding for the articles which especially struck their fancy, when the Phoenicians raised a shout and threw themselves upon them. The majority got away, but Io and some others were kidnaped, and the Phoenicians forced them on board and sailed off with them to Egypt. This is the Persian (as opposed to the Hellenic) story of how Io came to Egypt, and the Persians

---

[1] Her name is given in both the Persian and the Hellenic tradition as Io, daughter of Inachus. [AUTHOR.]

29

regard it as the first provocation on either side; but it was followed, according to them, by a raid on the part of some Hellenes[1] upon Tyre in Phoenicia, where they kidnaped the king's daughter, Europa. This made the parties even with one another, but fresh provocation was given, in which the Hellenes were the aggressors. They made a voyage in a warship to Aea in Colchis, on the River Phasis, and, not content with doing the business that had brought them there, they kidnaped the local king's daughter, Medea. The Colchian monarch sent an envoy to Hellas to demand satisfaction for the offense and the restitution of his daughter; but the Hellenes replied that, inasmuch as they had received no satisfaction from the Orientals for the kidnaping of the Argive princess, they were not disposed to offer them any in this case. Two generations later, however, Alexander, the son of Priam, was inspired by this story with the determination to kidnap a wife for himself in Hellas, in the assurance that satisfaction would in no case be exacted from him, since it had previously been refused by the other party. Consequently he kidnaped Helen, whereupon the Hellenes decided in the first instance to send a note demanding the restitution of Helen and satisfaction for the offense; but the other party met their representations by citing against them the kidnaping of Medea and pointing out that the Hellenes, who were now demanding satisfaction from others, had on that occasion refused to give satisfaction themselves or to make restitution when demanded. Up to this point they had confined their mutual offenses to kidnaping, but the Hellenes now incurred a heavy responsibility by taking the initiative in invading Asia before Europe had been invaded by the Orientals. Upon this the Persian historians comment that, while the kidnaping of women may be a crime, to insist upon taking revenge for it is a folly, and that the sensible course is to take no notice of it, since it is evident that the women would not have been kidnaped if they had not been willing victims. We Asiatics, they proceed, did not take it to heart when our women were kidnaped, while, for the sake of a Lacedaemonian woman, the Hellenes mustered a great armada, invaded Asia, and destroyed the power of Priam. From this time forth, they add, we have regarded the Hellenic world as hostile to ourselves.[2]

Holding this view of the facts, the Persians trace the origin of their feud with the Hellenes to the fall of Troy. In regard to Io, however, the Persian view is challenged by the Phoe-

[1] They have no record of their names, but presumably they were Cretans. [AUTHOR.]

[2] The Persians identify with themselves the continent of Asia and the nations inhabiting it, but regard Europe and the Hellenic world as alien. [AUTHOR.]

nicians, who maintain that she had not been kidnaped when she went with them to Egypt, but had had a love affair in Argos with the master of the ship, discovered that she was pregnant, could not face her parents, and therefore sailed off with the Phoenicians of her own free will, in order to escape detection. So much for the Persian and Phoenician stories. For my own part, I shall not commit myself to a definite opinion in this controversy, but shall take as my starting point the first historical character[1] who, to my knowledge, was guilty of aggression against the Hellenes. In the course of my narrative I shall devote as much attention to small countries as to great, for those which were great in the past have mostly become small, while those which were great in my time had been small before. Conscious as I am of the perpetual instability of human fortunes, I shall make no distinction in my treatment of the two.

THUCYDIDES OF ATHENS

(ca. 460–395 B.C.)

HISTORY OF THE PELOPONNESIAN WAR

(Oxford text, ed. by H. Stuart-Jones: Book I. chapters 1–23)

THUCYDIDES of Athens has written the history of the war between the Peloponnesians and the Athenians. He began to write as soon as war broke out, in the belief that this war would eclipse all its predecessors in importance. He drew this inference from the fact that both belligerents, when they started hostilities, had reached the highest degree of preparedness in every arm, while the rest of the Hellenic world was already taking sides—some countries intervening at once and others intending to follow their example. This war was, indeed, the greatest upheaval ever experienced by Hellas and by a part of the non-Hellenic world (it would hardly be an exaggeration to say: by the human race). It is true that the passage of time has rendered accurate research into the recent as well as the remote past impossible, but in the light of the earliest evidence that I consider trustworthy, I do not imagine that the past has produced either wars or other events on an important scale.

What is now called Hellas appears to have had no stable sedentary population until a comparatively recent date, and to have been subject in earlier times to migrations, in which populations were easily dislodged from their homes under

[1] Croesus, King of Lydia, ca. 560–546 B.C. [ED.]

pressure from some more numerous body of intruders. There was no trade and no security of intercourse by sea or by land. Each community lived at subsistence level by its own local production, without accumulating capital or investing it in the land, since none could foresee when the next invader would deprive them of their homes, which they had not yet learned to fortify. They also took it for granted that their bare daily bread would be as easy to gain in one place as in another. For these reasons they migrated readily, and therefore did not develop great manpower or great armaments. The richest territories, such as those now called Thessaly and Boeotia, most of the Peloponnese except Arcadia, and the best parts elsewhere, were particularly exposed to changes of population. The fertility of the soil produced accumulations of power, which resulted in ruinous civil disorders, and at the same time these countries were more eagerly coveted by foreigners. On the contrary, Attica, which enjoyed the longest unbroken immunity from civil disorders owing to the thinness of its soil, never lost its original population; and one of the strongest proofs of my contention that the comparative development of the other countries was retarded by migrations is to be found in the fact that the most important victims of war and civil disorders in the rest of the Hellenic world found an asylum, as refugees, at Athens, became naturalized there from remote antiquity and so still further increased the population, with the result that they subsequently overflowed from Attica and planted colonies in Ionia.

Another piece of evidence that impresses me with the feebleness of Antiquity is this: Before the Trojan War no united effort appears to have been made by Hellas; and to my belief that name itself had not yet been extended to the entire Hellenic world. In fact, before the time of Hellen, son of Deucalion, the appellation was probably unknown, and the names of the different nationalities prevailed locally, the widest in range being "Pelasgians." It was not till Hellen and his sons became a power in Phthiotis and were asked by the other states to intervene in their favor that these tended through intercourse to acquire one after another the name of "Hellenes." Evidently, however, a long interval elapsed before the name obtained universal currency, as may be inferred particularly clearly from Homer, a writer of much later date than the Trojan War, who nowhere applies the name to the whole race or to any except the followers of Achilles from Phthiotis, who actually were the first "Hellenes." He does not talk of "Non-Hellenes" [1] either—for the reason, I believe, that "Hellenes"

---

[1] In Greek βάρβαροι. [ED.]

had not yet been classified under a single name with which anything could be contrasted. In any case, the constituents of the Hellenic race (as the name spread, with mutual comprehension, from state to state until it eventually became universal) were prevented by weakness and lack of intercourse from embarking on any enterprise in common. Even the joint expedition to Troy was not made until they had taken to the sea.

The earliest builder of a navy known to tradition is Minos, who commanded the greater part of what is now the Hellenic Sea, ruled the Archipelago, and was the first to colonize most of the islands—expelling the Carian aborigines and installing his own sons as rulers. Presumably he cleared the seas of pirates as far as he was able, in order to attract revenue to his own treasury. In ancient times the Hellenes, as well as the non-Hellenic longshoremen and islanders, devoted themselves to piracy as soon as they began to develop maritime communications. The command was taken by men of considerable standing, for their personal profit and for the support of their dependents. They used to fall upon towns or village communities and plunder them, and this was their main source of livelihood. No disgrace as yet attached to the profession, which if anything conferred distinction, as is proved by the honor in which piratical talent is held among some continental[1] peoples down to the present day, and by the stock dialogue in early poetry.[2] They also raided one another on land, and to the present day there are many parts of Hellas in which the old ways survive—for instance, among the Southern Locrians, the Aetolians, the Acarnanians, and in all that region of the Continent. Among these continental peoples, the custom of carrying arms still survives from the days of piracy; for at one time the entire Hellenic world carried arms because they lived in the open and intercourse was insecure, and never parted with their weapons, any more than non-Hellenes do today. Such survivals in these parts of Hellas prove that similar customs once prevailed universally.

The Athenians were among the first to lay aside their arms and change to a more comfortable and refined way of living. The older men of the well-to-do class have only recently abandoned the luxuries of wearing linen shirts and fastening their hair in a bunch with gold grasshopper clasps. Among the kindred population of Ionia these fashions long retained their hold over the older generation. The simple dress which we

[1] *I.e.* peoples in the Balkan hinterland of the Hellenic Peninsula. [ED.]
[2] Crews coming to shore are invariably asked whether they are pirates, without any idea that they might be ashamed of the trade or that there might be anything insulting in the inquiry. [AUTHOR.]

wear today was first introduced by the Lacedaemonians, who reduced the whole outward standard of living to approximately the same level for rich and poor. They were also the first to take exercise naked, and to strip in public and oil themselves for this purpose. Originally, even at the Olympian Games, the athletes used to cover their nakedness with a loincloth while competing, and it is not many years since this practice has been given up. Among the non-Hellenic peoples of the present day, especially in Asia, when there are boxing and wrestling competitions, they still wear loincloths for the occasion; and it would be possible to point out many other similarities between ancient Hellenic and modern non-Hellenic life.

The towns most recently founded, after the conquest of the sea, had more available capital and were therefore built on the coast, or across isthmuses, with artificial fortifications, in the most favorable commercial and strategic positions. Owing to the long persistence of piracy, the earlier settlements avoided the neighborhood of the sea, not only on the islands but on the mainland (for they raided the non-seafaring coast-dwellers as well as one another), and they remain to this day on their original inland sites. The islanders, who were as active pirates as the rest, were Carians and Phoenicians, the majority of the islands having been colonized by these nationalities, as is confirmed by the evidence from Delos. When the island of Delos was reconsecrated by the Athenians during the late war, all the graves found in it were removed, and more than half of these proved to belong to Carians, who could be identified by the type of weapons interred with them and by the still prevalent Carian form of burial. After the building of Minos' navy, sea communications became more secure.[1] The coastal populations began to accumulate capital and to lead a more stable life; and they employed their surplus on protecting themselves with fortifications. The weaker found it profitable to accept the political domination of the stronger, and the more powerful used their surplus to reduce the smaller states to subjection. They had reached approximately this stage of development before they made their expedition against Troy.

In my opinion, Agamemnon was able to assemble his armada because he was the dominant power among his contemporaries rather than because the suitors of Helen were compelled to follow him by their oath to Tyndareus. Indeed, the best oral tradition of the Peloponnese records that Pelops first acquired power thanks to the funds which he brought with him from Asia to a poor country, upon which he thus suc-

---

[1] Minos cleared the islands of criminals, and this was the occasion on which most of them were colonized by him. [AUTHOR.]

ceeded in imposing his own name in spite of his being an immigrant. Still greater successes awaited his descendants, for when Eurystheus was killed in Attica by the Heracleidae, Atreus, who was Eurystheus' uncle on the mother's side and happened to have been banished from his father's house for the murder of Chrysippus, found himself in charge of Mycenae and its dominions, which Eurystheus had entrusted to him as a relation. When Eurystheus did not return, Atreus ascended the throne with the good will of the Mycenaeans, who were afraid of the Heracleidae.[1] Thus the Pelopidae surpassed the Perseïdae; and I imagine that it was this heritage, combined with naval predominance, that enabled Agamemnon to mobilize his forces, who were conscripts rather than volunteers. He appears to have furnished the largest contingent of ships himself and to have had enough to spare for the Arcadians, to judge by the evidence of Homer (if that is accepted as historical). In the *Delivery of the Sceptre,* too, the poet says that he "was lord of many isles and Argos all." But if he had been purely a land power without a navy he could not have dominated any islands except those adjoining his own coasts, which would not amount to many. What we know of the Trojan expedition may be used as evidence for the character of those that preceded it.

The smallness of Mycenae and the present insignificance of this or that town of the period is not sufficient evidence for discrediting the statements of the poets and tradition regarding the size of the armada. Supposing, for instance, that the town of Sparta were abandoned and nothing left but the public buildings and the foundations of the houses, I believe that remote posterity would be exceedingly sceptical of any correspondence between the actual power of the Lacedaemonians and their historical reputation. Actually they hold two-fifths of the Peloponnese and the suzerainty over the remainder, as well as over many allies beyond its borders, yet the town would give an impression of inferiority, because it has not been concentrated[2] or adorned with expensive public buildings, religious or secular, but remains a group of village communities in the primitive Hellenic style. On the other hand, if the same fate were to overtake Athens, the material remains of the town would probably give the impression that the Athenians were twice as powerful as they really are. It is therefore a mistake to be sceptical, or to judge states by their outward appearance rather than by their inward strength; and

---

[1] He already possessed prestige, and had ingratiated himself with the masses at Mycenae and in the other states of Eurystheus' dominions. [AUTHOR.]

[2] By the combination of a number of scattered villages into a single urban center, which was the historical genesis of the normal Hellenic city-state. [ED.]

it is safer to assume that the Trojan expedition surpassed its predecessors without attaining to modern dimensions—always supposing that the evidence of Homer may be taken as trustworthy. As a poet he presumably exaggerates, yet the inferiority remains, even on his showing. His figures are 1200 ships, with crews of 120 men in the Boeotian contingent and of 50 in Philoctetes', which I take to indicate the maximum and minimum size of vessels—at any rate, he makes no mention of size in other cases in his *Review of the Fleet*. He further indicates that crews and combatants were identical in describing the ships of Philoctetes, where he makes the oarsmen archers; and it is improbable that they carried many passengers except the kings and the superior officers—especially when they had to transport themselves and their war material across the open sea, and this in undecked ships of the primitive piratical build. If an average, then, be taken between the largest and the smallest vessels, the resulting figure for the total strength of the forces will not appear very high, considering that they represented a joint levy from the whole of Hellas.

The cause of this was weakness not so much in manpower as in money-power. Difficulties of commissariat limited them to such numbers as they estimated that the invaded country could support; and even when they had established their superiority in the field after landing, (and that they must have done, or they could not have fortified their camp), it appears that they did not employ their whole force in operations, but were driven by these difficulties of commissariat to have recourse to agriculture (in the Peninsula[1]) and to piracy. This dispersion of forces assisted the Trojans, who were a match for their combatant strength at any given moment, to hold out against them for the ten years; whereas, if they had brought supplies with them and had kept their total forces continuously in action, without dissipating them on piracy and agriculture, with their superiority in the field they would easily have taken Troy. As it was, they held their own with such a proportion of their total force as they were able to put into the line. Under modern conditions, they could have opened a regular siege and taken Troy with less time and trouble. Lack of money-power, however, was the weakness not only of previous epochs but of the Trojan War itself, which, although it enjoys greater renown than any enterprise that preceded it, is proved to have been in reality inferior to its reputation and to the fame with which poetry has invested it. Even after the Trojan War the Hellenic world remained subject to migrations

---

[1] The Gallipoli Peninsula. [ED.]

and resettlements which prevented steady development. Great unrest resulted from the delay in the return of the expeditionary force, and most states underwent revolutions, new states being founded by the consequent refugees. Sixty years after the fall of Troy the present Boeotians were driven out of Arne by the Thessalians and occupied what is now Boeotia but used to be called Kadmeis;[1] and, eighty years after, the Dorians, led by the Heracleidae, conquered the Peloponnese. It was only very painfully and slowly that Hellas quieted down and became sufficiently stable and settled to found colonies. Ionia and most of the islands were colonized from Athens, most of Italy and Sicily from the Peloponnese and a few places outside it; but all this colonization was later than the Trojan War.

As the Hellenic world became stronger and wealthier than it had been, despotisms were established,[2] public revenues increased, and Hellas built herself navies and took more decidedly to the sea. The Corinthians are said to have been the first to adopt modern methods of navigation, and triremes[3] are said to have been constructed at Corinth earlier than elsewhere in Hellas. The Samians appear to have had four vessels constructed for them by a Corinthian shipbuilder, Ameinocles, who went to Samos about three centuries before the termination of the late war. The earliest known naval battle was between the Corinthians and the Corcyraeans and occurred about 260 years before the date just mentioned. The position of Corinth on the Isthmus brought trade into the hands of her inhabitants from the earliest times, for the Hellenes inside and outside the Peloponnese originally communicated with one another by land more than by sea, and therefore across Corinthian territory. The Corinthians possessed money-power, as is proved by the early poets, whose epithet for the place is "wealthy." When seafaring became commoner in Hellas, the Corinthians acquired their fleet, put down piracy, established a market for sea-borne as well as for overland trade, and made themselves a power by their revenues. Later, the Ionians developed navies in the reign of Cyrus the First of Persia and his son Cambyses, and in their war with Cyrus they for some time commanded their own waters. In Cambyses' reign, Polycrates, despot of Samos, became a naval power and subjected a number of islands—including Rheneia, which he dedicated to Apollo of Delos. The Phocaeans, too, defeated

---

[1] A branch of them, settled there already, had sent the Boeotian contingent to Troy. [AUTHOR.]

[2] There had previously been patriarchal monarchies with fixed prerogatives. [AUTHOR.]

[3] Warships with an oar-power triple that of earlier types. [ED.]

the Carthaginians at sea when they were planting their colony at Marseilles. These were the strongest navies, and even these, though their date was many generations later than the Trojan War, appear to have employed few triremes and to have still consisted of "fifty oars" and longboats like the navies of the Trojan epoch. It was not till shortly before the Persian War and the death of Cambyses' successor Darius that triremes were constructed in considerable numbers by the despots in Sicily and by the Corcyraeans—the last important navies created in the Hellenic world before the expedition of Xerxes. The Aeginetans, Athenians and others possessed few ships and these mostly "fifty oars"; and it was at a comparatively recent date that Themistocles persuaded the Athenians, when they were at war with Aegina and the invasion of the Oriental was imminent, to build the ships with which they actually fought—ships, moreover, which were still not decked throughout.

That is the history of Hellenic navies in early and recent times. At the same time, nations that took the trouble to develop them acquired considerable power in money revenue and foreign dominion. They invaded and conquered the islands, especially those whose territories were not self-supporting. On the other hand, no war resulting in the accumulation of power occurred on land, such land wars as there were being between borderers. Distant military expeditions for permanent conquest were not yet made by the Hellenes, because the largest states had not yet brought the rest into subjection, while no joint campaigns on a footing of equality were undertaken by the independent units. There were merely local wars between neighboring communities. The early war between Chalcis and Eretria was the first instance of anything approaching a general division of the Greek world into two camps; and then the development of the different states was checked by various obstacles. The Ionians had made notable progress when Cyrus and the Persian Monarchy attacked them, after conquering Croesus and the countries west of the River Halys,[1] and reduced their states on the mainland. Darius afterwards made himself master of the islands as well, with the help of the Phoenician navy. The various despots, too, who had arisen in the Hellenic states, and whose egoistic outlook was limited to securing their personal comfort and their family fortunes, played as far as possible for safety in their foreign policy, and therefore produced no important results, except against communities within their local radius—the greatest powers built up by despots being those in Sicily. Thus

[1] Qyzyl Yrmaq. [ED.]

the Hellenic world was subjected for a long period to pressure from every direction, which precluded any conspicuous common achievement and reduced the individual states to a timid passivity.

However, the despots of Athens and the rest of Hellas (where despotic governments had for some time been prevalent) were most of them—and indeed the last of them except in Sicily—overthrown by the Lacedaemonians;[1] and not many years after their disappearance there followed the battle at Marathon between the Persians and the Athenians. Ten years from that date the Oriental a second time marched against Hellas with his Grand Army in order to enslave her, and in this crisis the Lacedaemonians, as the strongest Hellenic power, took command of the allies, while the Athenians met the Persian invasion by abandoning their town and evacuating on board ship, which resulted in their taking to the sea. The repulse of the Oriental was a common effort, but it was not long before the Hellenes liberated from Persia and the late allies were drawn into the two camps of Sparta and Athens, the greatest powers that had emerged—one on land and the other on sea. For a short time the comradeship in arms survived, and then the Lacedaemonians and the Athenians quarreled and went to war, involving their allies, while any other Greek states which quarreled thenceforth ranged themselves with the one group or the other. And so, from the time of the Persian War down to the late war, there was a perpetual alternation of truces and campaigns (against one another or against secessionists among their respective allies), which led them to perfect their armaments and improve their military technique by the training of active service. The Lacedaemonians did not impose financial contributions on the allies who rendered them military service, and confined themselves to ensuring that they should be governed on a narrow franchise in the interests of Sparta. The Athenians gradually took over the navies of their confederate states except Chios and the states in Lesbos, and assessed definite annual payments upon all of them, with the result that, at the beginning of the late war, the national armaments at their disposal were superior to the maximum strength of their confederacy at its prime.

Such are the results of my researches into the past—though in this field it is difficult to give credence to every piece of

---

[1] After the foundation of Lacedaemon by its present Dorian population, it was torn by internal disorders for an unparalleled number of years, but it was also the pioneer of reform and it has never fallen under a despot. For upwards of four centuries, reckoning back from the termination of the late war, the Lacedaemonians have lived under the same constitution, which has given them the power to interfere in the internal affairs of other states. [AUTHOR.]

evidence as it comes. Historical traditions, not excluding those of local events, are accepted with the same invariable lack of criticism by one mind from another. The majority of people at Athens imagine that Hipparchus was despot when he was assassinated by Harmodius and Aristogeiton, and do not realize that Hippias succeeded his father Peisistratus by right of primogeniture, and that Hipparchus and Thessalus were merely his brothers. This is because, on the day of the attempt, Harmodius and Aristogeiton suspected at the last moment that information had been given to Hippias by their fellow-conspirators. They therefore made no attempt upon Hippias, on the assumption that he was forewarned; but, in the expectation of imminent arrest, they determined not to risk their lives for nothing, and accordingly assassinated Hipparchus, whom they found in the act of organizing the Panathenaic Procession at the shrine of the Leocoreum. The memories of the past may be obscured by the passage of time, but many living institutions are equally misconceived by the entire Hellenic world. It is commonly supposed, for instance, that the Kings of Lacedaemon have two votes each instead of one, and that there is a "Pitane Battalion" there—a unit which has never existed. So little pains do the majority of people take to research into the truth and so ready are they to accept the first version that offers itself. Still, it is safe to draw substantially the conclusions that I have drawn from the evidence that I have cited, as contrasted with the poets' exaggerated rhapsodies or the entertaining rather than accurate compositions of the genealogists. There is really no means of verification in a subject of such antiquity that it has won its way into the misty region of romance, and in this field it may be regarded as sufficient if the salient features are established. The late war is a different matter. I am aware that while men are at war they are always of opinion that they are engaged in the greatest war in history, and that they have no sooner made peace than they succumb to the glamor of antiquity. But the facts of the late war speak for themselves and demonstrate that it surpasses its predecessors.

As regards the various speeches delivered before or after the outbreak of hostilities, I have found it impossible to preserve verbal exactitude in the cases in which I was my own reporter, and other persons from whom I have taken reports at second hand have had the same experience. My rule has been to reproduce what seemed to me the most probable and appropriate language for each occasion, while preserving as faithfully as possible the general sense of the speech actually delivered. As regards the material facts of the war, I have not been content to follow casual informants or my own imagination. Where I have not been an eye witness myself, I have investigated with the utmost accuracy attainable every detail that I have taken at second hand. The task has been laborious, for witnesses of the same particular events have given versions that have varied according to their sympathies or retentive powers. Possibly the public will find my unromantic narrative forbidding, but I shall be satisfied if it is favorably received by readers whose object is exact knowledge of facts which had not only actually occurred, but which are destined approximately to repeat themselves in all human probability. I have tried to produce a permanent contribution to knowledge rather than an ephemeral *tour de force*.

The greatest war before the last was the Persian War, and that was quickly decided by two engagements on sea and two on land. But the late war was greatly protracted and involved Hellas in more terrible catastrophes than she had ever before experienced in an equal period of time. Never before had so many towns been captured and devastated, some by non-Hellenes and others by the Hellenic belligerents themselves;[1] never had so many individuals been driven from their homes or massacred, some in the war itself and others in civil disorders. In addition to this, there were amply attested occurrences of calamities for which there were traditional precedents but few substantial examples, such as earthquakes, which set in with unparalleled range and violence, or eclipses, which occurred with greater frequency than had ever previously been recorded. There were also severe local droughts and consequent famines, while one of the worst scourges was the plague, which materially reduced the population. The war was the signal for the attacks of all these forces of nature.

The outbreak of war involved a breach of the Thirty Years' Peace which the Athenians and the Peloponnesians had concluded after the reduction of Euboea.[2] I shall give a preliminary account of the disputes by which this breach of the peace was brought about, in order that no reader may ever be at a loss to understand how the Hellenes came to be drawn into so formidable a struggle. The cause which I regard as fundamental hardly figures in the official versions, and that is the fear inspired in the Lacedaemonians by the aggrandizement of Athens, which in my opinion compelled them to take up arms.

[1] There were cases in which capture was followed by change of population. [AUTHOR.]

[2] By the Athenians in 446 B.C. [ED.]

After the negotiation of the treaty and the alliance between Sparta and Athens, by which the Ten Years' War[1] was concluded,[2] the signatories found themselves at peace; but Corinth and other states of the Peloponnese started to undermine the settlement, with the result that Lacedaemon was immediately involved in fresh troubles with her own allies. As time went on, the Lacedaemonians also became suspect to the Athenians, owing to their failure to execute certain points in the terms of agreement; and although for the first six and a half years they refrained from invading one another's territories, they lost no opportunity of injuring one another in other theaters. The truce remained precarious, until finally circumstances drove them into breaking the peace concluded after the first ten years and relapsing into open hostilities.

The history of this second phase of the war has been written—in chronological order by winters and summers—by the same Thucydides of Athens, down to the overthrow of the Athenian Empire by the Lacedaemonians and their allies and the occupation of the Long Walls and the Peiraeus.[3] The total duration of the war to this date was twenty-seven years, including the interval of armistice, which it would be a mistake to exclude from the reckoning. If any reader is inclined to disagree with me, he has only to examine this period in the light of the facts in order to realize that "peace" is a misnomer for it. The parties neither restored nor recovered all the places specified in their terms of agreement, not to speak of the violations of which both were guilty in connection with the Mantinean and Epidaurian wars and on other occasions; the allies of Athens on the Thracian littoral never ceased hostilities; and the Boeotians only made a truce for recurrent periods of ten days at a time. Including the first war (lasting ten years), the doubtful armistice that followed it, and the second war by which that armistice was terminated, the total number of years, calculating by seasons, works out, to within a few days, at the figure which I have mentioned; and, incidentally, believers in oracles are for this once justified by the event. I certainly remember the constant repetition in wide circles, from beginning to end of the war, of the saying that it was destined to last for thrice nine years. I lived through the whole

[1] 431–421 B.C. [Ed.]
[2] In Pleistolas' year of office at Sparta and Alcaeus' at Athens. [Author.]
[3] The author unhappily died before completing his project. [Ed.]

of it, and I was not only of an age of discretion, but took special pains to acquire accurate information. It was my fate to be exiled from my country for twenty years after my command at Amphipolis, and in this situation I was enabled to see something of both sides—the Peloponnesian as well as the Athenian—and to make a special study of the war at my leisure. I have now to relate the disputes that followed the conclusion of the first ten years' war, the breach of the treaty, and the course of the second war that ensued.

POLYBIUS OF MEGALOPOLIS

(*ca.* 201–120 B.C.)

WORLD HISTORY

(Teubner text, ed. by W. Büttner-Wobst; Book I. chapters 1–4)

IF previous historians had omitted to praise their own art, it might have been my duty to make a general appeal for the sympathetic reception of this branch of literature. The knowledge of past events is the sovereign corrective of human nature. This duty, however, is far from having been exceptionally or perfunctorily performed. It is actually the note on which almost all historians have begun and ended their work, when they have eulogized the lessons of history as the truest education and training for political life, and the study of others' vicissitudes as the most effective, or indeed the only, school in which the right spirit for enduring the changes of fortune can be acquired. It is evident, therefore, that no historian would be justified in reiterating what has been so often and so ably said before, and least of all the present writer. The events which he has chosen as his subject are sufficiently extraordinary in themselves to arouse and stimulate the interest of every reader, young or old. What mind, however commonplace or indifferent, could feel no curiosity to learn the process by which almost the whole world fell under the undisputed ascendency of Rome within a period of less than fifty-three years, or to acquaint itself with the political organization to which this triumph—a phenomenon unprecedented in the annals of mankind—was due? What mind, however infatuated with other spectacles and other studies, could find a field of knowledge more profitable than this?

The extraordinary nature and the supreme importance of the problem with which the present work is concerned are perhaps revealed most strikingly by a critical comparison between the supremacy of Rome and the most celebrated empires of earlier date which have hitherto absorbed the attention of historians. The relevant cases are the Persians, who temporarily acquired an extensive empire and dominion, but came near to losing not only their empire but their existence whenever they ventured beyond the bounds of Asia; the Lacedaemonians, who won the leading position in Hellas after a prolonged contest, and retained undisputed possession of it for barely ten years; and the Macedonians, who established their rule in Europe from the Adriatic to the Danube (an insignificant fraction of that continent, as it would now appear to us), and afterwards added to it the dominion of Asia by the overthrow of the Persian Empire. All these were reputed extensive and powerful empires in their day, yet they actually left the greater part of the habitable world outside their frontiers. They never attempted to contest the sovereignty of Sicily, Sardinia or North Africa, and they were virtually ignorant of the existence of the most warlike races in Europe, the nations of the West. The Romans, on the other hand, subjected not merely a portion, but practically the whole of the habitable world, and founded a power of such pre-eminence that no contemporary could resist it and posterity could not hope to surpass it. It is the object of the present work to throw light upon this phenomenon,[1] and also to demonstrate the numerous and important advantages offered to serious students by the "transactional branch"[2] of history.

The chronological starting point of the work is the Hundred and Fortieth Olympiad,[3] and the first transactions recorded are the following: In Hellas, the so-called Federal War, which started in an offensive alliance against the Aetolians between the Achaeans and Philip, son of Demetrius and father of Perseus; in Asia, the War of Hollow Syria between Antiochus and Ptolemy Philopator; in Italy and North Africa, the war between the Romans and the Carthaginians, usually known as the Hannibalic War. These transactions are continuous with the last recorded in the work of Aratus of Sicyon.[4] In previous periods the transactions of the habitable world took place in separate compartments, in which the projects

---

[1] The Greek text of this sentence is corrupt. [ED.]

[2] In Greek πραγματικός τρόπος — a technical term adopted if not coined by Polybius to characterize his own work. The substantive πράξεις from which πραγματικός is derived, is exactly equivalent to the word "transactions" as used by English historians a century ago. [ED.]

[3] An olympiad was a four years' cycle, measured by the recurrence of the Olympian Games. The one hundred and fortieth began in the late summer of the year 220 B.C. [ED.]

[4] The leading Hellenic statesman of his day (271-213 B.C.). [ED.]

attempted, the results attained, and the localities involved
were unrelated. But from this date onward history acquires
an organic character, the transactions of Italy and North Africa become involved with those of Hellas and Asia, and all
the currents set toward a single goal. This has decided the
writer to start his work at the date above-mentioned. The
defeat of the Carthaginians by the Romans in the Hannibalic
War was regarded by the latter as the decisive step in their
attempt at world power, and as soon as this step had been
achieved they were emboldened to stretch out their hands
over the rest of the world and to commit themselves to military intervention in Hellas and Asia.

If the two commonwealths which contended for world
power in this war had been objects of common knowledge, it
would perhaps have been superfluous to insert an introductory
section in order to explain the policies and resources that inspired them to embark upon enterprises of such magnitude.
Actually, however, the previous resources and transactions
of the Roman and Carthaginian states are so unfamiliar to
the majority of the Hellenic public that it has seemed essential
to preface this history with two introductory volumes.[1] This
will ensure that no reader will find himself at the commencement of my main narrative without an answer to the question: What policy was in the Romans' minds and what resources, military and economic, were in their hands at the
time when they embarked upon these projects, which resulted
in their becoming masters of the entire Mediterranean and its
littoral? These two introductory volumes will make it clear
that the means at the disposal of the Romans were admirably
adapted to the end of world power and world empire, as conceived and attained by them.

The coincidence by which all the transactions of the world
have been oriented in a single direction and guided toward
a single goal is the extraordinary characteristic of the present
age, to which the special feature of the present work is a
corollary. The unity of events imposes upon the historian a
similar unity of composition in depicting for his readers the
operation of the laws of Fortune upon the grand scale, and
this has been my own principal inducement and stimulus in
the work which I have undertaken. Otherwise, this field would
have proved far less attractive to my ambition. As it is, the
local wars and some of the transactions connected with them
have been taken up by a number of historians, while no one,
so far as I know, has even attempted to examine, from the

---

[1] A volume, in the original and literal sense of a roll of papyrus or parchment,
was a much smaller unit than one of our modern Western printed tomes. [ED.]

general point of view, the interrelation of events in their sequence, origins and results; and the realization of this has impressed me with the absolute necessity of not disregarding or passing over without remark one of the most admirable and instructive performances of Fortune. That mighty revolutionary, whose pawns are human lives, has never before achieved such an astonishing *tour de force* as she has staged for the benefit of our generation; yet the monographs of the historical specialists give no inkling of the whole picture, and if any reader supposes that a survey of the leading countries in isolation from one another, or rather, the contemplation of their respective local chronicles, can have given him an intuition into the scheme of the world in its general arrangement and setting, I must hasten to expose his fallacy. To my mind, the persuasion that an acquaintance with local history will give a fair perspective of the whole phenomenon is as erroneous as the notion that the contemplation of the *disjecta membra* of a once living and beautiful organism is equivalent to the direct observation of the organism itself in all the energy and beauty of life. I fancy that anyone who maintained such a position would speedily admit the ludicrous enormity of his error if the organism could be revealed to him by some magician who had reconstituted it, at a stroke, in its original perfection of form and grace of vitality. While the part may conceivably offer a hint of the whole, it cannot possibly yield an exact and certain knowledge of it; and the inference is that the specialists have a singularly small contribution to offer toward a true understanding of world history. The study of general contacts and relations and of general resemblances and differences is the only avenue to a general perspective, without which neither profit nor pleasure can be extracted from historical research.

WORLD HISTORY: PREFACE TO VOLUME IX.

(Teubner text, ed. by W. Büttner-Wobst; Book IX. chapters 1–2)

I AM aware that there is something forbidding about my work, that it is adapted to a particular class of readers, and that it is open to criticism on account of the monotony of its style. Almost all other writers, or at any rate the majority, introduce all the different branches of historical writing, and so attract a wide public to the perusal of their compositions. The story-lover is allured by the genealogical side; inquisitive and curious minds by the origins of states, the plantation of colonies and ethnological disquisitions such as are to be found in Ephorus; [1] and the politically-minded by that side which concerns itself with the transactions of peoples, states and rulers. It is to this latter side that I have addressed myself exclusively; and by grouping my whole work round this center I have adapted it, as I have said, to one special class of readers, at the cost of making it unattractive reading for the majority. The reasons which moved me to reject the other branches and to confine myself to the transactional side have been explained at greater length elsewhere, but there would appear to be no objection to summarizing them again in order to drive the point home for the benefit of my readers.

The fact is that the story of ethnology, origins, legends, genealogy and colonization has been told so often by so many writers that any historian who takes up the tale today is left to choose between the thoroughly dishonest course of repeating others' words as his own, or the straightforward but obviously fatuous alternative of confessing that the subject on which he is expending his thought and his literary abilities has already received adequate treatment in a monumental form at the hands of his predecessors. For this and other reasons I have left these branches on one side and have embraced the transactional branch—in the first place, because fresh material is perpetually accumulating and demanding a fresh record (since it is a logical impossibility for writers of the past to inform us of transactions of a later date), and secondly because it is a more instructive branch than any of the others. This has always been true, but never so true as at the present day, when the progress of knowledge and technique has reached such a point that every phenomenon presented by the development of events lends itself to something approaching scientific treatment in expert hands. I have therefore aimed less at the entertainment of the general reader than at the instruction of the serious student, and have accordingly addressed myself to this branch to the neglect of the others. In the conscientious student of my work I shall find the strongest witness to the justice of my contention.

---

[1] *Ca.* 405–335 B.C. [ED.]

DIODORUS OF AGYRIUM

(*ca.* 90–20 B.C.)

LIBRARY OF UNIVERSAL HISTORY

(Teubner text, ed. by F. Vogel: Book I. chapters 1–5)

THE authors of universal histories deserve the gratitude and recognition of their fellows for the spirit in which they give their labors for the benefit of the race. They have discovered the secret of imparting the fruits, without the perils, of experience, and therefore have knowledge of inestimable value to offer to the readers of their works. Toil and danger are the price of the practical wisdom which is bought by the experience of daily life, and we find that the legendary hero whose experiences were the most extensive had to suffer cruel misfortunes in order to

> *See the homes of many men and*
> *read the thoughts of their hearts,*

while History is able to instruct without inflicting pain by affording an insight into the failures and successes of others. We are further indebted to these authors for their efforts to marshal the whole human race, who are all members one of another, in spite of the barriers of space and time, in one magnificent array. In attempting this, they have constituted themselves nothing less than the servants of Providence. God, in His Providence, has related in a single system the evolutions of the stars of heaven and the characters of men, and maintains them in perpetual motion to all eternity, imparting to each the lot which Destiny assigns; while the authors of universal histories, in their works, record the general transactions of the world as though it were a single community, and pass the works of Providence through the grand audit of their clearinghouse.

It is a blessing to be given opportunity to improve ourselves by taking warning from the mistakes of others, and in all the chances and changes of this mortal life to be free to copy the successes of the past instead of being compelled to make a painful trial of the present. In ordinary life, the judgment of the older generation is always preferred by the younger on account of the experience which has come to them with time; yet the knowledge which comes by History surpasses individual experience in value in proportion to its conspicuous superiority in scope and content. For every conceivable situation in life the supreme utility of this study will generally be admitted. The young are invested by it with the understanding of the old; the old find their actual experience multiplied by it a hundredfold; ordinary men are transformed by it into leaders; men born to command are stimulated by the immortality of fame which it confers to embark upon noble enterprises; soldiers, again, are encouraged by the posthumous glory which it promises to risk their lives for their country; the wicked are deterred by the eternal obloquy with which it threatens them from their evil impulses; and, in general, the good graces of History are so highly praised that some have been stimulated by the hope of them to become founders of states, others to introduce laws contributing to the security of the race, and others to make scientific or practical discoveries by which all mankind has benefited. As a result of all these activities the sum of human happiness is increased, but the palm of praise must be rendered to History, who is the real cause of them all. History may claim to be the guardian of those who have a reputation to keep, the witness against those who have a reputation to lose, and the benefactress of all humanity. Even the entirely fictitious legend of Hell is a mighty instrument for turning the hearts of men to righteousness and the fear of God. How much greater, therefore, must we conceive to be the potential ennobling influence upon character of History, the prophetess of truth and wellspring of philosophy? Such is the infirmity of human nature that the lifetime of individuals is an infinitesimal fraction of eternity compared with the time that follows in which they are not. For those who have achieved nothing noteworthy in their lives, the death of the body involves the total extinction of existence; but for those whose abilities have won them glory, an eternal remembrance of their achievements is assured by the praises that resound from the divine lips of History; and surely the wise will find in immortal fame a fair reward for mortal toils. It is well known that Heracles devoted all the time that he spent in this world to the voluntary endurance of cruel and unceasing toils and dangers, in order that he might gain immortality as a benefactor of the human race; and the other saints who have obtained heroic or divine honors owe the glory which they have all earned to the immortality with which their attainments have been invested by History. All other memorials are transitory and exposed to destruction in many circumstances, but History, whose power extends to the limits of the world, has found in Time, the grand destroyer, a guardian of her everlasting tradition for future generations.

History is also a mistress of eloquence, the gift of gifts.

Eloquence raises the Hellene above the non-Hellene and the educated above the illiterate, and it is the only weapon which enables one man to prevail against many. In general, any proposition appears as it is represented by the ability of the spokesman, and we call good men "worthy of honorable mention," with the inference that this is the prize which they have won by their attainments. Of the several branches into which eloquence is divided, poetry affords pleasure rather than profit, legislation is punitive instead of being educative, and similarly the other branches either make no contribution to human happiness or produce a mixed crop of wheat and tares, while some of them are traitors to truth. In History alone there is not merely a harmony between the facts and their literary expression, but a combination of every utility. Know her by her fruits, and you will find her making for righteousness, denouncing evil, eulogizing the good, and, in a word, endowing those who study her with the sum of human wisdom.

The spectacle of the approbation with which historical writers are justly received has stimulated me to an equal enthusiasm for the subject; and a study of my predecessors in this field has inspired me with the strongest feelings of approval for their purpose. At the same time, I hardly feel that the full possibilities of instruction inherent in it have been realized in their works. The value of such works to the reader depends upon the introduction of the greatest possible number and variety of circumstances, and yet most historians confine their records to isolated wars waged by particular peoples or states, while few have attempted to record the general transactions of mankind from the earliest times down to their own day. Among this minority, again, some have stopped short of their own times; others have limited themselves to the transactions of the Hellenic world; others have rejected the legends of antiquity on account of the difficulty of the material; others have been cut off by destiny before they had succeeded in completing the program upon which they had embarked; and even among those who have embarked upon it, not one writer has carried his history beyond the Macedonian epoch. Some have terminated their compilations with the transactions of Philip, others with those of Alexander, others with the successors of Alexander in the first or the second generation; and although the transactions between the latter date and our own generation, which have been left untouched, are both numerous and important, the vastness of the subject has prevented any historian from attempting to deal with them within the limits of a single work. The consequence is that the record of human transactions is scattered through a number of works by different writers treating different periods, so that the subject as a whole is equally difficult to master and to remember.

After examining the compositions of the various writers to whom I have alluded, I determined to devote myself to a historical subject which combines the greatest potential utility with the least risk of wearying the reader. It was obvious to me that any historian who attempted, to the best of his ability, to trace the recorded transactions of the entire world from the earliest times to his own day as if he were dealing with a single country, would be imposing upon himself a formidable task, but that, at the same time, the work that would result from his labors would prove of the utmost value to the reading public. Such a work would constitute an immense reservoir from which everyone would find it possible to draw without difficulty what was relevant to his special field; while readers who attempt to thread their way through the labyrinth of existing historical works are confronted, in the first place, with the difficulty of obtaining access to the necessary books, while in the second place they find that the mastery of events eludes and evades them in the maze of heterogeneous published works. On the other hand, a treatment of the subject within the limits of a single work facilitates the task of the reader by providing him with a flowing narrative, the mastery of which is perfectly plain sailing. In short, the superiority of this branch of history over the rest is to be measured by the superior utility of the whole to the part and of continuity to discontinuity, not to mention the advantages of an accurate chronological setting over narratives in which not even the vaguest indication of date is forthcoming.

I was equally impressed with the utility of a work on the lines above-mentioned and with the sacrifices of labor and time involved, and I have accordingly devoted thirty years to the task, during which I have incurred considerable hardships and dangers in making extensive travels through Asia as well as Europe. I was determined to see with my own eyes as many places as possible, or at least the essential places, since lack of acquaintance with topography has frequently misled writers well above the ordinary level, and even some of the highest reputation. My principal resource in the execution of my project has been enthusiasm for the work—the spirit which enables human nature to accomplish apparent impossibilities—and, next to that, the materials for the study of my subject which are available in Rome. The supremacy of Rome, whose power extends to the ends of the earth, has afforded me innumerable resources and facilities during the long period of my residence there. My home is Agyrium in Sicily,[1] and my intercourse with the Latin-speaking settlers in the island has given me a thorough command of the Latin language, so that I have been able to derive accurate information of all the transactions of the Roman dominion from the national records, which have been preserved from an early date. As the starting point of my history I have taken the legendary origins of the Hellenic and non-Hellenic worlds according to the various local traditions, which I have spared no pains to investigate.

My program has now been completed, but before I present the results of my labors to the public, I must preface them with a brief table of contents of the work as a whole. My first six volumes contain transactions and legends previous to the Trojan War—the first three being non-Hellenic, while the rest are almost exclusively occupied with the ancient history of Hellas. In the eleven volumes that follow I have recorded the general transactions of the world from the Trojan War to the death of Alexander; while in the succeeding twenty-three volumes I have found room for all transactions between that date and the commencement of the Celto-Roman War, in which Gaius Julius Caesar, who commanded the Roman forces and whose achievements have won him divine honors, broke the resistance of the majority (including the most warlike) of the Celtic peoples and extended the dominion of Rome to the British Isles. The first transactions of this war occurred in the first years of the Hundred and Eightieth Olympiad, corresponding to Herodes' year of office at Athens.

These are the chronological limits of my work; but I have not attempted a definite chronology of events before the Trojan War, since no trustworthy table of dates for this period has reached my hands. Between the Trojan War and the Return of the Heracleidae I have followed Apollodorus of Athens in assuming an interval of eighty years; between the latter date and the First Olympiad I have reckoned an interval of three hundred and twenty-eight years, which I have based upon the reigns of the kings of Sparta; while between the First Olympiad and my terminal date, the commencement of the Celtic War, there are seven hundred and thirty years to be accounted for; so that the forty volumes to which the whole work extends cover a total period of eleven hundred and thirty-eight years, without including the period occupied by transactions previous to the Trojan War.

The object of this precise table of contents has been not only to give my readers a notion of my general plan, but to

[1] The prevailing language in Sicily at this time (and down to the eleventh century after Christ) was Greek. [ED.]

deter the publishing trade from their deplorable practice of mutilating works of which they are not the authors. The only favors that I have to ask are that successful passages in my work should be accorded a generous reception and that mistakes should receive correction at the hands of readers more competent than myself. This completes the account of my program, and I must now attempt to justify my promise by my performance.

DIONYSIUS OF HALICARNASSUS

(*Floruit* in the latter half of the first century b.c.)

THE ANCIENT HISTORY OF ROME

(Teubner text, ed. by C. Jacoby: Book I. chapters 1–8)

MUCH against my will, I find myself obliged to introduce those preliminary personal observations that are only too common a feature of prefaces to historical works. I have no intention, however, of enlarging upon my own merits, which would, I am well aware, prove singularly wearisome to my readers, or of attacking my fellow-writers, as Anaximenes and Theopompus have done in the prefaces to their histories. My motive is simply to explain the reasons which have induced me personally to embark upon this work, and to give some account of my sources of information. It is my conviction that anyone who proposes to bequeath to after generations some memorial that is destined to survive his own bodily existence, and especially a writer of historical works (the sanctuaries, as we believe, of that first principle of all wisdom and understanding, the Truth), is under an obligation in the first place to choose a good subject of a lofty character which will be truly profitable to the reader, and in the second place to devote the utmost care and industry to the task of providing himself with proper sources for his own composition. There are, of course, historical writers who have been led astray by the thirst for notoriety, no matter of what kind, or for opportunities to display their literary ability in a *tour de force,* and who have taken inglorious or trivial or unimportant events as the basis of their work. Such writers are neither admired by after generations for their learning nor celebrated for their abilities, but have simply contrived to implant in every mind that studies their works the impression that their personal aims in life are reflected in their publications—works of literature being naturally and universally regarded as mirrors of the author's personality. Writers, again, who choose fine subjects but reveal a slipshod and slovenly dependence upon hearsay in their execution obtain no credit for their choice, because it offends our susceptibilities to see the history of famous countries and rulers written in an offhand and slovenly manner. I regard these as the essential first principles for historical writers and have devoted considerable attention to both of them myself. For this reason I did not wish to leave them unmentioned, and I could find no place for them more suitable than the preface to my work.

It will not, I trust, require many words to demonstrate the excellence of the subject which I have chosen, the loftiness of its character or the wideness of the circle which may profit by it, if I may presuppose in my readers the most rudimentary acquaintance with general history. They have only to turn their minds to the empires of the past (whether exercised by city-states or by nations) of which we have a record, and to examine them first individually and then comparatively with a view to determining which of them acquired the widest dominions and performed the most brilliant achievements in peace and war, and they will find that the Roman Empire has immeasurably surpassed all its historical predecessors, not only in the extent of its dominion and the splendor of its achievements (which have never yet been celebrated worthily in literature), but in the length of its duration down to our own age. The ancient and semi-mythical Assyrian Empire dominated no more than a fraction of Asia; the Median Empire which overthrew it and rose to greater power lacked permanence and fell in the fourth generation; the Persians, who overcame the Medes and eventually established their dominion over almost the whole of Asia, met with limited success in their attempts to conquer the peoples of Europe and remained in power little more than two centuries; the Macedonian Dominion, again, which overthrew the mighty Persia and surpassed in extent all previous empires, enjoyed a transient prosperity and began to decline after the death of Alexander. In the first generation of his successors it was dismembered among a number of rival rulers, and its strength only held out for two or three generations longer before it collapsed through self-exhaustion and was finally swept away by Rome. Nor did even the Macedonian Empire establish a universal dominion over sea and land. It secured no footing in North Africa apart from the corner adjoining Egypt, and was far from subduing the whole of Europe, in which continent it did not advance farther north than Thrace or farther west than the Adriatic.

These were the highest points of power and prosperity to which previous empires of which there is a historical record had attained before they fell. As for the Hellenic powers, the extent of their empires and the period of their greatness was so insignificant compared with that of the empires abovementioned that they do not deserve to be brought into comparison with them. The Athenian Empire, which lasted sixtyeight years, was confined to the littoral, and to a mere fragment of that, between the Black and the Pamphylian[1] Seas, even at the zenith of Athens' naval power. The Lacedaemonians, whose empire was brought to an end by the Thebans before they had held it for a full thirty years, had only succeeded in extending their rule over the Peloponnesc and the rest of Hellas as far as Macedonia. It was reserved for Rome to establish her empire over the entire accessible land surface of the earth up to the limits of human habitation, as well as the entire sea—not merely the Mediterranean, but all the navigable waters of the Atlantic. Rome, first and alone of all powers recorded since the beginning of time, has established the sunrise and sunset as the boundaries of her dominion, and has maintained her power not for a brief interval but for a period unequaled by any other state or kingdom. Immediately after her foundation she began to assert her ascendancy over her numerous and warlike neighbors; none of her rivals escaped subjection; and this triumphal march has continued without interruption for seven hundred and forty-five years, down to the consulship of Claudius Nero[2] and Piso Calpurnius, who were elected in the Hundred and Ninety-third Olympiad. As soon as all Italy lay at her feet, she boldly aspired to world power; and when she had driven Carthage, the leading naval power, from the seas, and had overcome Macedonia, which had previously been regarded as the leading land power, she remained without a rival in either the Hellenic or the non-Hellenic world. The world-empire of Rome, thus established, has now reached the seventh generation, and there is hardly a nation that challenges even her dominion over itself, not to speak of her universal supremacy. I am surely absolved from any further demonstration of my original thesis that the subject which I have chosen is not unimportant and that the transactions which I have decided to narrate are neither trivial nor insignificant.

I must, however, devote a few preliminary words to explaining that my specialization in the *ancient* history of Rome has been a deliberate and a rational decision which I am in a posi-

[1] Gulf of Adalia. [ED.]
[2] His second tenure of the office in the year 7 B.C. [ED.]

tion to support by convincing arguments. Otherwise I am in danger of being condemned unheard by those captious critics whom nothing can please, and who will censure me for rejecting all the famous subjects presented to me by the history of Rome in order to devote myself to her undistinguished ancient period. The contemporary glory of Rome, they will tell me, derives from origins so humble and inglorious that they are unworthy of historical treatment. Her fame and grandeur date from her conquest of the Macedonian powers and her triumphal issue from the Punic Wars,[1] comparatively few generations ago. My answer is that the ancient history of Rome is still virtually a closed book to the Hellenic public. The majority have been misled by the false view, which is based on nothing but hearsay, that the founders of Rome were uncivilized vagrants and outlaws who were not even free-born; and that the secret of Rome's gradual advance to world dominion has not been her righteousness or her fear of God or any moral quality, but some blind, mechanical and immoral operation of Fortune, who has bestowed her greatest gifts upon her most unprofitable servants. In malicious circles it is the fashion to make this indictment in so many words and to blame Fortune for having imparted the privileges of the Hellenes to the lowest savages; and it is superfluous to speak of the general public when there are actually writers who have ventured to place this proposition on permanent record in their historical works. These writers have sacrificed truth and honor in order to gratify uncivilized monarchs of whom they had become the professional slaves and flatterers, and who hated the supremacy of Rome.

My object, as I have stated, is to eradicate these erroneous suppositions from the public mind and to implant the truth in their place in treating of the founders of Rome and of her early institutions and transactions. I shall accordingly explain in the present volume who her founders were, the dates at which they respectively foregathered, and the circumstances which led them to leave their ancestral homes, and I guarantee to demonstrate that they were not merely Hellenes but Hellenes of no mean or undistinguished stock. Their transactions in the period immediately after the foundation, and the institutions which enabled their descendants to acquire this mighty empire, will be described in the second and the succeeding volumes; and I shall do my best to omit nothing that deserves historical notice. It is my hope that the discovery of the truth may induce a proper appreciation of Rome in the minds of my readers, unless they are her fanatical and irrec-

---

[1] Punic = Phoenician, *i.e.* Carthaginian. [Ed.]

oncilable enemies. It is idle to resent what is a perfectly
natural subordination resting on the universal and eternal law
of nature, in accordance with which the weak are invariably
ruled by the strong; and it is equally idle to blame Fortune for
having lavished this great empire for this length of time upon
a state unworthy of the honor. One of the discoveries that
awaits my readers is the fact that, from the moment of her
foundation onwards, Rome has been fertile of moral greatness.
Whether in righteousness and the fear of God or in lifelong
self-control or in military prowess, the sons of Rome can bear
comparison with the sons of any other state, Hellenic or non-
Hellenic. My only fear is that the extraordinary and paradoxical character of the propositions which I have guaranteed to
prove may make my work invidious to my readers. However,
the glorious company of Roman empire builders remains entirely unknown to the Hellenic public, because it has found
no adequate historian. No accurate history of their achievements has so far appeared in Greek, if we exclude a few brief
and summary epitomes.

So far as I am aware, the first writer to touch upon the ancient history of Rome was Hieronymus of Cardia in his work
on the second generation of Alexander's successors. After him,
Timaeus of Sicily dealt with the ancient period in his general
history and devoted a special work to the war with Pyrrhus of
Epirus. In addition to the above-mentioned writers, Antigonus,
Polybius, Silenus and a host of others tried their hand with less
success upon the same events, each dealing with a fragment of
the story and basing his account on hearsay in lieu of accurate,
firsthand research. Nor is there anything to choose between
these works and the publications of the Roman authors who
have written the ancient history of their country in Greek,
the earliest of whom were Quintus Fabius and Lucius Cincius,
both contemporary with the Punic Wars. Each of these latter
historians is accurate enough in his description of events of
which he was a firsthand witness, but has given no more than
a cursory summary of the ancient history of Rome in the
period following her foundation. These considerations have
decided me not to leave without a record a great and hitherto
neglected period of history, an accurate account of which will
right an injustice and secure a happy result. In the first place,
good men and true, who have run their course, will be rewarded with eternal fame and the approbation of after generations, which transfigures human nature and enables men's
deeds to outlive their bodies; while, in the second place, the
living and the yet unborn descendants of those heroes will be
stimulated to prefer a life of noble ambition to a life of pleas-

urable ease, by the thought that those who have received a rich initial hereditary endowment ought to set themselves a high standard and never to show themselves unworthy of their ancestors. My own reward for having devoted myself to this work, with no thought of flattery but only of truth and justice (the true aims of all history), will be found first in the demonstration of my sympathy with all who take an honorable delight in the study of great and inspiring events; and secondly in the presentation to Rome herself of the best thankoffering which it is in my power to make in memory of the education and the other gifts which I have received from her during my sojourn as a stranger within her gates.

Having now given an account of my program, I have still to say something in regard to the sources to which I had recourse for the composition of this work. Readers already familiar with Hieronymus, Timaeus, Polybius or any of the other writers whom I have accused, just above, of superficiality, will have remarked the absence from their works of a great part of my own material, and they may conceivably suspect me of improvisation, or at any rate require to be satisfied in regard to the channels through which my information has reached me. I can best avert such suspicions from my readers' minds by offering some preliminary remarks upon the writings and records which I have taken as my basis. I landed in Italy at the moment when the Civil War had been brought to an end by Augustus Caesar in the middle of the Hundred and Eighty-seventh Olympiad.[1] Since that date twenty-two years have passed and I have never left Rome, where I have learned the Latin language, acquainted myself with the literature, and occupied myself continuously with studies bearing upon my present subject. Part of my information has been obtained orally from the leading Roman savants with whom I have come into personal contact, and part from the perusal of the historical works which enjoy the highest reputation among the Romans themselves, such as those of Porcius Cato, Fabius Maximus, Valerius of Antium, Licinius Macer, the Aelii, the Gellii, the Calpurnii and many other writers of distinction. These works (which resemble Hellenic local histories) form the basis which I have taken for my own. I need say no more about myself, and I have merely to mention the chronological limits of my work, its principal contents and its general plan.

I begin my story with the most ancient legends, which were omitted by my predecessors because they were difficult to establish without laborious research. I carry my narrative

[1] *I.e. ca.* 30 B.C. [ED.]

down to the beginning of the First Punic War, the date of which is the third year of the Hundred and Twenty-eighth Olympiad.[1] I give an account of all the foreign wars of Rome which fall within this period, as well as the civil disorders through which she passed, explaining the causes which produced them and the methods and reasons of their termination. I also deal with the successive constitutions of Rome both before and after the fall of the monarchy, and describe their workings. I discuss the most admirable of her institutions and the most celebrated of her laws. In short, I give a complete picture of the life of Rome in ancient times. The plan on which I have constructed my work differs equally from that of the exclusively military and the exclusively constitutional historian, and bears little resemblance to the chronicles published by the specialists on the local history of Athens. There is an inherent monotony in all these types of work which speedily offends the reader. In my own, I have attempted to combine the three branches of controversial, scientific and entertaining literature, in the hope that it may give equal satisfaction to publicists, to those whose interests lie in philosophical speculation, and to any readers who may be looking for a tranquil form of diversion in the study of history. I have now explained both the subject and the plan of my work.

(*Signed*) DIONYSIUS SON OF ALEXANDER, OF HALICARNASSUS
(Author of *The Ancient History of Rome*.)

THE GOSPEL ACCORDING TO St. LUKE

(The New Testament in the original Greek, ed. by B. F. Westcott and F. J. A. Hort (London, 1895, Macmillan). Chapter I. verses 1–4: Dedication to Theophilus)

EXCELLENCY,

Many witnesses before me have attempted to compose a narrative of the transactions that have been accomplished in our society, as the record has been handed down to us by the original eyewitnesses who devoted themselves to the task of preserving it; and this has decided me in my turn, after tracing back the whole course of events in detail to its earliest beginnings, to write a consecutive account for your benefit, in the hope of presenting you with exact information regarding the story in which you have been orally instructed.

[1] 265 B.C. [ED.]

FLAVIUS JOSEPHUS OF JERUSALEM

(A.D. 37–*ca.* 100)

THE JEWISH WAR

(Teubner text, Collected Works, Vol. V.,ed. by S. A. Naber:

Book I. chapters 1–16)

THE Judaeo-Roman War is the greatest war of our own times, and it would hardly be an exaggeration to add that it is the greatest of any wars on record between either city-states or nations. Nevertheless, its history has been written academically by authors who did not participate in the events themselves but have collected random and discrepant accounts of them by hearsay, while the firsthand witnesses have been tempted by their wish to flatter the Romans or by their hatred of the Jews to misrepresent the facts. Such works consist of alternative invective and encomium, without a vestige of historical accuracy, and this has induced me to offer to the public of the Roman Empire, in a Greek translation, a work of my own, originally composed in my native language [1] and published in the non-Hellenic Orient.[2] My name is Josephus son of Mathias. By descent I am a Hebrew from Jerusalem, by profession a priest. I saw service against the Romans in the initial phase of the war, and was a compulsory spectator of its latter stages.

This was, as I have remarked, an upheaval of the greatest magnitude, and it found the Romans in the grip of internal troubles, while the revolutionary element among the Jews, which was at its zenith both in funds and in forces, timed its rebellion to take advantage of the prevailing disorders. The consequent convulsions were so violent that the fate of the East hung in the balance between the two combatants, who had everything respectively to hope and to fear from the issue. The Jews hoped that the entire body of their compatriots beyond the Euphrates would join in their rising, while the Romans were harassed by attacks from their German [3] neighbors, unrest among their Celtic subjects, and the worldwide convulsions that followed the death of Nero, when the political situation produced a number of rival aspirants to the throne and the military were inspired by the hope of profit

[1] Aramaic. [ED.]
[2] Literally: "Among the non-Hellenes of the interior," *i.e.* beyond the eastern frontier of the Roman Empire, "the interior" being reckoned from the Mediterranean coast inward toward the centers of the surrounding continents. [ED.]
[3] In Greek "Galatian." [ED.]

with an enthusiasm for political change. I felt it a paradox that the truth concerning events of such importance should be suffered to remain unsettled and that the Parthians, the Babylonians, the most remote populations of Arabia, my own compatriots beyond the Euphrates and the inhabitants of Adiabene [1] should be accurately informed, through my labors, of the origin, vicissitudes and issue of the war, while the Hellenes and all Romans who did not serve in the campaign should have nothing better at their disposal than flattering or fictitious accounts which conceal the truth.

The writers to whom I have alluded have the audacity to arrogate the title of "histories" to works which are not only devoid of sound information but, in my opinion, entirely vicious in their aim. Their object is to magnify the Romans and to lose no opportunity of crushing and humiliating the Jews, though I fail to see what greatness there conceivably can be in overcoming an insignificant opponent. These gentlemen, however, are not abashed either by the long duration of the war or by the heaviness of the Roman casualties or by the great abilities of the Roman commanders, who, in my humble opinion, are robbed of the glory of their intense exertions in the siege of Jerusalem by the depreciation of their achievements.

It is far, however, from being my intention to enter the lists against the champions of the Romans and to blow my own compatriots' trumpet. In describing the performances of either side I shall maintain a strict objectivity, though I may devote my comment upon events to the expression of my subjective point of view and may give vent to my personal feelings in lamenting the misfortunes of my country. She fell because she was a house divided against itself; the hands of the Romans were forced by the tyrannical leaders of the Jews, and the fire was called down upon the Holy Temple by their doing. This is testified by Titus Caesar, who executed the work of destruction, but who, throughout the siege, showed consideration for the helpless population in the power of the revolutionaries and many times voluntarily postponed the storming of the city, in the hope that the protraction of the siege might induce a more reasonable frame of mind in those responsible. My strictures upon the tyrannical brigand element are prompted by anguish at the disasters in which they have involved my country. If any reader is inclined to make capital out of them

---

[1] In modern geographical terms: "The Iranis, the 'Iraqis, the most remote populations of Arabia, the Jewish colonies east of the Euphrates, and the inhabitants of the Mosul Vilayet"—i.e. the populations of the Middle East between India on the one side and the Roman Empire on the other, among whom Aramaic was the *lingua franca* of commerce and culture, as Greek was on the Roman side of the frontier. [ED.]

against me, I can only ask him to waive the conventions of history and to make allowance for my feelings, bearing in mind that Destiny had raised our city to a higher pinnacle of prosperity than any other in the dominions of Rome, only to hurl her down in the end into the lowest abyss of disaster. All the disasters of the human race that are recorded since the beginning of time pale into insignificance, to my mind, when compared with the disasters of the Jews, and the responsibility for this lies at no foreigner's door. In such circumstances it would have required a superhuman effort to suppress my feelings; but if any of my readers is so severe a judge as to be impervious to pity, I must beg him to credit the narrative of events to the account of the book and the lamentations to that of the author.

In reality, I should be justified in taking the offensive and censuring the conduct of Hellenic historians. In the presence of contemporary events of such importance that the wars of antiquity shrink into insignificance in comparison with them, they elect to remain critics, and offensive critics, of writers who venture into this arena (though they are as much inferior to them in conception as they may be their superiors in literary execution). They content themselves with writing the history of Assyria and Media, as if they could improve upon its presentment by the ancient historians, when in reality they fall as far below the latter in literary ability as they do in intellect. The ancients all devoted themselves to writing the history of their own times, in which their personal participation in events gave clarity to their presentment and every falsehood was certain of exposure by a public that knew the facts. To place on record events never previously related and to make contemporary history accessible to later generations is an activity deserving of notice and commendation. Genuine research consists not in the mere rearrangement of material that is the property of others, but in the establishment of an original body of historical knowledge to justify a new collocation of words. I, who am an alien, have spared no labor or expense in order to dedicate to the Hellenes and the Romans a memorial of their achievements; while they of the household, whose mouths are instantaneously open and their tongues loosed when there is money to be made at the Bar, find themselves gagged and bound when there is truth to be preserved and information to be collected by laborious research in the writing of history. That literary task they leave to weaker brethren who are not even acquainted with the transactions of the prominent personalities. The least that we Orientals can do is to pay some regard to historical truth, now that it is at a discount in Hellas.

THE ANCIENT HISTORY OF THE JEWS—A REPLY TO APION
(Dedicated to Epaphroditus)

(Teubner text, Collected Works, Vol. VI., ed. by S. A. Naber: Book I. chapters 1–59)

EXCELLENCY,

In my work on Ancient History, I conceive that I have sufficiently demonstrated to anyone who may be good enough to be my reader the extreme antiquity of our Jewish race, the pureness of its original stock and the circumstances in which it first settled in the country which still remains our home. This story, which extends over a period of five thousand years, I have taken from our sacred books and rewritten in Greek. Nevertheless, I find that a considerable portion of the public is sufficiently impressed by the malicious misrepresentations of certain of our enemies to be sceptical of my account of our ancient history, and to find evidence of the recent origin of our race in the fact that its existence is ignored by the most celebrated of the Hellenic historians. I have therefore felt myself obliged to make a brief contribution to this controversy, in order to expose the malicious intent and deliberate mendacity of our detractors, to correct the ignorance of their dupes, and to enlighten all who are genuinely concerned to know the truth in regard to our origins. In support of my own contentions, I shall cite the evidence of writers who are regarded by the Hellenes as the highest authorities in the whole field of ancient history, while I shall show how the writers who have slandered and misrepresented us may be confuted out of their own mouths. I shall attempt to explain the reasons why comparatively few members of our race have been mentioned by the Hellenes in their historical works, and I shall further point out the cases in which our history has not been ignored, to those readers who either are or profess to be unaware of them.

My first impulse is to express my astonishment at those who regard the Hellenes as the only trustworthy authorities from whom the truth regarding antiquity can be learned, while they consider us and all others to be unworthy of credence. As I see it, this is an exact inversion of the facts, if we are not to be guided by empty speculations but are to allow the facts to speak for themselves. In reality, you will find that the whole of Hellenic civilization is so recent that it might be described as a growth of yesterday or the day before. I refer to the foundation of the Hellenic states, to their material inventions, and to the codification of their law, but the activity with which they have concerned themselves almost last of all in Hellas is the writing of history. On the other hand, the Hellenes admit themselves (and they will not contradict me) that Egypt, Chaldaea and Phoenicia—to omit Judaea from the list for the time being—possess the most ancient and permanent historical records. All these nations inhabit regions singularly exempt from destructive atmospheric effects, and they have taken extreme pains to leave none of their transactions unrecorded, but to have them constantly enshrined by experts in public registers. On the contrary, the region in which Hellas lies has been exposed to innumerable ravages of nature which have obliterated the record of the past; her inhabitants have been constantly under the necessity of starting life afresh, on each of which occasions they have regarded their own epoch as the beginning of all things; and their acquisition of the art of writing was a belated and a painful process. Even those who claim the highest antiquity for its introduction boast that they acquired it from Cadmus and the Phoenicians. At the same time, it would be impossible to produce a written document, either from ecclesiastical or from public muniments, which has been preserved even from that period, considering the amount of speculation and discussion that has arisen over the question whether the art of writing was known to the generation which made the expedition to Troy, an event of a much later date. The view that our present method of writing was unknown to them is the more likely to be the truth, and certainly no undisputed example of writing older than the poetry of Homer is to be found in the Hellenic world. Homer is obviously later, again, than the Trojan War, and it is said that even he did not leave his poetry in written form, but that it was handed down orally and afterwards put together from the separate cantos, which would account for the numerous discrepancies which it contains. As for the pioneers of Hellenic historical writing, by whom I mean the school of Cadmus of Miletus, Acusilaus of Argos and the successors of Acusilaus whose names are preserved, they were scarcely anterior to the Persian invasion of Hellas. Moreover, the fathers of Hellenic speculation on astronomy and religion, such as Pherecydes of Syros, Pythagoras and Thales, are unanimously admitted to have sat at the feet of the Egyptians and Chaldaeans before they produced their own exiguous works. Yet the Hellenes, who regard these works as the most ancient of all, are sceptical of their attribution to their reputed authors.

In the light of all this it is surely unreasonable of the Hellenes to pride themselves on being the sole experts in ancient history and the sole depositaries of a truthful and accurate tradition. It is surely obvious from the internal evidence that the works of their historians are not based on any certain knowledge, but on their private conjectures in regard to the events. At any rate, more often than not the effect of their books is to confute one another, and they never hesitate to make the most contradictory statements on identical points. It would be officious on my part to instruct those better informed than myself in the discrepancies between Hellanicus and Acusilaus on points of genealogy, the corrections of Hesiod by Acusilaus, or the way in which the inaccuracy of Hellanicus on most points is exposed by Ephorus, that of Ephorus by Timaeus, that of Timaeus by his successors, and that of Herodotus by everybody. Even on points of local Sicilian history, Timaeus has not felt called upon to tell the same story as the school of Antiochus and Philistus or Callias; nor have the writers of Athenian chronicles followed one another on points of Athenian history, nor Argive historians on those of Argive history. It is superfluous, however, to speak of local and specialized history, when the most highly reputed historians are in disagreement regarding the transactions of the Persian Expedition. Even Thucydides, who is considered to be the most accurate historian of his time, is accused of inaccuracy on many points by certain critics.

Investigation would probably reveal a number of reasons for this striking degree of discrepancy, but I attribute the greatest effect to two causes which I shall proceed to mention. I will begin with that which I regard as the more decisive of the two. The fact that, from the outset, the Hellenes have never exerted themselves to keep public registers of current events is surely the fundamental reason for the confusion into which writers who have subsequently attempted to deal with ancient history have fallen, and for the license to commit inaccuracies which they have enjoyed. The registration of events was not only neglected in Hellas as a whole, but even at Athens, whose people are reputed to be indigenous and solicitous for culture, there is no trace of any such phenomenon. The most ancient public records at Athens are said to be the criminal legislation of Dracon, whose date is very little earlier than the reign of the despot Peisistratus. As for the Arcadians, their claim to antiquity is disposed of by the fact that they had barely succeeded in mastering the art of writing at an even later date than this.

The absence of any previously prepared foundation in the shape of public records, which would have instructed those who desired to know the truth and would have confuted the inaccurate, is thus the principal cause of the discrepancy between Hellenic historical writers; and, as a secondary cause, we must add the following. The Hellenes who aspired to authorship had no enthusiasm for the truth, though asseverations to the contrary were perpetually on their lips, but were concerned to display their literary ability. They accordingly adapted themselves to any method which offered them the prospect of outshining their rivals in this respect. Some of them had recourse to romance, some to the deliberate flattery of states or sovereigns, others specialized in the denunciation of transactions or of those who had recorded them, as a field in which they might hope to shine. In short, they persist in a practice which is the absolute antithesis of the historical spirit. The hallmark of veracious history is the consensus, on identical points, of all students and writers, while the Hellenic historians considered that the best means of establishing their transcendent veracity was to place themselves, in describing identical events, in a minority of one. For literary form and brilliance, we Orientals must undoubtedly yield the palm to the Hellenic historians, but not by any means for veracity in the treatment of ancient history, particularly when our respective local history is concerned.

In Egypt, then, and Babylonia the registration of events was entrusted to the charge of specialists—the priests in Egypt and the Chaldaeans in Babylonia—and of all the Orientals who had intercourse with the Hellenes, the Phoenicians made the most use of the art of writing for the conduct of their private affairs as well as for the record of public events. These facts are so universally admitted that I do not propose to insist upon them further. I shall pass now to our own ancestors and shall attempt to demonstrate, as briefly as I can, that they were as particular as their neighbors (I shall not go into the question whether they were actually more particular than they were) in keeping records; that they assigned the duty to the high priests and the prophets; and that down to our own day this practice has been maintained (and, I make bold to add, will be maintained hereafter) with scrupulous exactitude.

Not only did they place this department, from the outset, under the control of the picked men who attended to the service of God, but they took measures to preserve the race of the priests unmixed and pure. An aspirant to the priesthood must be born of a Jewish mother. Wealth and rank are irrelevant to the issue, and the candidate is required to prove his descent by establishing his genealogy from the archives and producing a number of witnesses. Nor is this practice confined to Judaea. Wherever there is a colony of our nation, an accurate marriage register is kept by the priests,[1] who send duplicates to Jerusalem, in which they enter the name of the wife's father and of her ancestors in previous generations, as well as the names of the witnesses. In the event of war, which has many times occurred before now,[2] the surviving members of the priesthood reconstitute the ancient records and examine the surviving women. Women who have been in captivity are not (for this purpose) readmitted, owing to the suspicion arising from the frequency of intercourse, in these circumstances, between them and non-Jewish males. The most striking testimony to our accuracy is the fact that the priests in our community can show an unbroken descent, for two thousand years, from father to son as entered by name in the records; while any individual affected by any one of the above-mentioned disqualifications is prohibited from serving at the altar or taking any part in the cult. This is not only natural but inevitable, when it is remembered that the right to make entries in the records is not left to the discretion of private individuals and that there is no discrepancy between the entries made, the privilege being confined to the prophets, who are acquainted with the most distant past by inspiration from God, and who record contemporary events with precision.

In our literature there is not an infinity of discrepant and irreconcilable volumes. The number is limited to twenty-two, which contain a record of all time and in which we legitimately repose our confidence. Five of them are the works of Moses, containing the laws and the tradition of the creation of Man down to the death of the author. From Moses' death down to the reign of Artaxerxes, the successor of Xerxes on the throne of Persia, the prophets who succeeded Moses have recorded the events of their own times in thirteen volumes. The remaining four volumes contain hymns to God and counsels for the conduct of human life. From Artaxerxes to our own times a detailed record exists, but it is not regarded with such implicit confidence as the earlier documents, since the succession of the prophets has not been so accurately preserved. The facts themselves sufficiently explain our attitude toward our na-

---

[1] I refer to the Jewish priests in Egypt and Babylon and any other part of the world in which priests of our nation are scattered. [AUTHOR.]

[2] For example, the invasions of the country by Antiochus Epiphanes, Pompeius Magnus and Quintilius Varus, and especially the events of our own time. [AUTHOR.]

tional records. During the vast period which has elapsed since their composition, no one has ventured either to add to them or to subtract from them or to transpose their arrangement. From his birth every Jew regards them instinctively as the decrees of God, which he faithfully observes and for which he cheerfully faces death, if called upon to do so. Many Jewish captives before now, on many occasions, have been known to endure tortures and horrible forms of death in public theaters rather than breathe a word contrary to the law and the records with which it is associated. Would any Hellene endure the like in his own person? He would not even undergo a minor discomfort for the sake of preserving all the works of Hellenic literature. The Hellenes regard these as mere words improvised according to the caprice of the writers; and in adopting this attitude toward their ancient literature they are certainly justified by the spectacle of certain contemporary Hellenic writers, who venture to relate the history of events in which they have not participated themselves and in regard to which they have made no effort to learn the truth from those in possession of the facts. In the very case of our own recent war, books entitled "histories" have been published by authors who have never visited the scene of events, nor so much as come near it at the time when the events were taking place, but have put together a few statements from hearsay as an excuse for this drunk and disorderly desecration of the name of history.

My own record of the war as a whole and of the incidental details is correct, since I was a firsthand witness of all the events. I was in command of our Galilaeans so long as resistance was possible, while after my capture I was a prisoner with the Romans. Vespasian and Titus compelled me to remain in constant attendance upon them under guard, at first in chains, though afterwards I was released and was sent from Alexandria, on the staff of Titus, to the siege of Jerusalem. During this period nothing was transacted that escaped my observation. The events in the Roman camp I sedulously recorded at first hand, while I was the only person present who could understand the reports of the deserters from the Jewish side. When all my material was in the proper state of preparation, I took advantage of a period of leisure at Rome to employ the services of collaborators to help me with the Greek language, and I thus wrote out my narrative. My confidence in the truth of my presentment was so abounding that I ventured to enlist Vespasian and Titus, who had been commanders-in-chief during the war, as my first witnesses. In other words, they were the first persons to whom I presented my work, copies of which I subsequently sold to many Romans who had taken part in the campaign and to many of our own countrymen, among those who have enjoyed a Hellenic education, including Julius Archelaus, His Highness Herodes, and His Most Excellent Majesty King Agrippa himself. All these distinguished persons testified that I was a sedulous champion of the truth, and they certainly would not have hesitated to speak out if ignorance or flattery had betrayed me into a confusion or omission of any of the facts. There are, however, certain persons of no consequence who have attempted to discredit my history and who have behaved like schoolboys to whom an exercise in scandalous and paradoxical denunciation had been set in class. The truth is that no one is justified in undertaking to record the truth for the benefit of others without first accurately mastering the facts himself, either by following the events in person or by ascertaining them from those who know. I flatter myself, however, that I have personally fulfilled these requirements in the case of both my works. My Ancient History, which is, as I have mentioned, a translation from the Holy Scriptures, is the work of one who is a priest by birth and who has been educated in the philosophy which those Scriptures embody. My History of the War is the work of a participant in many of the events and an eyewitness of nearly all of them, who may claim that nothing said or done in this connection has escaped his observation. I fail to see how those persons who have attempted to controvert my statement of the facts can be acquitted of audacity. They may profess to have had access to the memoirs of the commanders-in-chief, but they certainly were not also in touch with events on our, which to them was the enemy, side.

The above digression appeared to me unavoidable if I was to stigmatize the laxity of the professed writers of history; but I imagine that I have now made it sufficiently evident that the practice of recording the events of the past is an Oriental rather than a Hellenic tradition, and I shall pass on to a few preliminary remarks directed against the critics who attempt to prove the recentness of our existence as a nation from the fact that there is no mention of us (according to them) in the Hellenic historians. I shall then cite the evidence for our antiquity from the literature of other peoples, and shall demonstrate how utterly without foundation are the slanders that have been published against our race.

ARRIAN OF NICOMEDIA

(*ca.* A.D. 90–170)

ALEXANDER'S INVASION OF ASIA

(Teubner text, ed. by A. G. Roos: Book I. § § 1–3)

WHEREVER Ptolemy son of Lagus and Aristobulus son of Aristobulus give an identical account, in their works on Alexander son of Philip, I follow this with absolute confidence in its accuracy. Where they disagree, I choose the version which, in my judgment, is the more credible and at the same time the more interesting of the two. The historians of Alexander have each their own story to tell, and there is no historical character that has been treated by a greater number of writers or with a greater discrepancy between their results. Personally, I regard Ptolemy and Aristobulus as more trustworthy authorities than the rest—Aristobulus because he was King Alexander's companion in arms; Ptolemy for the additional reason that he was a king himself and would therefore have been more deeply disgraced than ordinary mortals by failing to tell the truth; and both alike because they wrote their works after the death of Alexander and were thus exempt from any necessity or incentive to misrepresent the facts. I have also included information drawn from other works, when it has appeared to me interesting in itself and not altogether untrustworthy, under the heading of unverified anecdotes. If any reader is inclined to wonder what induced me to embark upon this work in the wake of such a host of authors, I beg him to suspend judgment until he has examined all their works and acquainted himself with mine.

APPIAN OF ALEXANDRIA

(*ca.* A.D. 90–160)

STUDIES IN ROMAN HISTORY

(Teubner text, ed. by L. Mendelssohn: Vol. I. Introduction)

IN setting out to write the history of Rome, I feel it essential to prefix a survey of all the nations under Roman rule. . . .
[The survey follows.]

Although the Romans now rule all these mighty nations, it took them fully five hundred years of arduous struggles to achieve the thorough subjection of Italy alone. During the first half of this period they lived under a monarchy, while for the remainder—after they had expelled the kings and had taken a solemn oath never to tolerate monarchical government again—they maintained an aristocratic régime under the presidency of annually elected officers. The two centuries that followed the first five saw the aggrandizement of their Empire. The acquisition of their boundless power abroad and the conquest of the majority of their subject-nationalities fall within this period. Then Gaius Caesar (who had overshadowed his most powerful contemporaries, consolidated his ascendency and made effective arrangements for its preservation) imposed himself as supreme monarch, while retaining the existing constitutional names and forms. From that time to this the Roman Empire has continued under the sovereignty of individuals whom they do not call kings[1] but emperors,[2] a title originally attaching to their temporary military commanders. In reality, however, they possess all the attributes of kingship. These emperors have been in power for approximately two additional centuries, down to the present time—centuries during which the state has reached its highest point of organization and the public revenue its highest figure, while a long and stable peace has raised the whole world to a level of secure prosperity. A few more subject nations have been added by the emperors to those already under the Roman dominion, and others which have revolted have been reduced to obedience; but since the Romans already possess the choicest portions of the land and water surface of the globe, they are wise enough to aim at retaining what they hold rather than at extending their empire to infinity over the poverty-stricken and unremunerative territories of uncivilized nations. I myself have seen representatives of such nations attending at Rome on diplomatic missions and offering to become her subjects, and the Emperor refusing to accept the allegiance of peoples who would be of no value to his government. There are other nations innumerable whose kings the Romans appoint themselves, since they feel no necessity to incorporate them in their Empire. There are also certain subject nations to whom they make grants from their treasury, because they are too proud to repudiate them in spite of their being a financial burden. They have garrisoned the frontiers of their Empire with a ring of powerful armies, and keep guard over this vast extent of land and sea as easily as though it were a modest farm.

[1] Out of respect, I imagine, for their original oath. [AUTHOR.]
[2] In Greek "autokratores," the official equivalent of the Latin "imperatores." [ED.]

No other empire hitherto has either grown so great or lasted so long. The duration of the Hellenic empires could not be extended to any great number of years, even by adding together the figures for the successive ascendencies of Athens, Lacedaemon and Thebes, between the expedition of Darius, the occasion on which they have most cause to pride themselves, and the establishment of Philip son of Amyntas' supremacy over Hellas. Moreover, their struggles were not so much for the acquisition of empire as in pursuit of mutual rivalries, while the most glorious of them were fought in defense of their own liberty against the aggression of foreign powers. Those of them who sailed to Sicily in the hope of foreign dominion met with disaster, and any who crossed over to Asia retreated immediately, after accomplishing as little in this quarter as in the other. In general, the imperialism of the Hellenes, though they struggled desperately for supremacy, never secured a firm footing beyond the bounds of Hellas herself. They were wonderfully successful in postponing the evil day of defeat and enslavement, but from the time of Philip son of Amyntas and Alexander son of Philip they appear to me to have had a history of failure which has been unworthy of their past.

As for Asiatic imperialism, the achievements and qualities associated with it will not bear comparison with the most insignificant transactions of Europe, owing to the weakness and timidity of the Asiatic nations. This will become evident as my history proceeds, since it cost the Romans a very few battles to conquer all the nations of Asia that still remain under their rule, and this although the Macedonians were championing their cause. It was their wars in Africa and Europe that wore the Romans down. As for the Assyrians, Medes and Persians, the three greatest empires before Alexander son of Philip, their combined duration would not extend to the nine centuries that Rome has enjoyed up to the present, while the size of their dominions would not, I imagine, amount to one-half of that of the Roman Empire. I base this conjecture upon the fact that the Roman Empire stretches from the setting sun and the Western Ocean to the Caucasus Range, the River Euphrates and the Ethiopians of the interior, in which quarter it extends across Egypt and Arabia to the Ocean of the East. The Romans' boundary is the Ocean in which the divine luminary rises and sets, and they are masters of the Mediterranean and all its islands, as well as the oceanic isles of Britain. The Medes and Persians never extended their sea-power beyond the Pamphylian Gulf or over other islands than Cyprus and one or two small islands off Ionia. As for the Persian Gulf (which they did also command), what is the actual extent of its water-surface?

To turn to the Macedonian power—in the period before Philip son of Amyntas it was quite insignificant and occasionally under foreign domination, while Philip's career, though admirable as a monument of laborious endeavor, was confined to Hellas and the adjoining regions. In the time of Alexander, the Macedonian Empire dazzled the world by the scale, rapidity and success of its operations; but it lasted no longer than a brilliant flash of lightning, though, even after it had dissolved into a number of separate pashaliks,[1] the glory long pervaded the fragments. My own sovereigns[2] alone maintained an army of 200,000 infantry and 40,000 cavalry, 300 fighting elephants, 2000 armored cars, and 300,000 spare equipments. These were their land forces, while their navy consisted of 2000 punts and smaller craft, 1500 men-of-war (ranging from the one-and-a-half-class to the five-class), with a complete duplicate stock of spare fittings, and 800 houseboats with gilded sterns and gilded prows for active service, on board of which the kings themselves inspected the fleet. Finally, they had a fund of 740,000 Egyptian talents in their treasury. These are the figures to which the second king of Egypt after Alexander is shown by the royal records to have raised his armaments and forces, which he left on that permanent footing. No king ever surpassed him in fiscal ability, in the magnificence of his expenditure, or in the scale of his public works; yet many of the other pashaliks evidently did not fall very far behind. All of them, however, were worn out in the second generation by mutual attrition—internal disorder being the one malady that is fatal to great empires.

Time and wisdom have enabled the Romans to excel in the extent and the success of their imperialism. They surpassed all other nations in the valor, the endurance and the industry which they brought to the acquisition of their dominions. They permitted themselves neither to be elated by success until they had thoroughly established their supremacy, nor to be depressed by disasters, though there were occasions on which 20,000 or 40,000 or actually 50,000 of their fighting men perished on a single day. The city itself was often exposed to danger, and they suffered the simultaneous and continuous assaults of plague, famine and civil disorder without ever being diverted from their ambition, until they had built up

[1] In Greek "satrapies," a "satrap" being the ancient Persian equivalent of the modern Ottoman "pasha." [ED.]

[2] I.e. the Macedonian Dynasty of the Ptolemies, which ruled Egypt and many coasts and islands of the Levant between the death of Alexander and the conquest of Egypt by Augustus. [ED.]

their Empire to its present position through seven centuries of unrelieved toil and danger, and reaped at last that prosperity which is the reward of statesmanship.

This story, which fills a vaster canvas than the history of the Macedonian Empire (the greatest of any before Rome), has been written already by many Hellenic and Roman historians. When, however, I began to study it in order to obtain a complete picture of Rome's achievement in the case of each nation whom she encountered, I found myself perpetually transported by my authorities from Carthage to Spain; from Spain to Sicily or Macedonia, or to diplomatic missions or alliances in which other nations were involved; and then back again, in an unceasing round, to Carthage or Sicily, only to be removed once more from these theaters before the curtain had fallen. At length, for my own benefit, I assembled the separate parts—for example, all the campaigns, embassies and other transactions of the Romans in Sicily down to the date at which they established the present régime in the island; or, again, all their wars and treaties with Carthage, all the diplomatic missions exchanged between the two powers, and all the blows respectively delivered and received, down to the date at which the Romans razed Carthage to the ground, annexed the Berber nation, eventually colonized Carthage themselves and established the existing régime in Northwest Africa. I followed the same procedure in the case of every nation, with a view to ascertaining the respective achievements of the Romans in their regard—ascertaining, that is, the weakness or endurance of the conquered, the valor or good fortune of the conquerors, and all the incidental conjunctures and occurrences. In the belief that others may prefer, like myself, to study the history of Rome in this form, I am now writing it nation by nation, omitting all transactions with another nation that interrupt the narrative and transferring them to the section in which that nation is treated. I have felt it superfluous to date every event, but shall note the date of outstanding events at intervals. As regards nomenclature, the Romans originally possessed a single name for each individual, like all other nations. The number afterwards rose to two, and not long ago a third name, derived from some personal defect or quality, began to be added as a distinguishing mark in certain cases, just as some Hellenes used to bear surnames in addition to their names. I shall sometimes cite the full name, especially in the case of famous men, in order to identify them; but in ordinary cases I shall refer to my characters, whether famous or not, by the names which the Romans regard as the most distinctive.

In the first three of my volumes will be found collected the crowded tale of the Romans' transactions in Italy, and all three should be regarded as Italian, though the bulkiness of the subject matter has compelled me to make a division between them. The first volume describes the achievements of the seven kings in chronological order, and I have entitled it *Roman Studies—Book of Kings*. The next, which deals with the remainder of Italy except the littoral of the Ionian Gulf,[1] is called *Roman Studies—Book of Italy,* to distinguish it from the first. The last Italian nation with whom the Romans had to deal was the great and formidable confederacy of the Samnites in the hinterland of the Ionian Gulf, and the struggle lasted eighty years, until the Romans succeeded in subduing the Samnites also, as well as the neighboring nations who had been their allies and the Hellenic colonies along the southern coasts of Italy. This volume is distinguished by the title *Roman Studies—Book of Samnium*. The remainder are entitled, on the same system, *Roman Studies—Book of the Celts, of Sicily, of Spain, of Hannibal, of Carthage, of Macedon,* and so on. The order of their arrangement is determined by the relative date of the commencement of each war, even though the end of that particular nation may fall at a later date than that of many other nations who commence their story after it. The internal disorders and civil wars of Rome herself, from which she suffered more terribly than from any of her foreign complications, are divided into volumes corresponding to the leaders in each phase—Marius and Sulla, Pompeius and Caesar, Antonius and the second Caesar surnamed Augustus, of whom the two latter fought a first civil war in partnership against the murderers of the first Caesar and a second against one another. In this last civil war of the series, Egypt came under the dominion of Rome and Rome herself became a monarchy.

These are the volumes into which I have divided the different nations, and the leaders under whose names I have grouped the civil wars. The last volume will present a survey of all the military forces which the Romans maintain, all the revenue which they draw from each nation, or alternatively the excess of their local expenditure on garrisons and naval stations, and other information of the kind. An author aspiring to describe the greatness of Rome ought properly to begin by describing his own origin. The identity of the present writer is well known to many readers and has been indicated already by himself; but, for the sake of precision, he may mention

---

[1] That part of the Mediterranean which is bounded by the mouth of the Adriatic in the north and an imaginary straight line joining the southernmost points of Sicily and the Peloponnese on the south. [Ed.]

that he is Appian of Alexandria, that he has attained to a leading position at home, that he has pleaded in the Court of Appeal at Rome, and that he has subsequently been honored with a post in the imperial service. Any reader who may be curious to learn further details will find them in the author's own autobiography.

DIO CASSIUS COCCEIANUS OF NICAEA

(*ca.* A.D. 155–235)

HISTORY OF ROME

(Tauchnitz text, stereotyped edition: Vol. V. Book LXXII. chapter 23)

THE reason which led me to write the history of the violent wars and civil disorders that followed the death of Commodus was as follows. I had previously written and published a book on the dreams and portents which inspired Severus with the hope of attaining to the imperial office. This work was read by the Emperor himself in a copy presented to him by me, and he was gracious enough to reward me with a long and complimentary letter. This reached me late in the evening immediately before I went to bed, and in my sleep the composition of an historical work was enjoined upon me by a supernatural power. This was how I came to write the history of the period at which I have now arrived; and since this essay met with an extremely favorable reception from Severus himself as well as from the public, I was inspired at this point with the ambition to write a complete history of Rome. I accordingly determined not to leave my first essay as an independent fragment, but to embody it in this larger book, in order that I might write the whole story from the beginning down to whatever point Fortune might decree, as a bequest to posterity. Our Lady Fortune has fortified me for my work in reward for the reverent and bashful spirit in which I have approached her. In my weariness and travail she has restored me with her consoling dreams. She has given me bright hopes for the future and has assured me that I shall live to finish my work and that she will in no wise blot me out. She has been assigned to me, it seems, as my guardian angel in this life, and I am in corresponding measure her devotee. The collection of my materials for a work which covers the whole history of Rome from the beginning down to the passing of Severus has taken me ten years, and the writing of my narrative twelve more. What follows will be written as fast as the events unfold themselves.

HERODIAN THE SYRIAN

(*Floruit* in the first half of the third century after Christ)

HISTORY OF THE ROMAN EMPIRE AFTER THE DEATH OF MARCUS AURELIUS

(Teubner text, ed. by I. Bekker: Book I. chapter 1)

MOST writers who have occupied themselves with the composition of historical works and have been concerned to revive the memory of ancient events have solicited an immortal reputation for culture. Should they fail to express themselves, they feared to be numbered with the mighty multitude of the obscure; but in their narratives they have paid little regard to the truth and have devoted their principal attention to phrasing and euphony, in the confident assurance that, even if they trespass on the domain of legend, they will reap their personal reward from the charm of their style, while their statements of fact will not be subjected to severe scrutiny. Some have been induced by hostility or hatred toward despots, or by regard, whether interested or genuine, for kings, countries or individuals, to endow trivial and insignificant events with an exaggerated reputation by the brilliance of their literary art. For my own part, I have not been content to take at second hand some abstruse historical subject which my readers cannot control, but have collected the materials for my work with scrupulous exactitude at a time when the memory of the events which it records is still fresh in the minds of those who are to peruse it. It is also my hope that the study of the great events which have crowded so brief a period will not be without entertainment for future generations. A comparison of this period with the whole time that has elapsed since the Roman Empire became a monarchy in the age of Augustus will reveal the fact that, during the two centuries (approximately) which separate that epoch from the times of Marcus Aurelius, there have never been such a rapid series of changes on the throne nor such dramatic vicissitudes of foreign and civil war, nor such upheavals of nations and sacks of cities both in our world and in many uncivilized countries, nor such earthquakes and pestilential conditions of the atmosphere, nor such extraordinary careers of despots and emperors (careers for which few or no parallels are to be found in the records of the past). Some of these rulers retained their power for a considerable length of time, some for a more transitory period, while others had barely enjoyed the title and honor for the brief span of a day before they went down to destruction. For the space of sixty years the Roman Empire was partitioned between a greater number of rulers than the times required, with strange and dramatic consequences. Such of those rulers as were well advanced in years may have been enabled by their experience of affairs to safeguard their own interests and those of their subjects; but others who were in their first youth were inconsequent in their private lives and revolutionary in their administration. These differences of age and authority inevitably declared themselves in differences of behavior, and I shall now proceed to relate the history of these events in detail, taking the separate rulers in chronological order.

EUNAPIUS OF SARDIS

(*ca.* A.D. 350–405)

CONTINUATION OF THE HISTORY OF DEXIPPUS—SECOND EDITION[1]

(Teubner text=*Historici Graeci Minores*, ed. by L. Dindorf: Vol. I. p. 207)

THE history of Dexippus of Athens is arranged under the years of the annual officers of Athens since their first institution, with notices of the corresponding Roman consuls, although the narrative itself begins before either consuls or officers were heard of. The characteristic feature of Dexippus' work is to omit the early period which enters into the domain of poetry, which he surrenders to pens more capable than his of imposing upon the reader, while he himself collects the more substantial evidence that presents itself as time goes on, and concentrates it in a form more susceptible of historical accuracy and genuine criticism. He forces his narrative into a chronological mold by grouping it into Olympiads and into the Athenian years of office into which each Olympiad falls. The approaches with which he prefaces his book are replete

[1] From which the author partially expurgated the attacks which in the first edition he had made against Christianity. Dexippus, of whom Eunapius was the continuator, was a celebrated Athenian historian and man of action of the third century after Christ. [ED.]

with beauty, and he displays, as he proceeds, a stately interior by removing all legendary and archaic ornaments (which he returns, like an old-fashioned drug that has lost its popularity, to the apothecaries who first prescribed it). As he surveys the Egyptian epoch, and as he presses on to the earliest dated years of office in each country and notices the founders and fathers of History, he allows it to appear, if he does not asseverate in so many words, that he has always been anticipated by his predecessors in the introduction of unhistorical elements. His own compact and concentrated narrative is like a general perfumery store, into which a picturesque and convenient assortment of historical goods is imported direct from a vast variety of makers. All events that are of historical interest from the general point of view or in connection with the lives of particularly distinguished individuals are indefatigably surveyed and arranged in Dexippus' work, which he concludes with the Emperor Claudius II.[1] Dexippus reckons up such and such a number of Olympiads with the corresponding consuls and Athenian officers, having taken a full millennium as his ground plan. He seems haunted by a fear of failing to supply his readers with a sufficiently extensive vista of years.

Having made this work my study, I have been enabled to learn and appreciate from the example of Dexippus himself the serious dangers involved in writing History in the form of an annual chronicle, specially when the author himself confesses to his readers that his chronology is not exact but is a subject on which opinions differ, and when he roundly accuses himself, as Dexippus does, of having produced a confused narrative teeming with contradictions (like a meeting without a chairman) through having committed himself to the chronological method. The Boeotian proverb "This is not music" has been constantly singing in my ears; and I have also reminded myself that the ideal aim and object of History is to record events in the light of the truth with the minimum of subjectivity, and that rigid chronological calculations, breaking in like uninvited witnesses without being called for, are of no value for this purpose. What does chronology contribute to the wisdom of Socrates or to the brilliance of Themistocles? Did summertime ever make these great men what they were? Were they ever observed to grow and shed their moral qualities like foliage according to the season of the year? Or may we assume that at least their innate and inherent qualities were in every case exercised and preserved in their activities without

[1] A.D. 268-270. [ED.]
That is, with the first year of his reign, in which that reign began and ended—Claudius having thus ruled the Empire for one year only, though some authorities treat him to a second. [AUTHOR.]

intermission or interruption? If so, what bearing has it upon the true object of History to be seized of the fact that the Battle of Salamis was won by the Hellenes at the rising of the Dog Star? Or how is the historical education of the reader improved by the knowledge that on such-and-such a day so-and-so was born, who afterward became a famous poet or musician? If the ultimate criterion of historical values is the power to survey a boundless vista of events in a short space of time by a rapid course of reading, and to anticipate the wisdom of age in the days of our youth through a knowledge of the past, which is equivalent to the knowledge of good and evil, then I am convinced that the purpose of History is directly frustrated by writers who ruin the wholesome and nutritious diet that she offers with an exotic dressing of superfluous and irrelevant episodes, and who taint the sweet waters of their story with a brackish style. There may possibly, however, be this much to be said for indulgence in superfluous knowledge: that, as Dexippus himself remarks, chronologies are almost invariably discrepant, while there is no variation in the household stories of musty antiquity. What figure is so widely celebrated in the Republic of Letters as that of Lycurgus the Lacedaemonian? Everyone is familiar with the testimony of Heaven by which Lycurgus was explicitly proclaimed divine on account of his legislative activities. Yet no writer who has related this legend agrees with any other in regard to the date at which the legislation was enacted. They are like surveyors of a building, column or other architectural monument, who all concur with one accord in the fact of its existence, but have filled volumes with elaborate discussions regarding the date of its construction. That model of accuracy, Thucydides, actually records that the great and celebrated war of which he is the historian experienced a recrudescence, the origin and occasion of which was a disagreement between the parties in dating the capture of certain towns; and the historian himself is unable to arbitrate accurately and conclusively upon the relative justification for the rival pleas. As soon as he comes down to a question of days, he betrays in spite of himself the vanity and inutility of chronological studies and researches.

After considerable internal debate and reflection on the lines indicated above, I arrived at the conclusion (which I recommend equally to all enthusiasts for chronology) that the accurate observation of days and seasons is the business of land-agents and accountants, and also, of course, of the star gazers and others avowedly engaged on mathematical studies. I must accordingly warn my readers in good time that, while I have embarked upon the task of recording past and contemporary events with sufficient confidence in my own abilities, I have repudiated, as uncongenial to the spirit of History, any obligation to date by the year or the day, since I regard the reigns of emperors as more scientific chronological units. My readers will find it recorded that such-and-such an event occurred in such-and-such a reign, but I leave it to others to trip airily into the false pretense of assigning a year or a day. When I express confidence in my own abilities, I mean that I am following authorities who were by a long way the most cultivated minds of our day and who set an inspiring example of saving from oblivion the public events of our own time and of the interval that separates it from the point where Dexippus' history ends—a period which had not previously been favored with any notable historian. In this undertaking, which is common to myself and to my predecessors, I have taken as my central point the reign of the Emperor Julian, which overlapped with my own lifetime.

This emperor was reverenced as a god by all mankind. . . .

[At this point the manuscript becomes corrupt.—ED.]

CONTINUATION OF THE HISTORY OF DEXIPPUS—PART II.

(Teubner text=Historici Graeci Minores, ed. by L. Dindorf: Vol. I. p. 215)

IN the preceding chapters the events that fill the interval between the terminal point of Dexippus' work and the times of Julian have been described as adequately as has been possible in so summary a treatment. Herewith my story approaches the hero who has been its objective from the beginning, and compels me to immerse myself in his career with all the passionate love that I bear to him. Not that I ever saw him or enjoyed the privilege of personal contact. While Julian was on the throne the present writer was quite a child. But the universal emotion of Mankind and the unanimity of the tribute which is paid to his memory have an extraordinary and irresistible effect in inspiring devotion. How could I be silent on a subject upon which no one else could bring himself to keep silence? How refrain from taking up a tale that welled even from the lips of the unlearned and ignorant, who treasured my hero's golden age as a theme of surpassing sweetness? The ordinary man did not feel the same compulsion to express this general emotion in literary form; but in my case the most distinguished and celebrated figures in the literary world refused to excuse me from a task from which I should gladly have excused myself. They pressed me with encouragement and with offers of assistance, and the Emperor Julian's most intimate friend, Oribasius of Pergamum, whose training in natural science has made him an excellent medical consultant and a still more wonderful practitioner, testified in plain language that it would be a crime on my part not to undertake the task. Oribasius proceeded to compose, for my guidance, a detailed memorandum of the Emperor's transactions, all of which he knew with the thorough knowledge of a firsthand witness; so that I found myself deprived of all excuse to shrink from the labor, even if I had desired to do so.

MARCUS THE DEACON

(*Floruit ca.* A.D. 375–425)

LIFE OF PORPHYRIUS, BISHOP OF GAZA

(Teubner text, ed. by members of the Philological Society of Bonn: chapters 1–3)

THE struggles of holy men and their divine longing and enthusiasm are a sight that rewards the eyes of the beholder. They have only to be seen in order to inspire admiration. At the same time, considerable instruction may be obtained from the story as told at second hand, when it is instilled into the souls of the readers from minds accurately acquainted with the facts. Though firsthand evidence is more credible than secondhand evidence, the latter also carries conviction when it is derived from trustworthy authorities. If the record of instructive events had remained untampered with and falsehood had not been sown among the truth, it would have been superfluous to write works on the subject. The truth sown in the hearts of each generation by oral tradition would in that case have been sufficient for the purposes of edification. As it is, time corrupts the record, either through lapse of memory or through deliberate tampering with the story, and it is this that has constrained me to undertake the present work. My object is to save the memory of so holy a man as Saint Porphyrius from being obliterated by the passage of time. The record of his achievements is a veritable prophylactic for those who read of them; and it is paradoxical that dramatic and other authors should spend their literary abilities upon witticisms and old wives' tales, while we leave the memory of holy men to oblivion, without an effort to save them from what is the last fate that they deserve. I tremble to think what a crime I should be committing if I failed to enshrine in permanent literary form the career of a man so well-beloved of God—the career of an enthusiast for the Heavenly City—from which a true understanding of life may be obtained. I shall relate his wars and contests not only against the leaders and champions of idolatry, but against an entire population possessed by madness in all its forms. The saint remembered the words of the blessed apostle, in which he says: "Put on the whole armor of God, that ye may be able to withstand in the dreadful day, and, having accomplished all things, to stand." This was the armor with which the apostle aforesaid girded himself when he entered upon his conflicts; and Porphyrius, who was faced with a struggle as severe as that of the apostle, against equally numerous and formidable opponents, was crowned with as glorious a victory as his. The trophy of this victory was erected in the heart of the enemy's country, in the shape of the holy Church of Christ which the saint founded in Gaza. The power which won it was not his human nature, but the wisdom which drew down the heavenly grace upon this passionate lover of Christ, who was prepared to do and suffer all things in His cause. How many bitter attacks at the hands of his enemies did not this wonderful character withstand? How many tricks and sneers did he not endure? The whole story of the great man would take too long to tell, and many features in it both are, and are widely regarded as being, of doubtful authenticity. I shall therefore confine myself to the narration of a few facts which I personally remember from the long period of my residence with him, when I was privileged to enjoy the society of that blessed and awe-inspiring soul whose true companions were the angels. This saint endowed with every quality of perfection is entitled to the praise of all Mankind, and while I am aware that the qualities of such a character are far beyond the reach of words, I am encouraged by his holy prayers to feel that the attempt must be made. There will be nothing pretentious in the language with which I shall clothe his beautiful story. Fine writing can add no ornament to the careers of men of his character. On the contrary, the perfection of their conduct ennobles the very words in which it is recorded. I am accordingly encouraged, in my own case, by the prayers of the saint aforementioned, to approach this literary task. Through the mediation of those prayers, I pray for the grace and assistance of Our Lord Jesus Christ to enable me, by whatever means I may, to describe the perfection of that holy man; and I beg of the readers of this work not to be incredulous of its contents. I was an eyewitness of Porphyrius' perfection as his fellow-lodger, fellow-traveler and fellow-victim of persecution down to the last day of his life here on earth.

PROCOPIUS OF CAESAREA

(*ca.* A.D. 500–565)

HISTORY OF THE WARS OF JUSTINIAN

(Teubner text, Collected Works, Vol. I., ed. by J. Haury:
Book I. chapter 1)

PROCOPIUS of Caesarea has written the history of the various wars waged by Justinian, Emperor of the Romans, against the non-Romans of East and West. His object has been to save achievements of the first magnitude from being exposed, without a record, to the victorious onslaught of infinite time, which threatens to hurl them into the abyss of oblivion, where the memory of them shall utterly vanish away. In the author's belief, the preservation of this record will have equally important and beneficial effects upon the present and upon future generations, in the event of Mankind being subjected a second time in the course of history to the pressure of a similar situation. Parties inspired with a will to war or inclined to embark upon any trial of strength have valuable lessons to learn from the results presented by research of this type, which, in revealing the course of similar struggles in the past, is able to throw a certain light upon the probable issue of the present (on the assumption that the situation is wisely handled). The author feels himself especially qualified to write this work for the sole and sufficient reason that, as the confidential adviser of General Belisarius, he was privileged to participate personally in almost all the events in question. To his mind, the proper ornament of journalism is brilliance, of poetry romance, and of history truth; and for this reason he has not suppressed the dark side in discussing even his most intimate friends, but has described in detail the conduct of all his characters (whether creditable to them or the reverse) with conscientious accuracy.

To an unprejudiced mind it will be evident that the events of these wars are at least as striking and imposing as any in history. They have been responsible for occurrences of a more extraordinary character than any of which a record survives, except (possibly) from the point of view of a reader who insists upon giving the palm to antiquity and refuses to be impressed by anything in the contemporary world. The first example that occurs to my mind is the affectation of alluding to modern troops as "archers" and reserving such appellations as "hand-to-hand combatants" or "men-at-arms" to the warriors of antiquity, in the confident assumption that in our day these military qualities are extinct. Such assumptions merely betray a superficiality and an utter lack of experience in those who make them. It has never crossed their minds that the archers in Homer, whose arm is cast up against them as an opprobrious epithet, had no horseflesh between their knees, no lance in hand, and no shield or body-armor to cover them. They went into action on foot and were compelled to take cover, either by posting themselves behind the shield of a comrade or by "leaning against a tombstone"—a position which precluded them equally from extricating themselves in defeat and from pursuing a retreating enemy, and, above all, from fighting in the open. Hence their reputation for playing an underhand part in the game of war; while, apart from that, they took so little pains with their technique that, in shooting, they only drew the bowstring to the breast, with the natural result that the missile was spent and ineffective by the time that it reached its target. This was undoubtedly the level at which archery stood in earlier times. By contrast, modern archers go into action equipped with cuirasses and knee-boots and with their quiver on their right side and their sword on the other, while some troopers have a lance slung over their shoulders and a small handleless [1] shield of just sufficient diameter to cover the face and neck. Being admirable horsemen, they are trained to bend their bow without effort to either flank when going at full gallop, and to hit a pursuing enemy in their rear as well as a retreating enemy to their front. They draw the bowstring to the face, to the level (approximately) of the right ear, which imparts such force to the missile that its impact is invariably fatal and that neither shield nor cuirass can resist its momentum. Some people, however, who choose completely to ignore the existence of these troops, persist in an openmouthed adulation of antiquity and refuse to admit the superiority of modern inventions. Misconceptions of this kind are, of course, powerless to rob the late wars of their superlative interest and importance.

[1] *I.e.* presumably slung on the elbow and not gripped in the fist. See the equestrian figure, in high relief, of King Khosru II, of Persia (reigned A.D. 591–628) at Taq-i-Bustan, reproduced in E. Herzfeld's *Am Tor von Asien* (Berlin, 1920, Reimer). [Ed.]

Unpublished History

(Teubner text, Collected Works, Vol. III. Part I., ed. by J. Haury: Unpublished History, Book I., Preface)

In my *Military History of the Roman People* up to the present date, I have arranged my description of events under the respective chronological and geographical heads to the best of my ability. In the remainder of my work I shall adopt a different principle of composition and shall set down everything that has actually occurred in every part of the Roman Empire. The reason for this change of method is that, so long as the authors of these events remained alive, it was impossible to record them in a proper manner. It was impossible, in the first place, to elude the army of spies or to escape destruction by a terrible death, if once detected, while no confidence could be placed in the loyalty of even the most intimate relations. I was accordingly compelled to suppress the causes of many of the facts mentioned in my previous volumes, and my task in the present section of my work will be to explain facts hitherto passed over in silence, as well as the unexplained causes of facts already set forth.

In embarking upon this second and almost insuperably difficult attempt to write the biography of Justinian and Theodora, I find my faculties paralyzed by the thought that the contents of the present work are bound to appear neither trustworthy nor credible to future generations, especially when I consider how Time's ever-rolling stream instills the weakness of age into every story. I am genuinely afraid of acquiring the reputation of a romancer and of being classed among the dramatic authors rather than the historians. I have, however, one cause for confidence which prevents me from flinching under the burden of my task, and that is the existence of witnesses to the truth of my story. The present generation are thoroughly well-instructed witnesses of the events in question, and I may leave it to their competent hands to convey to my readers of the future their own belief in my veracity.

There is, however, a further consideration which has long restrained me whenever I have been seized with ardor for this literary task. I suspected that its accomplishment might be detrimental to future generations. The most heinous crimes are precisely those which it is most desirable to conceal from the knowledge of posterity, if despots are not to aspire to repeat them, as they will undoubtedly do if they come to their knowledge. The rulers of the day are usually so unimaginative that they find it a godsend when the worst side of their predecessors is revealed for their imitation, and their line of least resistance is invariably to repeat the sins of the past. Eventually, however, I was induced to record the history of the events here related by the reflection that the despots of the future will also receive from them certain salutary lessons—the first being that retribution for their sins is not unlikely to overtake them, as it overtook the persons of my story; while in the second place their conduct and character will be recorded for all eternity, a consideration which may possibly check their impulse to transgress. The dissolute career of Semiramis and the frenzy of Sardanapalus and Nero would not, after all, have been known to a single individual in after generations if the record had not been bequeathed to them by contemporary historians; and it is worth remembering in this connection that the story may not prove altogether unprofitable to the possible future victims of despots in similar circumstances. Sufferers usually derive consolation from the knowledge that they have not been alone in their misfortunes. I shall therefore proceed with my narrative, in which I shall describe first the misconduct of Belisarius and afterwards the misconduct of Justinian and Theodora.

AGATHIAS OF MYRRHINA

(A.D. 536/537–ca. 582)

HISTORY OF HIS OWN TIMES

(Teubner text=*Historici Graeci Minores,* ed. by L. Dindorf, Vol. II., p. 132: Book I., Preface)

A GLAMOR of success surrounds the triumphs and trophies of war, the destruction and aggrandizement of states, and all the marvelous pageant of great events. Such prizes bring glory and pleasure to their fortunate winners, and yet, when those winners have departed this life and passed into the other world, they do not find it easy to carry their achievements with them. Oblivion breaks in and covers them, until she has distorted the true course of events; and when even the witnesses have departed in their turn, the knowledge of the facts is extinguished with them and dispersed into nothingness. Mere memory is thus an unprofitable illusion that possesses no permanence or power to keep abreast with time in its eternal prolongation. In my belief, the heroes who have deliberately risked their lives for their country or taken the burdens of others upon their shoulders would never have done what they did in the certainty that, when they had reached the height of human achievement, their fame would perish with them and would dissolve into nothing within the short span of their own lifetimes, unless what can only be regarded as a divine providence had fortified the weakness of human nature by introducing the blessings and the hopes that flow from the art of History. It is not, I imagine, the olive or the parsley crown that has inspired the victors of Olympia to strip in the ring, nor the mere desire for the immediate profits of prize money that has prompted the best soldiers to commit themselves to the well-foreseen and unmistakable dangers of war. The prize for which both have labored has been glory untarnished and imperishable, and this can only be reaped through the immortality conferred by History, whose method bears no resemblance to the ritual of Zamolxis and the follies of the Getic creed,[1] but is truly divine and immortal and is the sole means of enabling mortal beings to live forever. It would be far from easy to give an exhaustive catalogue of the blessings with which History fills the life of Man, but I can convey them in a word by expressing the opinion that she certainly does not yield the palm to Political Philosophy, and is possibly the greater benefactress of the two. Political Philosophy is an unbending and unapproachable governess, who issues her orders and lays down her regulations regarding the proper objects to seek and to shun. Her persuasions are never without an element of compulsion; whereas History relies as far as possible upon charm, seasons her lessons with a rich variety of illustrations, and presents in literary form the instances in which men have gained credit by the exercise of wisdom and righteousness and those others in which they have been led into a false step by some adverse decision or chance, until gently and imperceptibly she implants in their souls the qualities which best adorn them, and which strike the deeper and the more lasting roots for being congenial in character and voluntarily received.

As a result of prolonged consideration and reflection upon these prerogatives of History, I had felt it incumbent upon me to pay her a high tribute of admiration and to eulogize the benefactors of humanity who had already achieved the production of historical works, but I felt no obligation to set my hand to this task myself nor even to experiment in it. From boyhood, my first love had been Heroic Poetry, and I

---

[1] Zamolxis was the apocryphal prophet of the Getae or Dacians, a nomadic tribe which migrated (probably in the seventh century B.C.) from the great Eurasian steppe into the Danube valley between the Balkans and the Carpathians, bringing with it a bizarre doctrine of immortality which interested the Hellenes. [ED.]

delighted in the conceits which are the condiments of the poetic art. I am, in fact, the author of several short pieces in hexameters entitled "Daphniaca," which are embroidered with amatory romances and replete with other attractions of the kind. It also appeared to me at one time a praiseworthy and not ungraceful task to make as complete a collection as possible of recent occasional verse which was not yet public property, but was hummed on a few lips with little regard for correctness, and to prepare a revised and properly arranged edition. I have been successful in executing this project besides a number of other literary enterprises, which, although they can scarcely be said to have had a practical object, may possibly possess a certain attraction and charm of their own. Poetry, after all, is a holy and a supernatural thing. Souls are fired by it with enthusiasm (as the philosopher[1] whose father was Ariston might express it) and bring offspring of surpassing beauty to birth, if they are genuinely inspired and possessed by the divine frenzy. It was therefore my intention to devote my time to Poetry and never voluntarily to abandon these vivacious and delightful pursuits, but to follow the precepts of Delphi and to "know my own business."[2]

I happened, however, to have been born into a generation in which great wars broke out unexpectedly in many parts of the world, a number of uncivilized peoples migrated to new homes, and the life of the entire human race was upheaved by a series of obscure and incredible events with extraordinary *dénouements*, by violent oscillations of fortune, and by the extermination of races, the enslavement of populations and the settlement of others in their place.[3] The spectacle of these and other similar portents inspired me with a certain misgiving as to whether I might not be sinning against the light in leaving unrecorded and unmentioned, so far as I was concerned, events of such supreme interest and importance which might have a positive value for posterity. I arrived at the conclusion that it would not be beyond my province to make some kind of experiment in historical writing, in order that my whole life might not be spent upon romance and the curiosities of literature, but might bear some practical fruit as well. This impulse of mine was further strengthened and stimulated by pressure and encouragement from many of my friends, particularly from the younger Eutychianus, while the initiative in the matter was taken by a high official in the Civil Service whose excellent character, acute intellect and

---

[1] Plato. [ED.]

[2] The famous inscription at Delphi was "Know thyself." [ED.]

[3] A pedantic reminiscence of a passage in the preface of Thucydides. [ED.]

finished education made him the brightest ornament of the house of the Florii. This gentleman, who had my interests at heart and had devoted much attention to my advancement both in literary reputation and in worldly affairs, persisted in pressing me and in holding out high hopes of success. He would not allow me to regard the project as difficult or beyond my powers, nor to be disheartened by the novelty of the experience like a landsman embarking on his first voyage. He recommended to me as the truer view that History was not far removed from Poetry, and that the two arts were sisters in the same family, with nothing, conceivably, except the versification to distinguish them from one another. I was to consider myself equally at home in both camps and was to make my move and set to work with corresponding confidence and energy. My friend's incantations fell upon willing ears; to hypnotize me into acquiescence was no difficult task; and this is how I came to undertake the present work. I trust that the result may be worthy of my enthusiasm, and may correspond as nearly as is practicable to the importance of the events recorded.

I have first to follow the usual practice of historical writers and to explain my identity. My own name is Agathias, my birthplace Myrrhina, my father Memnonius, my profession the Law and the Bar. The Myrrhina to which I refer is not the country town in Thrace, nor any other place in Europe or Africa which may happen to bear the name, but the ancient Aeolian colony in Asia, situated at the mouth of the River Pythicus, which flows from the country of Lydia and discharges into the innermost recess of the Eleatic Gulf. I trust to repay her for my nurture as completely as in me lies by publishing a new and detailed history of all her celebrated achievements from one generation to another. For the time being, I must beg her to accept my tribute graciously and favorably and in consonance with the enthusiasm with which it is offered, and I must pass to public events of major importance.

In character, my work will not resemble that of some of my contemporaries. There are, of course, others at the present time who have already set their hands to the same task, but for the most part they have paid slight regard to the truth or to the narration of occurrences as they were actually shaped by Fortune, and have elected instead to flatter and compliment a number of persons in high places in so transparent a fashion that no one would believe them, even if they happened occasionally to tell the truth. The experts declare, however, that the exaggeration of an individual's merits is the function of journalism, and journalism alone; while History, though she too does not refuse in principle to pay a tribute to successful achievement, declines, I conceive, to accept this as her aim and characteristic. Where the physiognomy of the events suggests praise or blame, History is not at liberty to strain or embroider the facts. Yet these authors, who purport to be writing History and allow this to be indicated in the professions of their title-page, have been convicted, under examination, of playing fast and loose with the name which they have arrogated to their work. In dealing with the living (whether these happen to be sovereigns or other men of mark), they not only eulogize them in their account of their achievements (which would be a comparatively venial fault), but they allow it to become obvious to every reader that their sole concern has been to exceed the necessary minimum in praising and glorifying their heroes. On the other hand, in dealing with the dead, whatever their true character may have been, they either vituperate them as criminals and scourges of society or take the milder course of ignoring them and denying them all mention of their existence. This is their notion of consulting their momentary interests and securing personal profit by subservience to the powers of the day. They fail to realize that even those whom they honor with their praises are not particularly gratified by the attention, considering how little such threadbare flattery can possibly contribute to the establishment of their reputations. These authors must write as inclination and habit may counsel them, but I am resolved, in my case, to make the truth my first consideration, whatever the consequences may be.

I shall record transactions of public interest in the Roman and the greater part of the non-Roman world down to the present date (omitting nothing of importance), and I shall not confine my narrative to the actions of persons who may happen to be still alive, but shall devote more space, if anything, to persons now departed. Although, therefore, my entry into the historical field only dates from the time posterior to the death of Justinian, when the younger Justin had succeeded to the imperial office, I shall nevertheless go back to the antecedent period and shall make it my own business to research into any events in which no other historian has anticipated me. The greater part of the occurrences of Justinian's time have already been recorded in detail by Procopius of Caesarea,[1] and I may accordingly pass them over, on the safe assumption that they have received adequate treatment at his hands. My own task is to take up the story where Procopius leaves it, to the best of my ability. . . .

[1] The lawyer. [AUTHOR.]

[A table of contents of Procopius' History follows.]

The events noticed in the preceding table bring the story down to the twenty-sixth year of the reign of Justinian,[1] and this (if I am not mistaken) is the point at which Procopius has concluded and terminated his work. I shall therefore now proceed to the sequel, which has been my objective from the outset.

HISTORY OF HIS OWN TIMES: PREFACE TO VOLUME III.

(Teubner text=*Historici Graeci Minores,* ed. by L. Dindorf, Vol. II. p. 236: Book III. chapter 1)

IN the preceding volume I have discussed the institutions of Persia, her complicated political revolutions, and the essential points (as I see them) in regard to Chosroes and his dynasty. In spite of the considerable space which I have devoted to this digression, and of its comparatively slight connection with what precedes, I trust that it will not be felt superfluous or unprofitable, but that my readers will agree with me in finding in it a happy combination of charm and instruction. My intention, as far as in me lies, and my earnest endeavor is "to mingle the Graces with the Muses," but I am constantly drawn in another direction by the cares of this world, and follow the lead of necessity against all my inclinations. My historical work is the most important and sublime occupation that man can have; it is a loftier thing than any worldly business; and yet (to paraphrase the sweet singers of Boeotia) it is forced into the second rank in life's pilgrimage, and I am debarred from living the perfect life in the world of my desire. I ought to make a leisurely study of the literature of the past in order to take it as my model; I ought to appreciate and investigate in detail the various accumulations of historical material, and to keep my mind free to consecrate itself to these activities. Instead, I sit in chambers, where from morn to dewy eve I master innumerable briefs and go through innumerable papers. I am exasperated by the clients who pester me, and I am equally desolated when they do not pester me enough, since I am unable to earn my daily bread without toil and trouble. Yet, however hard the battle, I will not cease from mental strife so long as the passion sustains me, however invidious it may be to aim too high or "to try to find room in a pot for a pottery." Critics may write off my work as the spurious and misconceived embryo of a mind distracted

[1] A.D. 552. [ED.]

by too great a diversity of interests, yet I may at least hope to be one of those unmusical singers who give intense pleasure to themselves. It is time, however, to return to my narrative, for if I indulge in further digression I may be convicted of drifting into an offense against taste.

MENANDER THE GUARDSMAN

(*Floruit* in the latter half of the sixth century after Christ)

HISTORY OF HIS OWN TIMES

(Teubner text=*Historici Graeci Minores*, ed. by L. Dindorf, Vol. II. p. 1)

MY father Euphratas, who was a native of Byzantium, never enjoyed the advantage of a superior education, while my brother Herodotus was driven by his first taste of a legal education into rebellion against the legal career. My own conscience would not allow me to abandon the study of the law until I had completed my course, and I accordingly did so to the best of my ability; but I never went into serious practice. I did not find the work in court congenial, and still less so the regular attendance in chambers and the effort to produce a favorable impression upon clients by intellectual brilliance. I accordingly neglected my career for the highly undesirable pursuits of frivolity and dissipation. My heart was in the "rows" between the colors,[1] the excitement of the Races and the pageant of the Ballet. I also entered the Ring, and ran my folly so hard upon the rocks that I stripped my coat, and with it my common sense and all the decencies of life.

This continued until the imperial crown was assumed by Maurice, who not only displayed a paternal solicitude for his subjects, but was a lover of literature and such an ardent reader of poetry and history that he used to spend the greater part of the night in the pursuit of these interests, and consequently to encourage indolent intellects and to stimulate them by financial inducements. At that time the painful pinch of insufficient means, which was the penalty for drifting as my fancy led me, was forcing me to reconsider the advisability of my fruitless dissipations. I eventually resolved to give some point to my life by turning my energies to the present work, for which I have taken as my initial date the death of my predecessor Agathias. . . .

[1] The two parties (Blue and Green) which backed the different horses entered for the races, and which were so elaborately organized that, in the sixth century after Christ, they were a political power in Constantinople. [ED.]

I build my hopes of success upon the interest of my subject rather than the distinction of my style; for I cannot conceivably have attained to that level of culture which would justify my embarking upon literary composition, considering the careless and irregular life which I have led hitherto.

THEOPHYLACTUS SIMOCATTA[1] THE EGYPTIAN (*ca.* A.D. 560–630)

UNIVERSAL HISTORY: DIALOGUE BETWEEN PHILOSOPHY AND HISTORY

(Teubner text, ed. by C. de Boor)

Philosophy. What is this, daughter? Do solve for me this problem of which I am longing to learn the secret, with the light of truth as my golden thread to guide me through a far from legendary labyrinth. I find the approaches of speculation excessively difficult to negotiate.

History. Philosophy, queen of the universe, if it is really suitable that I should be your teacher and you my pupil, I will answer as intelligently as I am capable of doing. I agree with the philosopher of Cyrene[2] in my desire not to be ignorant of anything worth knowing.

Philosophy. I should like to ask you, daughter, by what precise means you were brought to life again yesterday or the day before; but my words are checked once more, as though a bearing-rein were choking me into silence, by the thought that most induces diffidence. Am I being deluded by a conjuring trick? You had been dead, my child, so long— ever since the imperial court was invaded by the steel-clad Calydonian despot,[3] the semi-savage ogre, the Cyclops, the Centaur who has disgraced the majesty of the purple and has degraded the imperial throne into a prize of debauchery. His other crimes I cannot mention if I am to spare my own decency or the dignity of the reader. On the same occasion I, too, was banished from the imperial precincts and could find no refuge in Attica, where my sovereign Socrates had been put to death by the Thracian Anytus. In the fullness of time, the Heracleidae[4] brought salvation, restored the constitution, purified the palace of the pollution, and at last established

---

[1] "Snubnosed Cat." [ED.]
[2] Perhaps Aristippus, perhaps Callimachus. [ED.]
[3] The Emperor Phocas, who reigned A.D. 602–610. [ED.]
[4] *I.e.* Heraclius and his family, who overthrew Phocas and succeeded him. [ED.]

me again in the imperial demesne. The imperial residence echoes with my voice as I intone my ancient Attic melodies. All is now well with me; but how, daughter, were you saved, and by whom?

History. Queen, are you unacquainted with the great high priest and president of the whole habitable world?[1]

Philosophy. Why, daughter, he is my oldest friend and my peculiar treasure.

History. Then, queen, you have discovered for yourself the answer to your query. It was he who raised me from the tomb of illiteracy and breathed into me the breath of life. I was an Alcestis, and he restored me with all the strength of a protective Heracles. With princely generosity he took me in and robed me in shining garments and adorned me with a necklace of gold. This coiffure, on which you see perched a golden grasshopper,[2] was also dressed for me by my marvelous benefactor, who irradiated me with my present glow of reason, offered me a pulpit benevolently erected for my use, and made me free to speak the truth without fear of danger.

Philosophy. Daughter, I admire the noble hierophant for the magnanimity which he displays. How steep the ascent of achievements that he has scaled, until he has taken his seat upon the lofty peak of Theology and has made his dwelling upon the summit of all the virtues. Yet he does not despise sublunary successes, and his life is devoted to the highest activities of the intellect, for he cannot bear that even this earthly world should remain in chaos. May all my lovers do me as much credit as he. Assuredly, if Thought does not philosophize on earth in incorporeal form, she has become incarnate and is dwelling in the likeness of man among men.

History. How beautifully, queen, you have woven the wreath of your eulogies; but, if you please, will you sit for a little while at the foot of this plane tree? Its branches spread invitingly, and the height and shadiness of this willow are equally admirable.[3]

Philosophy. Lead the way, daughter, and offer the ready reader a preface as a starting point for the story. I will give my mind to you like any king of Ithaca, and will not stop my ears, but will listen to your Siren-voice as you tell your tale.

History. Queen, I will obey and will set the lyre of History aquiver. Condescend to be my bow—the most musical bow that lyre could have. You are an Ocean of knowledge and

---

[1] The Oecumenical Patriarch of Constantinople, Sergius. [ED.]

[2] A meaningless allusion to a passage in the preface of Thucydides. [ED.]

[3] A fatuous reminiscence of Platonic dialogues. [ED.]

a Tethys of eloquence. In you all grace resides, "like some isle engirdled by the boundless sea."

UNIVERSAL HISTORY: PREFACE

(Teubner text, ed. by C. de Boor: Book I.)

IT was proper that Man should be adorned by his own discoveries as well as by the endowments of Nature, because there resides within him the divine and marvelous principle of Reason. By Reason he has learned to reverence and worship God and to contemplate the mirrored reflection of his own nature, and has put off his ignorance of his own physical organization. By Reason, men converge toward one another, advance from the outer surface to the inner mind, and unravel the mysteries of their own creation. Reason has showered innumerable blessings upon men and is an admirable collaborator with Nature. What Nature has left undone, Reason has completed to perfection—beautifying one thing for the sight, sweetening another for the taste, tightening or slackening some things for the touch, harmonizing others for the ear, enchanting the soul and attracting its attention by the magic of melody. Has not Reason, again, the best claim to be the inventor of the arts? Out of wool she has woven the close-knit cloth; out of wood she has carpentered the farmer's plow handle, the seaman's oar and the soldier's shield and buckler which are his very present help in war. Most important of all, Reason has arranged the infinite variety of History to delight the reader and to educate the soul. For inquiring souls there is nothing more attractive than History, as is sufficiently demonstrated by a story in the pages of Homer.

The son of Laertes was enjoying hospitality at the court of King Alcinous after having been recently cast ashore by the surf of the sea, and Odysseus had been overwhelmed with kindness. The naked and battered victim of shipwreck had been offered shining raiment to gird about his loins; he was an honored guest at the royal table; and the stranger was thus presented with freedom of speech and permission to unfold his story. The Phaeacians took such delight in the study of History that they dismissed the cup that cheers, transformed the banquet into a theater, distended their ears and gazed open-mouthed at the narrator without being in the least irritated by the length of his story—and this though the majority of the incidents kept their eyes downcast, as the company were thrilled by perilous adventures until they lived them over again.

The human mind is a greedy and insatiable feeder when it is feasted upon extraordinary tales, and this explains why the poets were the first to gain prestige as an educational force. The poets have found the souls of men inquisitive and eager to learn and perpetually thirsting for strange stories, and so for their benefit they manufacture romance, clothe their material in style, camouflage their mendacity with rhythm, and set off their jugglery with the magic girdle of meter. Such was the power of their wizardry that they were regarded as theologians, and the Gods were thought to visit them and through their mouths to lay bare to men the secrets of their hearts and the achievements or misfortunes which had occurred in their own lives. History will accordingly be found to be the universal teacher of Mankind, who lays before us what we should attempt and what we should leave alone as being unlikely to succeed. It is apparent that her counsels give to soldiers the mastery of their art, since she knows how to dispose forces and how to baffle the enemy by *ruses de guerre*. She makes them quicker to foresee the disasters of others by the signpost of their predecessors' mistakes, while in successes she increases their prosperity by building up lofty summits of achievement from small beginnings. For the old, she is a nurse and an unbroken reed; for the young, she is an admirable and supremely intelligent tutor, who powders the head of youth with the hoariness of experience and thus anticipates the gradual knowledge that comes by time. I am resolved to throw myself into her embraces, even though the enterprise be greater than my powers in view of the vulgarity of my style, the imbecility of my ideas, the awkwardness of my phraseology and the unskilfulness of my composition. If any reader should find here and there a touch of felicity in my narrative, he must attribute it to chance, for most certainly it will not be due to the competence of the writer.

PART TWO
The Philosophy of History

SECTION I.—MUTABILITY

LEAVES AND MEN

(HOMER: Oxford text: *Ilad,* Book VI. lines 146–149)

MARK ye the leaves, for men are like thereto.
  When leaves by winds into the dust are whirled
Soon the green forest buddeth millions new,
  And lo, the beauty of spring is on the world.
So come, so pass, all that are born of man.
                                    GILBERT MURRAY

MORTALITY

(HERODOTUS: Book VII. chapters 44–46)

WHEN they arrived at Abydos,[1] Xerxes wished to review his army. An observation platform of white marble had been constructed beforehand upon an eminence in the neighborhood,[2] and from this station, which commanded a view of the shore, Xerxes surveyed the land forces and the fleet. As he surveyed them, he was overtaken by the desire to witness naval maneuvers, and when these were carried out and the Phoenicians of Sidon were victorious, he was delighted with the maneuvers and with the whole expedition. When he saw the surface of the Dardanelles covered by the fleet and all the headlands and the lowlands in the territory of Abydos swarming with troops, Xerxes proceeded to congratulate himself, but after that he wept. His tears were noticed by his uncle Artabanus, who had originally expressed his opinion so frankly in a sense unfavorable to the campaign against Hellas. Per-

[1] The town commanding the Narrows of the Dardanelles on the Asiatic side. [ED.]
[2] It had been constructed by the people of Abydos under a previous order from the king. [AUTHOR.]

99

ceiving that Xerxes had begun to weep, Artabanus taxed him with it. "Sire," he said, "there is an extraordinary inconsistency in your behavior now and a moment ago. First you congratulate yourself and then you weep."—"I was struck with pity," Xerxes answered, "at the thought of the brevity of all human life, when I realized that, out of all these multitudes, not a single individual will still be alive a hundred years from now."—"In life," replied Artabanus, "we have other experiences more pitiable than that. Our lifetime is indeed as brief as you say; and yet there is not a single individual, either in this army or in the world, so constitutionally happy that in this span, brief as it is, he will not find himself wishing, not once but many times over, that he were dead and not alive. The blows of misfortune and the ravages of disease make even the shortest life feel long; and so death comes as a blessed release for Man from an evil existence, while God is proved an envious God in his dealings with Man by the taste of sweetness in life with which he tantalizes him."

THE ATHENIAN DISASTER IN SICILY
(416–413 B.C.)

(THUCYDIDES: Book VI. chapter 24–26 and 30–32; Book VII. chapters 43–44 and 84–87)

THE DECISION

NICIAS, throughout his speech, had estimated the requirements of the campaign at a high figure, with the idea that he would either deter the Athenians from it altogether or would at any rate have succeeded in reducing the risk to a minimum if he were still compelled to sail. The Athenians, however, were not cured of their eagerness for the expedition by the burdensomeness of the armaments entailed, but felt the impulse more strongly than ever, and the result of Nicias' speech was the exact opposite of his intention. His advice was approved as offering an ample margin of insurance for the safety of the expedition.

A veritable passion for the adventure took possession of all alike. The older men imagined that they would either conquer their objectives or that, at the worst, a force of this strength would be immune from disaster; the men of military age were inspired by a longing to see and study strange lands and by a confidence that they would return in safety; while the masses [1] and the private soldiers looked forward to earning money in the immediate future and to acquiring new dominions from which pay in perpetuity would be forthcoming. The intense eagerness of the majority reduced individual dissentients to passivity, for fear of being considered unpatriotic if they recorded a hostile vote. Eventually, a private member rose to remonstrate with Nicias for his unwarrantable prevarications and delays, and called upon him to declare once and for all, in this assembly of his countrymen, what armaments the country was to vote him. Much against his will, Nicias replied that, subject to further consultation with his colleagues at greater leisure, his provisional estimate of the forces required was not less than a hundred warships (the number of actual Athenian ships, suitable for use as transports, to be determined later, and the remainder to be levied from the Allies), and a minimum combined total of five thousand Athenian and Allied infantry, which should, if possible, be exceeded. The rest of the armaments which they were to provide for the expedition, and which were to include native and Cretan archers and slingers and any other arm which might be considered essential, were to be of proportionate strength. He had no sooner finished speaking than the Assembly voted the generals full powers, with authority to settle the strength of the forces and all the details of the expedition at their own discretion. Preparations were begun forthwith, contingents were demanded from the Allies, and troops were conscripted in Athens. The country had just recovered from the plague and from the continuous war; the Armistice had recruited her manpower from a new generation, and had accumulated a reserve in the treasury; and therefore little difficulty was experienced in regard to ways and means.

* * *

THE START

It was midsummer when the expedition to Sicily set sail. The majority of the Allies, the grain ships, the merchantmen and the rest of the flotilla had been given their *rendezvous,* for an earlier date, at Corfù, with the intention that the whole fleet should cross the Adriatic from that point to the heel of Italy in a single convoy. The Athenians themselves and any Allied nations who happened to find themselves at Athens went down to the Peiraeus on the day appointed, and proceeded to man their ships for the voyage. They were accompanied

---

[1] Who served as oarsmen in the fleet. [ED.]

to the port by practically the entire population of the city, both citizens and aliens. The natives, who were seeing off their respective friends, relatives or sons, as the case might be, went with mingled sensations of hope and sorrow—hope of the conquests which they might make and sorrow at the thought that they might never see their friends again, considering the distance from home of their objectives. At this point, when they were on the verge of parting from one another in perilous circumstances, they realized the risks more vividly than at the time when they had voted for the expedition. They were encouraged, however, by the evidence of their eyes, when they saw the strength of the expeditionary force collectively and in detail. As for the aliens and the remainder of the crowd, they came as spectators of what was universally regarded as an imposing and extraordinary enterprise; for this was the most extravagant and magnificent armada of Hellenic forces that had ever, up to that time, set sail from the shores of a single country. In actual numbers of vessels and troops, the expedition which sailed with Pericles to Epidaurus and subsequently with Hagnon to Potidaea [1] was not inferior. It included four thousand native Athenian infantry with three hundred cavalry and a hundred warships, fifty Lesbian and Chian warships and large additional Allied forces. Their objectives, however, were near at hand and their equipment was poor, while the present armada was expected to see long service, and was therefore provided with every requirement of both arms for operations on either element. The fleet had been brought to perfection at vast expense both to the captains [2] and to the state. The Treasury gave each sailor a drachma *per diem*, and supplied the hulls—sixty fast vessels and forty transports, with picked crews. The captains gave bonuses to supplement the official pay of the first class and the ordinary seamen, [3] provided expensive ensigns and fittings, and spared no pains in any instance to make their own ship excel above all others in speed and smartness. The land forces were conscripted by a careful process of selection, and there was keen competition between individuals in the matter of arms and equipment. A spirit of emulation reigned among the troops themselves in their respective services, and the expedition was regarded as a demonstration of the strength and power of Athens for the benefit of the rest of Hellas rather than as an

---

[1] In the spring and the summer of 430 B.C. respectively. [ED.]

[2] The "captains" of Athenian warships did not usually command them when on commission, but were private citizens who fitted up the hulls and paid the crews out of their own pockets as a kind of "super tax." [ED.]

[3] The first class seamen were usually Athenian citizens, lower ratings usually resident aliens. [ED.]

operation of war. The total sum exported from Athens on this occasion would have been found to reach an impressive figure if a calculation had been made of the public expenditure of the state and the private expenditure of the individuals serving. The public expenditure included the military chest of the high command, as well as the preliminary outlay; while the private expenditure had to cover not only the cost of the personal outfit (and, in the case of captains, the cost of what they had spent already, and would have to spend subsequently, upon their ships), but also that of the stores which, in the expectation of so long a campaign, every individual would naturally provide for himself over and above his pay. The sensation which the Armada created was due to its stupendous audacity and its brilliant display no less than to its crushing superiority of force over the prospective enemy, but chiefly to the fact that it was the greatest and most ambitious overseas expedition that had ever been attempted.

When the ships had been manned and all the equipment which they intended to take with them was at last on board, the call for silence was sounded on the bugle and the prayers customary before weighing anchor were offered up—not in each ship separately, but by all in unison, conducted by a herald. Cups were filled[1] from end to end of the Armada, and libations were poured from golden and silver goblets by the soldiers[2] and officers. The prayer was taken up by the crowd on shore, in which the citizens were joined by sympathetic foreign spectators. Then the military cheer was given, the religious service was concluded, and the anchors were weighed. The ships started in line ahead and raced as far as the island of Aegina, whence they made their best speed to Corfù, which was the *rendezvous* for the rest of the flotilla.

* * * *

THE LAST ATTACK

Demosthenes[3] decided that it was impossible to approach and scale the Heights by daylight without being observed. He therefore gave orders that rations for five days should be

---

[1] Literally "mixed," since the Hellenes ordinarily diluted wine as we do spirits. [ED.]

[2] *I.e.* the heavy infantry transported on the warships, who belonged to a wealthier class than the crews. [ED.]

[3] The Athenian second-in-command, who had just arrived with reinforcements for Nicias when the siege of Syracuse by the original expeditionary force was on the point of failure. The heights which Demosthenes now attempted to capture command Syracuse in much the same way as the Heights of Abraham command Quebec. [ED.]

served out to the troops; took over all the engineers, with supplies of ammunition and of materials required for fortifying a new position in the event of success; paraded the entire army in the early hours of the night under his own command, with Eurymedon and Menander as his colleagues; and advanced against the Heights, Nicias remaining in reserve within the Athenian lines. They struck the Heights at Euryelus, where the first expeditionary force had originally scaled them, took the Syracusan pickets by surprise, attacked and captured the Syracusan post established at this point and inflicted casualties upon the garrison. The majority of the garrison, however, immediately scattered in the direction of the three cantonments which had been established on the Heights in outworks of the main line, and which were held respectively by the Syracusans, the other Sicilian Hellenes and their non-Sicilian allies. The fugitives brought information of the attack and reported it to the six hundred Syracusan troops who were in the front line on this sector of the Heights. These troops immediately moved forward in support, but were met by Demosthenes and the Athenians and were forced to retire after offering a vigorous resistance. The Athenians immediately continued their advance, in order to push on to their objectives before their *élan* was expended; while other detachments, detailed for this purpose when the attack was first launched, proceeded to capture and disorganize the traverse previously constructed by the Syracusans, the garrison of which failed to hold its ground. The Syracusans, their allies and the force commanded by Gylippus[1] now began to move forward in support from their cantonments; but the audacity of the night attack had taken them by surprise; they were in a state of panic when they came into collision with the Athenians, and at first they were overpowered and compelled to retreat. In the course of their advance, however, the Athenians were abandoning their formation, partly on the assumption that the battle was already won, and partly in an effort to dispose as quickly as possible of all enemy forces which had not yet been engaged and which might find an opportunity to re-form if there were any slackening in the Athenian attack. At this critical moment the Boeotians first arrested the Athenians' advance, delivered a counterattack, forced them to retreat, and turned the retreat into a rout.

When this occurred, the Athenians so completely lost their discipline and their presence of mind that it has not been easy to obtain any consecutive account of what followed from either side. Even in operations by daylight, which are less

[1] The Spartan military attaché at Syracuse, who saved the situation. [Ed.]

confusing, the individual combatants find it difficult to follow the general development of the action beyond their own immediate sector, and precise information is therefore hardly to be expected from participants in the only night operations of the late war in which considerable forces were engaged. Although there was a bright moon, there was only the low visibility characteristic of moonlight, which enables the eye to discern a human form in its field of vision without enabling it to identify it with any confidence as a friend's. Masses of infantry belonging to both armies were maneuvering in a confined space, and on the Athenian side some troops were already giving way, while others were still advancing victoriously in the first impetus of their attack. A considerable portion of the Athenian reserves had also either just scaled or were in the act of scaling the heights, so that they did not know what points to take as their objective. From the moment that the rout had begun, the troops in front had completely lost their formation, and the noise made it difficult to distinguish friend and foe. The Syracusans and their allies were cheering vociferously[1] to one another to follow up their victory, while engaging all who came into collision with their lines. The Athenians were attempting to establish contact with one another, and were treating all troops approaching from the opposite direction as enemy forces, although actually they might be friends already in retreat towards the rear. They were also constantly challenging one another for the password, which was their only means of mutual identification, but which threw their own ranks into confusion when everyone was challenging at once. Incidentally this betrayed the Athenian password to the enemy, while it was not so easy for the Athenians to discover theirs, since as victors they had kept their formation and were therefore able to identify one another more easily. In consequence, whenever the Athenians encountered a weaker body of the enemy, the latter escaped through their knowledge of the Athenian password, while whenever the Athenians failed to answer the enemy's challenge, they were annihilated. They suffered most of all, however, from the cheering, which created confusion owing to its similarity on the two sides. Whenever a cheer was given by the Argives, Corcyraeans and other Dorian[2] contingents serving with the Athenians, the Athenians fell into a panic, and the same thing happened among the enemy. When once

---

[1] In the dark there was no other practicable method of communication. [AUTHOR.]

[2] "Dorian" was the name of one group of Greek dialects spoken in the Hellenic world, in which it corresponded to such groups as "Romance" or "Teutonic" in modern Europe. [ED.]

their formation had been lost, friends and fellow-countrymen came into collision with one another at a number of points in the line, until eventually they not only lost their nerve, but actually came to blows and could only be parted with difficulty. In their flight from the pursuing forces, many met their death by throwing themselves over the cliffs, owing to the narrowness of the way down from the Heights; and although the majority of the survivors who reached the plain succeeded in escaping to the camp,[1] a certain number of the newcomers [2] lost their way and wandered over the country until they were overtaken by daylight, when the Syracusan cavalry cut them off and annihilated them.

• • •

THE LAST STAND

With the return of daylight, Nicias set his forces in motion, and the Syracusans and their allies attacked him, as before, with converging volleys of missiles. The Athenians pushed forward towards the River Assinarus, partly under the pressure of converging attacks from a powerful cavalry supported by other arms, from which they expected some relief if they succeeded in crossing the stream, and partly under the stress of exhaustion and the stimulus of thirst. When they reached the bank they threw themselves in, and all discipline was at an end. Each individual soldier was determined to be the first to cross, and the attacks of the enemy were already making it difficult to cross at all. Forced, as they were, to proceed in a huddled mass, they stumbled over and trampled upon one another, and some of them were killed instantaneously by the points of their weapons, while others were tangled in the baggage and carried away by the stream. The opposite bank of the river, which was precipitous, was lined by the Syracusans who showered missiles from above upon the Athenians, most of whom were drinking greedily and jostling one another in the hollow bottom of the river. The Peloponnesians came down to close quarters and began a butchery, especially of those in the river. In an instant the water had been fouled, but nevertheless the majority continued to drink it, mudded and bloodstained as it was, and even fought to reach it. Eventually, when the corpses were piled in heaps in the river and the force had been cut to pieces—the main body in the riverbed

---

[1] Especially the troops belonging to the original expeditionary force, who were better acquainted with the topography. [AUTHOR.]

[2] Members of Demosthenes' second expeditionary force, which had only recently arrived. [ED.]

and the fugitives by the cavalry—Nicias surrendered personally to Gylippus, whom he trusted more than he did the Syracusans, and begged him and the Lacedaemonians to do what they liked with his own person, if only they would stop their butchery of his men. After this, Gylippus ordered that quarter should be given; all survivors not secreted by their captors (as a large number were) were rounded up as prisoners; and the three hundred men who had broken through the cordon of pickets during the night were captured by troops dispatched in pursuit. The percentage of the Athenian force officially collected as prisoners was not large, while the number of those spirited away was so great that all Sicily was filled with them, the reason being that, unlike Demosthenes' force, they had not become prisoners by a formal capitulation. A very high percentage was actually killed outright, for the terrible carnage of this action was never exceeded on any other occasion in the late war. Considerable numbers had also been killed previously in the frequent engagements that had accompanied the march. Nevertheless, many succeeded in saving themselves—some immediately, and others by escaping at a later date, after having been reduced to slavery. These found an asylum at Catana.

The Syracusans and their allies now concentrated their forces, provided for the transport of the captured material and of as many of the prisoners as possible, and marched back to the city. All Athenian and Allied citizens who had been captured were deposited in the quarries as being the safest method of internment, with the exception of Nicias and Demosthenes, who were put to death—against the will of Gylippus. Gylippus looked forward to bringing the enemy commanders to Sparta as a crowning personal triumph. Although one of them, Demosthenes, ranked among Sparta's greatest enemies in virtue of the events at Pylos and in the island of Sphacteria,[1] the other counted, in the same connection, as one of her greatest friends. It was thanks to the exertions of Nicias, in persuading the Athenians to make peace, that the Lacedaemonians captured in the island had secured their release. In return for this service the Lacedaemonians were kindly disposed towards him, and it was largely owing to his confidence on this account that he had surrendered to Gylippus. Certain Syracusans, however, who had been in correspondence with him, were afraid, it was said, of his making revelations under torture which might trouble their momentarily smooth waters; while others, particularly the Corinthians, were afraid of his utilizing his wealth in order to

---

[1] Where he had captured a Peloponnesian force in 425 B.C. [ED.]

purchase his escape by bribery and so living to disturb their peace again. These parties persuaded the allies to concur in his being put to death, the motive for the crime being substantially as I have described it. Of all Hellenes in my generation he least deserved such a fate, considering the strictness with which his life was regulated on the highest principles.

The prisoners in the quarries were barbarously treated at the beginning by the Syracusans. Overcrowded as they were in a narrow shaft, they were still tormented at first by the sun and the stifling heat, to which they were exposed without a roof to cover them, while the sudden advent of the cold autumn nights, with their violent change of temperature, upset their systems and generated disease. The overcrowding compelled them to perform all their bodily functions in the same place; the corpses of the victims who succumbed to their wounds, to the change of temperature and to other causes, were heaped upon one another; and intolerable stenches arose. In addition they were afflicted with the pangs of hunger and thirst,[1] and were spared no single one of the sufferings inevitably entailed by imprisonment in such a death trap. For some seventy days they had to endure this life, promiscuously herded together. At the end of that period they were all sold into slavery, except the Athenians and those Sicilian and Italian Hellenes who had joined the expedition. An accurate figure for the total number of prisoners would be difficult to give, but it was certainly not less than seven thousand.

This tragedy, which was the most colossal that occurred in the late war (and, in my opinion, in all recorded Hellenic history), conferred unparalleled glory upon the conquerors and inflicted unparalleled disaster upon the victims. They were utterly defeated in every way; there was nothing on the small scale in any of their sufferings; fleet, army and everything else was annihilated in the literal sense of the word, and few returned to see their homes out of the many who had left them.

THE BURDEN OF MACEDON

(POLYBIUS: Book XXIX. chapter 21)

THE fate of Macedon has often vividly recalled to my mind the words of Demetrius of Phalerum.[2] In his work on Fortune,

---

[1] Their daily ration, over a period of eight months, was half a pint of water and a pint of cereals. [AUTHOR.]

[2] An Athenian philosopher and statesman, who governed Athens in the Macedonian interest from 317 to 307 B.C. [ED.]

in which his object is to indicate unambiguously to his fellow-men the mutability of this principle, Demetrius interrupts his narrative of the epoch of the overthrow of the Persian Empire by Alexander in order to make the following observations:

"In order to realize the baffling character of Fortune there is no necessity to take account of vast periods of time extending over many generations. The past half century provides a sufficient example. Supposing that, fifty years ago, some divinity had foretold the future to the Persians and the King of Persia or to the Macedonians and the King of Macedon, do you imagine that they would ever have believed that at the present date the very name of Persia—at that time mistress of almost the entire habitable world—would be utterly blotted out, while the Macedonians, whose name was previously unknown, would have the world at their feet? In my belief, however, this is only one of the signs and wonders by which Fortune is perpetually demonstrating to Mankind her power, her incommensurability with human life, and her revolutionary practice of disconcerting human reason. In setting Macedon in the seat of mighty Persia, she has signified the fact that her investiture of Macedon with the insignia of empire is equally revocable and contingent upon her discretion."

In the case of Perseus[1] this eventuality has actually come to pass. The words of Demetrius have proved themselves inspired and prophetic; and, now that my own narrative has brought me to the epoch of the overthrow of the Macedonian Kingdom, I feel that, as a firsthand witness of the event, I should not be justified in passing it over without pointing the moral myself and giving his due to Demetrius. To my mind, there is a supernatural prescience in his dictum. He has accurately anticipated the course of events almost a century and a half in advance.

THE BURDEN OF ROME

(POLYBIUS: Book VI. chapter 57)

THE disintegration and transformation to which everything in the Universe is exposed may really be taken for granted as a self-evident corollary to the Uniformity of Nature. There are, however, two possible processes by which the disintegration of any given type of commonwealth may be effected—one external and the other internal; and while the external process

[1] The last King of Macedon, who was conquered and deposed by Rome in 168 B.C. [ED.]

is not amenable to scientific study, the internal obeys fixed laws. I have already described the successive phases of political development, and the transitions from one phase to the other, sufficiently to enable readers capable of drawing the logical deductions from the present inquiry to forecast the future for themselves. In my opinion, the future is clear. In the case of any commonwealth which has repelled a series of acute dangers and has subsequently attained to a position of undisputed predominance and supremacy, it is evident that the violent influx of prosperity will produce a more extravagant standard of living and an excessively keen competition between individuals for office and other objects of ambition. As these tendencies develop, a process of deterioration will be initiated by the thirst for office and the reproach of an undistinguished career, as well as by the pretentiousness and extravagance of the standard of living. The nominal responsibility for this transformation will attach to the masses, when they are inspired with a sense of injustice by the material greed of some of their masters, and with a false conceit by the insincerity of others in pursuit of a political career. At this point the masses become so intensely exasperated and so completely guided by passion that they repudiate all subordination to or even equality with the upper classes and identify the interests of the community with their own. When this point is reached, the commonwealth acquires the flattering appellations of Liberty and Democracy, while it is subjected to the appalling reality of the "despotism of the crowd."

THE FULFILMENT OF SCRIPTURE

(POLYBIUS: Book XXXVIII. chapter 22;[1] PROCOPIUS:
Book V. chapter 22 [12-22])

CARTHAGE: 146 B.C.

CARTHAGE had flourished for seven centuries since her first foundations; she had been mistress of broad lands and islands and seas; she had rivalled the greatest empires of the world in the scale of her armaments and her revenues and in the number of her elephants and ships; and she had surpassed them all in energy and courage, for, even after she had completely disarmed, she had held out for three years against a terrible war and a terrible blockade. When Scipio saw this great and an-

---

[1] At second hand, from the paraphrase of the original which is given by Appian—*Roman Studies: Book of Africa*, chapter 132. [ED.]

cient city meeting her end forever in utter annihilation, he is
said to have burst into tears and not to have concealed the
fact that he was weeping for the enemy. For a long time he
remained wrapped in his own thoughts; he realized that cities
and nations and empires were destined, by God's providence,
to pass away; he remembered that this had been the fate of
Ilion, a city prosperous in its day; the fate of the Assyrian and
the Median and the Persian Empires, which each in turn had
been the greatest in the world; the fate of the Macedonian
Empire, the most recent and most brilliant of them all. Then,
whether deliberately or unconsciously, he repeated aloud the
lines:

> A day of doom shall dawn, and on that day
> Shall Holy Ilion's city pass away,
> And Priam, that great spearman, and the host
> Of Priam's people in their proud array.

Polybius, whose pupil Scipio had been, asked him in so many
words what he intended by the quotation, and Scipio is said
to have thrown aside all reserve and to have uttered the name
of his own country, on whose behalf he was filled with fore-
boding by his vision of the destinies of Man.[1]

· · ·

ROME: A.D. 537

MEANWHILE a second attack, which I shall proceed to describe, was delivered by the Goths against the Aurelian Gate.
Outside this gate, and about a stone's throw from the *enceinte*
of the city, there stands the mausoleum of the Emperor Hadrian, which is one of the wonders of the world. It is built of
Parian marble, and the courses are laid without any interstice
between the blocks or any filling of inferior material between
the outer and inner faces. It has four symmetrical sides, each
nearly a stone's throw in length and rising higher than the city
wall. On the summit there are statues of men and horses,
carved in the same marble and of exquisite workmanship.
This mausoleum was regarded as an outwork of the city and
was accordingly enclosed by the ancients, and incorporated in
the fortifications, by the construction of two curtain walls running to the mausoleum from the *enceinte*. In fact, the mausoleum is like a lofty bastion flanking the gate in this sector. . . .
The Goths proceeded to deliver their assault upon the Aure-

[1] Polybius has recorded this at first hand. [APPIAN.]

lian Gate and the Tower of Hadrian. They did not employ artillery, but brought up quantities of ladders. They hoped to put the enemy out of action more effectively by a concentrated discharge of small-arms, and thus to overpower the insufficient garrison without difficulty. They advanced under cover of their shields, which were fully as large as those in use among the Persians, and succeeded in arriving within close range of the opposing force before they were detected, by taking cover behind the cloister which runs to the sanctuary of Peter the Apostle. They broke cover and opened their attack with such suddenness that the defenders were unable either to bring into play their "throwers" [1] (a weapon which can only hit targets at its own elevation) or even to reply to the assailants with their small-arms, which were rendered ineffective by the shields. The Goths pressed their attack, swept the battlements with their missiles, and were on the point of setting their ladders to the walls. The defenders of the mausoleum found themselves almost encircled; whichever way they turned, they were enfiladed from the flank or rear; and for some moments they were at their wits' ends how to extricate themselves without disaster from their perilous situation. It was not long, however, before they recovered their presence of mind sufficiently to break up the majority of the statues, which were of colossal proportions, lift the massive marble fragments in both hands, and hurl them down perpendicularly upon the heads of the enemy, who momentarily broke under their impact. . . .

DEATH THE LEVELER

(PLUTARCH OF CHAERONEA (*ca.* A.D. 46–125), *Parallel Lives,*
Teubner text, ed. by C. Sintenis: Vol. III. pp. 270–4
= *Life of Pompeius Magnus,* chapters 77–80)

WHEN the plan of seeking asylum in Egypt had carried the day, Pompeius and his wife sailed from Cyprus in a Seleucian warship, his suite accompanying him partly on other warships and partly on board merchantmen. After an uneventful passage across the open sea, he received information that King Ptolemy was encamped at Pelusium with armed forces and was conducting military operations against his sister. He accordingly made Pelusium, after sending a representative to the king in advance to explain his position and to ask for assistance. Ptolemy himself was quite a child, but his all-powerful

---

[1] *I.e.* the heavy artillery, which slung large masses of stone. [ED.]

minister Pothinus summoned the Council of State, in which a Privy Councillor was another name for a creature of Pothinus, and declared the debate open to all members present. It was a sufficient outrage that the fate of Pompeius Magnus should be debated by a eunuch like Pothinus and a paid elocution master like Theodotus of Chios and an Egyptian like Achillas, who were the principal Councillors in this noble company of chamberlains and valets; and while he waited for this tribunal to deliver its verdict, Pompeius, whose dignity forbade him to owe his life to Caesar, was forced to ride at anchor in the offing. The Council as a whole was divided in opinion between two motions, one in favor of refusing admission to Pompeius and the other of inviting him and offering him hospitality. Theodotus, however, elected to advertise his dialectical and forensic ability by condemning both motions as involving excessive risks. If they offered hospitality, they would have Caesar for their enemy and Pompeius for their master; if they refused asylum, they would be held responsible by Pompeius himself for having ejected him and by Caesar for having failed to arrest him. The best course was to summon the individual and then to put him out of the way— a solution which would ingratiate them with one of the two rivals and relieve them from all fear of the other. The orator is reported to have added, with a smile, that "Dead men do not bite."

The Council adopted Theodotus' motion and entrusted its execution to Achillas. This personage took with him an old officer of Pompeius' named Septimius, an ex-non-commissioned officer named Salvius and three or four orderlies, and rowed out to Pompeius' ship. As it happened, all the most distinguished members of his suite had come on board in order to learn what action was being taken; and when they saw nothing resembling the brilliant reception with royal honors upon which Theophanes [1] had anchored his hopes, but a few individuals rowing out to them in a single fishing boat, they suspected that the discourtesy was significant and advised Pompeius to back oars and stand out to sea while they were still out of range. By this time, however, the boat had arrived sufficiently close for Septimius to forestall them by rising to his feet and saluting Pompeius in Latin with the title of "General." Achillas also greeted him in Greek and invited him to trans-ship into the fishing-boat. He explained that there was a long stretch of shoal water full of submerged sand banks which a vessel with the draft of a warship would be unable to negotiate. At this juncture, the crews of some of the

---

[1] Pompeius' Mitylenaean secretary. [ED.]

Egyptian naval vessels were observed to be going to their quarters, while infantry were occupying the line of the shore, so that it appeared too late to escape, even if they changed their minds, and there was the further consideration that the mere betrayal of uneasiness would give any would-be murderer an excuse for executing his nefarious design. So Pompeius bade adieu to Cornelia, whose grief already anticipated her husband's end, and gave orders for two non-commissioned officers, one of his freedmen called Philip and an attendant of the name of Scythes to precede him on board. Achillas and his party were already greeting him from the boat, when he turned to his wife and son and repeated the lines of Sophocles:

> Who merchandises with a despot, he
> Is straight his slave, how free soe'er he be.

These were the last words which he spoke to his family before he embarked.

Although the distance from the ship to the shore was considerable, not a single friendly remark was addressed to him by his fellow passengers, until he looked at Septimius and said to him: "I am surely not mistaken in recognizing you as an old companion in arms?" Septimius only nodded in answer without adding a word or making any gesture of friendship. A second period of silence followed, during which Pompeius was studying a speech in Greek which he had written out in a little notebook and intended to address to Ptolemy. As they approached the shore, Cornelia, who, with her friends on board the warship, was watching in an agony of anxiety to see the development of events, began to take courage when she saw a large body of the royal troops assembling at the landing place as if they were to form a guard of honor. At this moment Pompeius, who was taking Philip's hand to assist him to his feet, received a first swordthrust in the back from Septimius, which was the signal for Salvius and Achillas to draw their weapons. Pompeius pulled his cloak over his face with both hands, uttered one groan and received the blows unflinchingly, without saying a word or committing an act that was unworthy of his character. He was in his sixtieth year, and met his death on the day following his birthday.

When the party on board the ships witnessed the assassination, they sent up a wail which was audible from the shore and hastily weighed anchor to secure their own salvation. A fresh breeze favored them as they stood out into the open sea and deterred the Egyptians from their first impulse to pursue them. The assassins cut off Pompeius' head and threw the body naked out of the fishing boat on to the shore, where they left it exposed to the curiosity of the crowd. Philip kept watch over it until they had feasted their eyes to their fill, and then washed it in the sea and wrapped it in some of his own underclothing. Finding himself without any of the other requisites, he looked round the shore and found the remains of a little fishing boat which, though decayed, were sufficient to furnish the bare minimum of fuel necessary for the consumption of a naked and mutilated corpse. While he was collecting these into a pile, he was accosted by an old man of Roman nationality, who in his early youth had served in Pompeius' first campaigns, and who said to him: "As I see, sir, that you are proposing to bury Pompeius Magnus, may I ask who you are?" When Philip told him that he was Pompeius' freedman, the old man rejoined: "But you must not monopolize this honor, and I beg you to accept my assistance. This is not only a sacred duty but an unexpected privilege for me, which will partly console me for my exile from home. The painful experiences through which I have passed will have brought me the one reward of performing with these hands the last offices for the greatest general under whom Romans have ever served." This was how Pompeius received the rites of burial. On the following day Lucius Lentulus arrived from Cyprus, in ignorance of what had occurred, and was coasting along the shore when he saw a corpse burning on a pyre and Philip standing beside it. Before he was able to distinguish who they were, he called: "Who is it who has fulfilled his destiny and found his rest in this forlorn place?" And then, after a short interval, he added, with a groan: "Perhaps it is you, Pompeius Magnus." A few minutes later he went ashore, was placed under arrest, and suffered the fate of his leader.

This was the end of Pompeius. When, not long afterwards, Caesar arrived in an Egypt reeking with the pollution of this abominable crime, he turned away in disgust from the individual who came to present him with Pompeius' head, and wept when Pompeius' seal was placed in his hands. The device on the seal was a lion bearing a sword. Achillas and Pothinus were put out of existence by Caesar himself, while the king was defeated in action in the neighborhood of the Nile and was never seen again. Theodotus the "uplifter" escaped Caesar's justice by fleeing from Egypt and becoming an outcast and a vagabond. Eventually Marcus Brutus, who had taken Caesar's life and had come into power, discovered Theodotus in Asia Minor and put him to death with every refinement of torture. The remains of Pompeius were conveyed into the hands of Cornelia and were buried by her at Albano.

A CIRCUMVENTION OF TIME

(POLYBIUS: Book VI. chapter 52¹⁰–54⁴)

THE Italians possess an innate superiority over the Phoenicians and Berbers, both in physical strength and in animal courage; but they also enormously stimulate the development of their young men in this direction by the training that they give to them. The description of a single institution will suffice as an example of the efforts made by the Roman commonwealth to breed men prepared to endure all things for the sake of winning honor and glory in the sight of their countrymen.

When any of their distinguished men departs this life, the funeral ceremony includes a procession in which the corpse—usually erect and exposed, or more rarely recumbent—is carried in state to the so-called "Rams" [1] in the *piazza*. The whole people gathers round, and the platform is ascended by a speaker [2] who delivers an oration upon the character of the deceased and his career. By this recital a vivid remembrance of the past is aroused in the minds of the public, including those who have no personal connection with the dead as well as those who have shared in his achievements, and the sympathy thus created is so intense that the fatality is felt as a public loss which is not confined to the mourners. Later, when the funeral is over and the customary rites have been performed, they place the likeness of the deceased, enclosed in a miniature shrine of wood, in the place of honor in his ancestral mansion. This likeness is a bust designed with a minute and conscientious realism in modeling and in contour. The whole series of likenesses is unveiled on the occasion of public festivals and decorated with scrupulous devotion; and whenever a distinguished member of the house departs this life, they parade these likenesses in the funeral procession, selecting individuals with the closest possible resemblance to the original, both in height and in profile, for the honor of wearing them. These impersonators assume the appropriate uniforms—white with a scarlet border, if the original was a consul or a praetor; scarlet throughout, if he was a censor; and white shot with gold, if he had celebrated an official triumph or attained some equally signal honor. The impersonators themselves ride in carriages, preceded by the Rods and Axes and the other insignia which ordinarily accompany high offices of state, in accordance with the official rank actually attained in his career

[1] A platform decorated with the rams of captured Carthaginian warships. [ED.]

[2] The son of the deceased, if he survives him and happens to be in Rome, or, failing a son, some other relative. [AUTHOR.]

116

by the individual impersonated. When they arrive at the platform they all take their seats in order of precedence on ivory thrones, and it is not easy to imagine a spectacle which would make a happier impression upon a young man of good character and wholesome ambition. Who would not be affected by seeing the likenesses of the revered and celebrated men of the past gathered together before his eyes in all the animation of real life? What spectacle could be more impressive? And then the speaker who is to deliver the funeral oration does not confine himself to the individual just deceased, but proceeds, after exhausting his immediate theme, to recite the successes and achievements of his predecessors, beginning with the earliest there represented. By this perpetual commemoration of the glorious dead, the fame of all who have distinguished themselves by any noble action is immortalized, and the story of those who have deserved well of their country becomes a household word which is handed down to posterity. Most important of all, young men are stimulated to endure all things for the sake of the common weal, by the hope of winning the fame that does not fail to attach itself to those who deserve it.

SECTION II.—PRIDE, DOOM AND THE ENVY OF THE GODS

(Hybris, Ate, Phthonos)

THE AUTHORIZED VERSION

(HERODOTUS: Book VII. chapter 10; δ^2—ϵ)

Artabanus to Xerxes:

"In my experience, good judgment is more valuable than any other accomplishment. Even if something goes amiss, the soundness of the original judgment remains unaffected and its frustration is due to Fortune. Conversely, bad judgment may reap a windfall if Fortune elects to favor the result, but it remains bad judgment none the less. You observe how God blasts with his thunderbolt the animals that overtop their fellows, and how he cannot bear them to show off, while the little animals never irritate him; and you also observe how he invariably directs these shafts of his upon the highest houses and the tallest trees. God loves to cut short everything that overtops its kind. In this way, a great army is destroyed by a small army in certain circumstances—as, for instance, when God in his envy sends down panic upon them, or thunder. Then they perish, and their last state is unworthy of their first. God suffers no one to be proud except himself."

THE WISDOM OF SOLON

(HERODOTUS: Book I. chapters 32–34)

CROESUS was so much exasperated by Solon's observations regarding human happiness that he exclaimed: "My dear sir, is *my* happiness so abjectly insignificant to your Athenian mind that you actually place me lower in the scale than private individuals?" "Sire," replied Solon, "I know for a fact that the Godhead is invariably envious and destructive, and then you question me regarding human life! The passage of time provides many unwelcome spectacles and many unwelcome experiences. I estimate the natural term of human existence at seventy years. These seventy years amount (omitting intercalary months) to 25,200 days; or, alternatively, if every second year is reckoned as one month longer, in order to keep the calendar year and the astronomical year in correspondence, the number of intercalary months, over a period of seventy years, amounts to thirty-five, containing 1050 days. Out of all these days which go to make up the seventy years and which amount in all to 26,250, not one day brings forth anything remotely resembling the offspring of another; and therefore, Sire, Man is nothing but Misfortune. I imagine that you personally are immensely rich and that you have a vast number of subjects; but I cannot yet give you the title which is the object of your question, before I hear that you have been fortunate in your end. The millionaire is not in the least degree more prosperous than his neighbor who lives from hand to mouth, unless Fortune so far favors him as to guide him to a happy end without a shadow on his horizon. Many multi-millionaires are unprosperous, and many men of moderate means are fortunate. The unprosperous millionaire has two advantages, and two only, over the real man of fortune, whereas the latter has innumerable advantages over the unprosperous millionaire. The millionaire is better equipped for satisfying his desires and for bearing the blow of a great catastrophe, but the following advantages over him are enjoyed by the other. The catastrophes and desires for which he is not so well equipped as the millionaire are averted from him by his good fortune, and, over and above the blessings of a perfect physique, immunity from illness, freedom from troubles, a family of fine children, and a fine personal presence are added unto him. If he succeeds in crowning these blessings by meeting a good end, then, Sire, he is the object of your search, or in other words, the man who deserves to be called happy. Until I see his end, however, I must suspend judgment and call him not 'happy' but 'fortunate.' The entire list of blessings above mentioned cannot possibly, of course, be combined by any given human being, any more than a given piece of land can be a self-contained unit of production. The piece of land will possess one requisite and lack another, and the best piece will be simply the piece that possesses the greatest number. Similarly, the individual human being is not a self-sufficient unit, but will possess one requisite and be deficient in another; and the man who possesses the greatest number of requisites over the longest period, and eventually meets a gracious end, will have, Sire, in my judgment, a right to the title in question. In order to appraise any phenomenon, the attention must be directed upon the circumstances in which it meets its end. To many people God has given a glimpse of happiness in order to destroy them root and branch."

These observations of Solon's did not at all commend themselves to Croesus, who dismissed the philosopher with contempt, as a man of no intelligence whatever, for his principle of discounting present values and appraising every phenomenon by its end. After the departure of Solon, however, Croesus was overtaken by a heavy retribution from God—presumably because he had ventured to regard himself as the happiest of all Mankind.

THE PARABLE OF POLYCRATES

(HERODOTUS: Book III. chapters 39–43 and 122–125)

POLYCRATES son of Aeaces made himself master of Samos by a *coup d'état*. At the beginning he divided the country into three and gave portions to his brothers Pantagnotus and Syloson; but afterward he killed the former, banished Syloson, the younger, made himself master of the whole of Samos, and proceeded, by an exchange of presents, to establish an *entente* with Amasis, king of Egypt. In little or no time Polycrates rose to be a power whose prestige extended throughout Ionia and the rest of Hellas. Whatever objective he selected for his expeditions, they were invariably successful. He disposed of a hundred "fifty oars" and a thousand archers; and he looted all comers without discrimination, it being a favorite remark of his that he would be giving more pleasure to a friend by restoring what he had taken than by never taking it at all. He captured numerous islands and many continental towns. One of his exploits was to defeat and take prisoner the entire navy of the Lesbians, who had come to the assistance of Miletus. These prisoners excavated, in chains, the whole length of the moat that surrounds the town wall of Samos. However, the vast success of Polycrates did not exactly escape the eye of Amasis, but engaged his earnest attention, and, when it continued to increase by leaps and bounds, Amasis finally wrote him the following letter, which he dispatched to Samos:

"Amasis offers the following observations to Polycrates. The prosperity of a friend and ally is agreeable news, but your vast successes do not please me, because I know for a fact that the Deity has an envious disposition. My general ideal, for myself as well as for those in whom I take an interest, is to succeed in some things and to fail in others, and so to pass through alternations of fortune in the course of a career rather than to enjoy unbroken success. I have never yet heard of anyone who enjoyed unbroken success without eventually coming to a bad end and being cut off, root and branch. Take my advice and insure against our successes in the following way. Search your thoughts until you find the object on which you set the greatest store and the loss of which will cause you the keenest pang, and then get rid of that object so effectually that it shall never again be seen by human eyes. If thereafter you do not find your successes alternating with failures, continue to seek a remedy along the lines that I have suggested."

Upon reading this, Polycrates realized that Amasis was offering him good advice, and he began to search his thoughts to discover which of his treasures he would be most chagrined to lose. His search led him to fix upon a gold-mounted emerald signet ring, set by Theodore son of Telecles of Samos, which he habitually wore. He decided to get rid of this ring, and took the following steps to that end. He manned a "fifty oar," went on board her, and then ordered her to stand out into the deep sea. When he found himself far out from the island, he took off the ring and cast it into the deep sea in the sight of the whole ship's company. After this performance he returned to port, went home, and was exceedingly sorry for himself. Five or six days afterwards, however, he had the following experience. A fisherman had caught a fine large fish, which he thought a suitable present for Polycrates. Accordingly he brought it to the door, requested a personal interview with Polycrates, and, when he obtained it, presented the fish with the following speech:"Sire, though I have to live by my labor, I did not feel justified in taking this fish that I have caught to market. It seemed to me worthy of you, Sire, and of your empire, and so I have brought it as a present for you." Polycrates, who was delighted at the speech, replied to him: "You have indeed done well, and I am your debtor twice over for your gift and for your words. I invite you to dine with me." The fisherman went home deeply gratified, but when the servants cut the fish open, they found lodged in its stomach—Polycrates' ring! As soon as they had espied it and picked it out, they brought it in triumph to Polycrates, and presented it to him with an explanation of how it had been found. The occurrence struck Polycrates as supernatural, so he wrote all that he had done and all that had come of it in a letter, which he addressed to Egypt. When Amasis read the letter from Polycrates, he realized that it is impossible for one human being to extricate another from the destiny awaiting him, and that no good end could be awaiting Polycrates, whose success was so unbroken that he recovered even what he had thrown away. In view of this, he sent a note to Samos denouncing the *entente*. His object in making this *démarche* was to save his own feelings from being harrowed, as they would be for a friend and ally, when Polycrates was overtaken by such a crushing disaster.

• • •

Oroetes,[1] who had taken up his quarters in the town of Magnesia-on-Maeander, sent the Lydian Myrsus son of Gyges on a mission to Samos. Oroetes had read Polycrates' mind, for Polycrates was the first Hellene in historical times who aspired to the command of the sea.[2] Oroetes divined this aspiration, and made his envoy the bearer of the following note:

"Oroetes offers the following observations to Polycrates. I

[1] The Persian Satrap, or Pasha, of Lydia, the present Vilayet of Aidin. [Ed.]
[2] Leaving out of account Minos of Cnossus and any others who may have commanded the sea before him. In the non-legendary epoch Polycrates was the first, and he had serious hopes of establishing his dominion over Ionia and the islands. [Author.]

hear that you have important projects on hand, but that your financial resources are unequal to your ambitions. I have a proposal to make, your acceptance of which will mean success to you and salvation to me. I have positive information that King Cambyses is plotting to put me to death. Extricate my person and my treasure from this situation, and part of that treasure shall be yours, if you will leave a portion to me. Then, as far as finance is concerned, you will be master of all Hellas. If you distrust my statements in regard to the treasure, send your most confidential adviser, and I will give him ocular proof."

The contents of this letter delighted Polycrates and captivated his will. He was vastly enamored of money, and he dispatched his Samian secretary Maeandrius son of Maeandrius on a preliminary mission of inspection.[1] As soon as Oroetes heard that the investigator was on his way, he took steps to cheat him by filling eight chests with stones, except for a shallow space immediately below their rims, and covering the stones with a layer of gold. The chests were then padlocked, and were held in readiness to be produced for the benefit of Maeandrius, who duly came and inspected them and made his report to Polycrates.

Polycrates immediately prepared to make the journey himself, ignoring the equally emphatic warnings of his diviners [2] and his friends, as well as the vision which appeared in a dream to his daughter. She dreamed that she saw her father suspended in mid air and being washed by Zeus and anointed by the Sun. This vision made her do everything in her power to prevent her father from going to visit Oroetes, and she went so far as to deliver herself of unfortunate [3] expressions as he was on his way to his "fifty oar." Polycrates retorted with the threat that, if he returned safe and sound, she need not expect an early marriage—whereupon the girl prayed that his words might be fulfilled, for she would gladly wait for a husband as the price of not losing her father. Polycrates, however, insisted on sailing for Oroetes' country in the teeth of all advice, and he took with him a numerous suite, which included the physician Democedes son of Calliphon of Croton, the best practitioner of his time. Upon his arrival at Magnesia, Polycrates met with a shocking fate, which was quite unworthy of his

[1] It was this Maeandrius who, not long afterward, dedicated in the temple ot Hera at Samos the magnificent fittings of Polycrates' state rooms. [AUTHOR.]
[2] They professed to foretell the future by examining the configuration of the bones and intestines of sacrificed animals. [ED.]
[3] "Unfortunate" in the technical sense of "ill-omened." It was a popular Hellenic belief that, at critical moments, the spoken word had a supernatural, or rather mechanical, effect in determining the course of events. [ED.]

character and ambitions.[1] After putting him to death[2] (the
details of which I shall pass over), Oroetes crucified his
corpse; and Polycrates, as he hung there upon the cross, fulfilled his daughter's vision faithfully. He was washed by Zeus
when it rained, and he was anointed by the Sun when he
exuded moisture from his own body. This was the end of Polycrates' innumerable successes.

THE REVISED VERSION

(AESCHYLUS OF ATHENS (525/524–456/455 B.C.): Works, Oxford
    text, ed. by A. Sidgwick: *Agamemnon*, lines 750–781)

A GREY word liveth, from the morn
    Of old time among mortals spoken,
That man's Wealth waxen full shall fall
Not childless, but get sons withal;
And ever of great bliss is born
    A tear unstaunched and a heart broken.

But I hold my thought alone and by others unbeguiled;
'Tis the deed that is unholy shall have issue, child on child,
Sin on sin, like his begetters; and they shall be as they were.
But the man who walketh straight, and the house thereof,
    tho' Fate
Exalt him, the children shall be fair.

But Old Sin loves, when comes the hour again,
    To bring forth New,
Which laugheth lusty amid the tears of men;
Yea, and Unruth, his comrade, wherewith none
May plead nor strive, which dareth on and on,
    Knowing not fear nor any holy thing;
Two fires of darkness in a house, born true,
    Like to their ancient spring.

But Justice shineth in a house low-wrought
    With smoke-stained wall,
And honoureth him who filleth his own lot;
But the unclean hand upon the golden stair

---

[1] With the single exception of the despots of Syracuse, not one of the Hellenic
despots has been comparable to Polycrates in magnificence. [AUTHOR.]

[2] Oroetes liberated the Samian members of Polycrates' suite and told them to
thank him for having made them free men; but he retained possession of the
aliens and slaves, whom he treated as chattels. [AUTHOR.]

With eyes averse she fleeth, seeking where
  Things innocent are; and, recking not the power
Of wealth by men misgloried, guideth all
  To her own destined hour.

[Translated by GILBERT MURRAY.]

THE DAY OF JUDGMENT

(XENOPHON OF ATHENS (*ca.* 430–354 B.C.): *A History of Hellenic
    Affairs,* Oxford text, ed. by E. C. Marchant: Book II. chapter
    2³⁻⁴)

AT Athens the disaster [1] was announced by the arrival of the
Paralus,[2] and a wail spread from the Peiraeus through the
Long Walls into the city, as the news passed from mouth to
mouth. That night no one slept. Besides mourning for the
dead, they mourned far more bitterly for themselves, for they
expected to suffer the fate which they had inflicted upon the
Melians (who were colonists of the Lacedaemonians) when
they had besieged and captured their town, and upon the
Histiaeans, the Scionians, the Toronians, the Aeginetans and
many other Hellenic peoples. Next morning they held an assembly, in which it was decided to block up all the harbors
except one, to clear the fortifications for action, to dispose
troops to man them, and to put the city into a thorough state
of defense for the eventuality of a siege.

THE TITAN IN HARNESS

(POLYBIUS: Book VI. chapter 56)

THE point in which, to my mind, the Roman constitution
evinces its greatest superiority is the attitude adopted toward
Religion. In my belief, a disposition that is reprobated in
other countries is actually the keystone of the Roman system,
by which I mean Superstition. At Rome, this feature has been
artificially exaggerated and introduced into private life as well
as public affairs to the utmost extent conceivable. Doubtless
many readers will find this extraordinary, but in my opinion
the Romans have done this deliberately with a view to the

---

[1] The battle of Aegospotami, in the Dardanelles, in which the last Athenian
fleet had been annihilated by the Peloponnesians in 405 B.C. [ED.]
[2] The *Paralus* and the *Salaminia* were the two fastest sailers in the Athenian
Navy, and were employed to carry dispatches. [ED.]

masses. If a community exclusively composed of intelligent beings were a practical possibility, such a policy might conceivably be unnecessary; but in fact the masses everywhere are unstable and instinct with such anti-social passions as irrational temper and homicidal fury, and there is therefore no means available for holding them in check except unseen terrors and the mummery of Superstition. From this point of view, I feel that there was nothing random or irresponsible in the policy of our forefathers when they introduced among the masses the conceptions of Religion and the notions regarding Hell, and that it is far more irresponsible and irrational of the present generation to expurgate these ideas. One of the many unfortunate consequences of this false step may be seen in the fact that, in Hellenic countries, when even so trifling a sum as one talent of public money is entrusted to persons in official positions, the latter are controlled by ten countersignatures and as many seals and twice that number of witnesses and are still incapable of being faithful to their trust; whereas, in Rome, public men handle vast sums of money in the administration or on diplomatic missions upon the sole security of their personal oath, and are still faithful to their duty. In other countries, it is rare to find an individual who keeps his hands off the public purse and can show a clean record in this respect. In Rome it is equally rare to see anyone convicted of such malpractices.

RATIONALISM

(PROCOPIUS: Book V. chapter 3⁵⁻⁸)

AT this juncture the Christian high priest [1] of Rome was visited by a mission from Byzantium, consisting of Hypatius the priest [2] of Ephesus and Demetrius of Philippi in Macedonia. The mission had reference to a point of doctrine on which the Christians differ and dispute among one another; but, although I am instructed in the controversy, I have no intention of discussing it. The attempt to research into the nature of God appears to me to be an aberration of disordered minds. The human intellect is unequal, I take it, to the exact comprehension even of human affairs, and therefore *a fortiori* to that of problems relating to the nature of God. On such questions I propose to maintain a prudent reserve, and shall only remark that

---

[1] *I.e.* archbishop. [ED.]
[2] *I.e.* bishop. [ED.]

I am not a disbeliever in accepted principles. Personally, however, I hesitate to make any statement about God except that he is morally perfect and materially omnipotent. I leave it to others, priests or laymen, to formulate in words the theological knowledge which they believe themselves to possess.

SECTION III.—EVOLUTION

DEGENERATION

(HESIOD OF ASCRA: Teubner text, ed. by A. Rzach: *Works and Days,* lines 109–201)[1]

IN the beginning, a Golden Race of mortal men was made by the immortal dwellers on Olympus. These men lived in the days of Cronus, when he was king in Heaven. They lived like Gods with hearts free from care, without part or lot in labor and sorrow. Pitiful old age did not await them, but, ever the same in strength of hand and foot, they took their pleasure in feasting, apart from all evils. When they died, it was as though they were overcome by sleep. All good things were theirs, and the grain harvest was yielded by bountiful Earth of her own accord—abundantly, ungrudgingly—while they, in peace and goodwill, lived upon their lands with good things in abundance. Now after this race had been hidden by Earth, they became good spirits by the will of great Zeus—spirits above the ground, guardians of mortal men, givers of wealth (for they have gotten even that prerogative of kings).

Again, a second race far worse, a Race of Silver, was made thereafter by the dwellers on Olympus—a race not like unto the Golden either in body or in mind. For a hundred years the child was nurtured at his good mother's knee, playing, a helpless infant, in his home; and when they reached their manhood and the measure of it, short was the time that they lived, and that in pain through their folly. They could not refrain from baneful outrage upon one another, and they would not serve the immortals or make sacrifice upon the holy altars of the blessed Gods after the lawful manner of men in all their dwelling places. These, in the end thereof, were put away by Zeus son of Cronus in his wrath, because they would not pay

---

[1] Mr. F. M. Cornford's translation has been followed with a few alterations, mostly in the order of words, and these most likely for the worse. [ED.]

their honors to the blessed Gods of Olympus. Now after this race also had been hidden by Earth, they gained among mortals the name of blessed ones beneath the ground—second in glory; and yet, even so, they too are attended with honor.

And Father Zeus made yet a third race of mortal men—a Race of Bronze, in no wise like unto the Silver, fashioned from the ash-shaft,[1] mighty and terrible. Their delight was in the grievous deeds of Ares and in the trespasses of Pride. No bread ever passed their lips, but their hearts in their breasts were strong as adamant, and none might approach them. Great was their strength and unconquerable were the arms which grew from their shoulders upon their stalwart frames. Of bronze were their arms, of bronze their houses, and with bronze they tilled the land. (Dark iron was not yet.) These were brought low by their own hands and went their way to the moldering house of chilly Hades, nameless. For all their mighty valor, Death took them in his dark grip, and they left the bright light of the Sun.

Now when this race also had been covered by Earth, yet a fourth race was made, again, upon the face of the All-Mother, by Zeus son of Cronus—a better race and more righteous, the divine race of men Heroic, who are called Demigods, the race that was aforetime upon the boundless Earth. These were destroyed by evil War and dread Battle—some below Seven-Gate Thebes in the land of Cadmus, as they fought for the flocks of Oedipus, while others were carried for destruction to Troy in ships over the great gulf of the sea, for the sake of fair-haired Helen. There they met their end and Death enfolded them; and then, apart from Mankind, they were granted a life and a dwelling place by Zeus son of Cronus, who made them to abide at the ends of the Earth. So there they abide, with hearts free from care, in the Isles of the Blessed beside the deep eddies of Ocean Stream—happy Heroes, for whom a harvest honey-sweet, thrice ripening every year, is yielded by bountiful Earth.

O would that I had not tarried to live thereafter with the fifth race, but had either died before or had been born after; for now in these latter days is the Race of Iron. Never by day shall they rest from travail and sorrow, and never by night from the hand of the spoiler; and cruel are the cares which the Gods shall give them. The father shall not be of one mind with the children nor the children with the father, nor the guest with the host that receives him, nor friend with friend, nor shall brother cleave to brother as aforetime. Parents shall swiftly age and swiftly be dishonored, and they shall reproach

---

[1] Ash was the wood from which spear-shafts were made. [Ed.]

their children and chide them with cruel words. Wretches that
know not the visitation of the Gods! Such as these would not
repay their aging parents for their nurture. The righteous man
or the good man or he that keeps his oath shall not find favor,
but they shall honor rather the doer of wrong and the proud
man insolent. Right shall rest in might of hand and Ruth shall
be no more. The wicked shall do hurt to his better by use of
crooked words with oath to crown them. All the sons of sor-
rowful Man shall have Strife for their helpmate—harsh-voiced
Strife of hateful countenance, rejoicing in evil.

And then, at long last, shall those spirits go their way to
Olympus from the wide-wayed Earth, with their beautiful faces
veiled in white raiment, seeking the company of the immortals,
and leaving behind them the company of men—even the
spirits of Ruth and Retribution. Pain and grief are the portion
that shall be left for mortal men, and there shall be no defense
against the evil day.

ACHIEVEMENT

(SOPHOCLES OF ATHENS (495/494–406/405 B.C.): Cambridge
text, ed by R. C. Jebb: *Antigone,* lines 332–375)

WONDERS are many, but none there be
  So strange, so fell, as the Child of Man.
He rangeth over the whitening sea,
  Of the winds of winter he makes his plan;
About his going the deeps unfold,
  The crests o'erhang, but he passeth clear.
Oh, Earth is patient, and Earth is old,
  And a mother of Gods, but he breaketh her,
To-ing, fro-ing, with the plough-teams going,
  Tearing the soil of her, year by year.

Light are the birds and swift with wings,
  But his hand is round them and drags them low;
He prisons the tribes of the wild-wood things,
  And the salt sea-swimmers that dart and glow.
The nets of his weaving are cast afar,
  And his Thought in the midst of them circleth full,
Till his engines master all beasts that are.
  Where drink the horses at the desert pool,
That mane that shaketh for his slave he taketh,
  And the tireless shoulder of the mountain Bull.

Speech he hath taught him and wind-swift thought
  And the temper that buildeth a City's Wall,
Till the arrows of winter he sets at naught,
  The sleepless cold and the long rainfall.
All-armèd he: unarmèd never
  To meet new peril he journeyeth;
Yea, his craft assuageth each pest that rageth,
  And help he hath gotten against all save Death.

The craft of his engines hath passed his dream,
  In haste to the good or the evil goal.
One holdeth his City's Law supreme
  And the Oath of God in his inmost soul;
High-citied he: citiless that other
  Who striveth, grasping at things of naught,
On the road forbidden. From him be hidden
  The fire that comforts and the light of thought!
                                    GILBERT MURRAY

THE WHEEL OF EXISTENCE

(PLATO OF ATHENS (427–348/347 B.C.): Collected Works, Oxford
text, ed. by J. Burnet, Vol. I.: *Politicus*, pp. 269 c4–270 A; (271
c4–272 A; 272 D6–273 E4; 274 B-D)

Dramatis Personae: STRANGER *and* YOUNG SOCRATES

Stranger. Here is the story. This Universe is sometimes conducted on its path and guided in its orbit by God, while at
other times, when the cycles of its appointed time have arrived
at their term, it is released from control by God and proceeds
to revolve in the opposite direction by itself (which it can do,
because it is a living creature endowed with intelligence by
the Being who originally constructed it). The tendency toward
this reverse motion is inevitably innate in the Universe . . .
in virtue of the principle that perpetual self-consistency and
self-identity are properties confined to the divine order of
existences, to which Matter, by its nature, does not belong.
That which we call the Heavens and the Universe has been
endowed with many blessings by its Begetter, but these blessings do not include freedom from a material ingredient. For
this reason it is impossible for the Universe to be permanently
exempt from change, though up to the limits of its capacity it
does its utmost to move with a constant and unvarying rhythm
in the same locus, and has therefore been allowed (when it

changes) to revolve in the reverse direction, as being the slightest possible deviation from its proper motion. Perpetual self-rotation, however, is beyond the capacity of almost every being except that by which all things that move are conducted, and this Being is precluded from moving them sometimes in one direction and sometimes in the opposite. From these various premises it follows that the Earth neither rotates itself perpetually nor is entirely and perpetually rotated by God in two contrary revolutions, and again that there are not two Gods rotating it with contradictory purposes, but that (as has just been stated and is the only remaining alternative) it is sometimes conducted by a divine cause outside itself, in which phase it receives an access of vitality and a renewal of immortality from its Creator, while at other times it is released from control and moves by itself. It is released at a juncture which enables it to pass through many hundred thousand reverse revolutions—a feat made possible by the infinitesimal size of the base upon which its vast mass moves with perfect equilibrium. . . .

Young Socrates. Tell me about the life which you ascribe to the reign of Cronus. In which of the two periods does it fall? It is, of course, evident that the changes in the course of the stars and Sun occur in both periods.

Stranger. You have followed my argument admirably; but the spontaneous generation of all things for the use of Man, concerning which you ask me, is entirely foreign to the motion now prevailing, and is one of the phenomena of the previous period. In the previous period, the whole circular motion itself, in the first place, was controlled and superintended by God, and the same superintendence was provided locally by the assignment of all the parts of the Universe to other controlling deities. Living creatures, too, according to their kinds, were taken in charge by divine spirits, and each of these good shepherds was efficient in every respect to care for the creatures under his particular charge, so that there was no savagery, no preying upon one another, and no war or discord among them at all. The other features of this dispensation are too numerous to relate, but the story current among the human race regarding the spontaneous production of the means of livelihood has arisen for the following reason. God himself at that time shepherded and watched over Mankind, just as now Man, who stands out like a God from among his fellow creatures, acts as the shepherd of other races lower in the scale. When God was shepherd, there was no state and no ownership of women and children. All human beings came up into life again out of the Earth, without any recollection of their previous experience. All the historical conditions of life were absent, while on the other hand they enjoyed fruits in abundance from trees and other plants, which were not the product of cultivation, but were raised spontaneously by the Earth herself. For the most part they camped in the open without clothes or bedding, the climate having been tempered so as to do them no injury, and they found soft couches in the grass which was produced by the Earth in abundance. . . .

When, however, the period of this dispensation had been completed and a change was due, or, in other words, when the entire earthborn race had been exhausted, because each soul had accomplished its tale of births and had been seeded in the Earth the number of times respectively ordained, at that point the Helmsman of the Universe abandoned control of his rudder and retired to his observation post, and the Universe was set rotating in the reverse direction by Destiny and innate Desire. Forthwith, all the local Gods who shared the authority of the Great Spirit realized what was happening and successively abandoned control of those parts of the Universe which were under their immediate charge. Then the Universe, as it reversed its motion, experienced the shock of two contrary momenta, which were simultaneously beginning and coming to an end. It quaked to its depths with a terrible convulsion, which worked fresh havoc among every race of living creatures. Afterwards, with the lapse of time, the Universe began to emerge from this tumult and disorder, to obtain relief from the seismic storms, and to settle down into its own habitual rhythm, in which it exercised control and authority, over itself and all that was therein, and followed the instructions of its Creator and Father to the best of its recollection. At the beginning it performed its functions with comparative precision, and then with growing clumsiness as it approached the final phase. The cause of this degeneration was the material element in its composition, which was one of the original ingredients in its nature and which had been in an utterly chaotic state before the present order of the Universe was imposed upon it. By its Constructor it has been endowed with all good qualities. On the other hand, from its previous condition it has inherited in itself and reproduces in its living creatures everything evil and unrighteous. So long as the Universe enjoyed the co-operation of the Helmsman in breeding its living creatures, it implanted in them only trifling defects with a predominance of good; and when it parts company with him, it always performs its functions best during the phase least far removed from its release. As time goes on, however, and forgetfulness invades it, the malady of its original disharmony begins to gain the upper hand, until in the final phase it breaks out openly. Then the Universe receives into its composition only a trifling element of good and so predominant an admixture of the opposite that it becomes in danger of involving itself and all things therein in a common destruction. At this point, therefore, God, who had originally set it in order, perceives the straits into which the Universe has fallen and—anxious lest it may break up under the tempestuous blows of confusion and may founder in the fathomless gulf where all things are incommensurable—he again assumes control of its rudder, reverses the tendencies towards sickness and dissolution which had asserted themselves in the previous period when the Universe had been left to itself, sets it in order, corrects that which was amiss, and endows the Universe with immortality and eternal youth. . . .

We have now arrived at the goal towards which my story has been striving from the outset. I will pass over the animals, because it would take me far too long to enumerate and account for their transformations, and I will confine myself to Man, whose case can be more shortly stated and is more relevant to the point. When Mankind had been deprived of the care of the Spirit who had been our shepherd, the majority of wild beasts that were fierce by nature turned savage, while Man himself became weak and defenseless. In consequence he was harried by the wild beasts, and in this first phase he was destitute of all equipment and resource, since his spontaneous food supply had failed before he had been taught, by the stress of necessity, to provide for himself. For all these reasons, Man found himself in the direst straits, and this is the origin of those legendary Gifts of the Gods with which we have been presented, together with the instruction and training necessary for the use of them—fire from Prometheus, the arts and crafts from Hephaestus and his consort, and seeds and plants from other benefactors. Every stone in the foundations of human life has been hewn from this quarry. The watch (aforementioned) which had been kept over Man by the Gods had now suddenly failed, and he was forced to live by his own efforts and to keep watch over himself, exactly like the Universe as a whole, which we ever imitate and follow in the alternating phases of our life and growth.

CYCLES OF CIVILIZATION

(PLATO: Collected Works, Oxford text, Vol. IV.: *Timaeus*, pp. 21 E–23 C)

Critias loquitur:

In the Egyptian Delta, round the head of which the channel of the Nile divides, there is a department called Sais, with a departmental capital of the same name.[1] The people of this town have a patron goddess whose name in Egyptian is Neith—corresponding, as they aver, to the Hellenic Athena. The Saites claim to be strongly Athenophil and to be in some sense specially related to the Athenian nation. Solon (according to his own account) had traveled to Sais and had been received there with distinguished honors. During his stay he had taken opportunities of consulting the leading experts among the priests upon Ancient History, and had made the discovery that he himself and all his fellow Hellenes were in a state of almost total ignorance on the subject. On one occasion he sought to lead them into a discussion upon Antiquity by entering upon an exposition of the most ancient traditions of Hellas relating to the so-called primeval Phoroneus and Niobe, whence he descended to the period after the Deluge, narrated the legendary history of Deucalion and Pyrrha, recited the genealogies of their descendants and attempted to supply a chronological basis for dating the events in his story. This drew from an extremely aged priest among Solon's interlocutors the words: "Solon, Solon! You Hellenes are perpetual children. Such a thing as an old Hellene does not exist."—"What do you mean?" rejoined Solon. "All of you," continued the aged priest, "are young in mind. Your minds contain no thoughts handed down from Antiquity by ancient tradition and no knowledge hoary with age. There is a reason for this, which I will explain. A series of catastrophes in a variety of forms has befallen, and will continue to befall, the human race, the greatest being those effected through the agency of fire or water, while the others, which are of less violence, are produced by an infinity of different causes. In Hellas you have a tradition that Phaethon, the child of the Sun, once harnessed his father's chariot but proved incompetent to drive it along his father's course, with the result that he burnt up everything on the face of the Earth before his own career was cut short forever by the thunderbolt. Although this tradition has been dressed in a legendary form, it preserves the scientific fact that, at immense intervals of time, there is a declination in the orbit of the

[1] The native town of King Amasis. [AUTHOR.]

heavenly bodies revolving round the Earth and a catastrophe which overtakes life on this planet in the shape of a vast conflagration. At this juncture the inhabitants of regions with a mountainous relief, a high altitude or an arid climate pay a heavier toll than those of riverain or maritime zones; and on these occasions we in Egypt are rescued by the Nile, our unfailing savior, from a quandary from which he is immune himself. There are other occasions on which the Gods cleanse the Earth with a deluge of water, and in these circumstances the shepherds and herdsmen on the mountains survive, while the inhabitants of your towns in Hellas are swept away to sea by the rivers. In Egypt, however, water never descends upon the fields from above—not even in these diluvial epochs—but rises from below by a law of Nature which never varies. Thus, for the above reasons, the traditions preserved in Egypt are the most ancient in the world, the scientific truth being that in every locality where there are not prohibitive extremes of heat or cold, the human population is subject to periodic increases and decreases. Glorious or important or in any way remarkable events in the history of Hellas or of Egypt itself or of any other region within our field of knowledge are consequently recorded and preserved in our shrines here in Egypt since a remote antiquity. On the other hand, human society in Hellas or elsewhere has always just arrived at the point of equipping itself with written records and the other requisites of civilization, when, after the regular interval, the waters that are above the firmament descend upon you like a recurrent malady and only permit the illiterate and uncultivated members of your society to survive, with the result that you become as little children and start again from the beginning with no knowledge whatever of Ancient History either in Egypt or in your own world. Let me tell you, Sir, that the genealogies which you have recited in your account of your Hellenic past are scarcely above the level of children's fairy tales. In the first place, you have only preserved the memory of one deluge out of a long previous series, and in the second place, you are ignorant of the fact that your own country was the home of the noblest and the highest race by which the *Genus Homo* has ever been represented. You yourself and your whole nation can claim this race as your ancestors through a fraction of the stock that survived a former catastrophe, but you are ignorant of this, owing to the fact that, for many successive generations, the survivors lived and died illiterate."

THE CONTINUITY OF HISTORY

(POLYBIUS: Book III. chapters 31–32)

No doubt there are a few uncritical dilettanti who will feel that I have gone into unnecessary detail in discussing the origins of the Hannibalic War. My reply will be that, if any such critic supposes himself competent to deal without assistance with any situation, in that case a knowledge of the antecedents, while still a desirable ideal, may conceivably not be a necessity. If, however, any mere human being would shrink from making this claim in regard to any affairs, either private or public, being conscious of the fact that, even if he were momentarily successful, no sensible person could be justified in taking present circumstances as a basis for future expectations—if the real facts are these, then I maintain that they make an acquaintance with the past not merely a desirable ideal but an absolute necessity. How could anyone whose personal rights or whose country's rights were being violated find champions and allies; or how could anyone who was anxious to secure an object or anticipate a competitor encourage his prospective collaborators to set to work? How, again, when satisfied with the objects in view, could he be justified in stimulating those whose efforts he was enlisting for the support of his own policy and for the safeguarding of its results, if he knew nothing whatever of the previous record of the individuals involved? Everyone normally adapts his words and actions to the situation of the moment and plays the corresponding part with sufficient adroitness to make the policy of the particular individual hard to divine, and to obscure the truth in an appalling number of cases. The actions of the past, however, are put to the test by the actual course of events and therefore shed real light upon the aims and attitudes of individuals, revealing in some of them the existence of goodwill, good intentions and practical helpfulness in our regard, and in others the opposite dispositions. From such examples it is frequently possible, in many situations, to discover who will sympathize with our sorrows and our grievances, and who will justify us—possibilities which add greatly to the resources of human life in both public and private affairs. For this reason, writers and readers of History ought to concentrate attention less upon the bald narrative of transactions than upon the antecedents, concomitants and consequences of any given action. If you abstract from History the "Why" and the "How" and the "Wherefore" of the particular transactions and the rationality or the reverse of its result, what is left of her ceases to be a science and becomes a *tour de force,* which may give momentary pleasure, but is of no assistance whatever for dealing with the future.

The implication of this is that those critics who regard my work as difficult to obtain and difficult to read owing to the number and size of the volumes, are laboring under a misapprehension. It is immeasurably easier both to obtain and to read from cover to cover a series of forty volumes woven in one continuous length, and to follow clearly the transactions of Italy, Sicily and North Africa from the time of Pyrrhus to the fall of Carthage, and the transactions of the rest of the world from the flight of King Cleomenes of Sparta, without a break, down to the battle between the Romans and Achaeans at the Isthmus of Corinth, than it is to obtain and to read the compositions of the specialists. Apart from the fact that they are many times more voluminous than my own record, it is actually impossible for readers to obtain from them any certain information—first, because the majority of these writers give discrepant versions of identical events, and in the second place because they ignore the contemporaneous transactions in other fields, in spite of the fact that the comparative method of study and analysis transforms the investigation of every detail as compared with the results obtained by the method of dissection in compartments. Another reason is that they are quite incapable of so much as touching the fundamental points, for, as I have just said, the essential elements in History are the consequences and concomitants of action and, above all, its causes. We observe that the War of Antiochus arises out of the War of Philip, the War of Philip out of the War of Hannibal, the Hannibalic War out of the Sicilian War, while the intervening events, numerous and complicated though their various aspects may be, are all oriented towards the same central theme. All these facts can be learned and understood from the writers of General History, but not from those who write the history of particular wars, like the Wars of Perseus or the War of Philip, in isolation—unless anyone, in reading the bare accounts of the battles, imagines that he has also acquired from these writers' works a clear understanding of the morphology of the war as a whole. That, however, would be an entire hallucination, and I conceive that my own history differs from the works of the specialists as profoundly as learning with the mind differs from mere hearing with the ear.

THE UNIVERSALITY OF HISTORY

(POLYBIUS: Book V. chapter 31⁶–33)

As I think I have already explained, I have undertaken to record, not some particular group of events, but those that have occurred throughout the world, and it is hardly an exaggeration to say that I have projected my historical work upon a larger scale than any of my predecessors. It is proportionately incumbent upon me to expend the utmost possible forethought upon my treatment and arrangement, in order that the composition of my work may be lucid both in general outline and in detail. In turning now to the kingdoms of Antiochus and Ptolemy, I shall therefore retrace my steps for a short distance in an attempt to find an acknowledged and familiar starting point for the narrative that I am about to introduce—an attempt which is my most essential duty as a historian. In their proverb "The starting point is half the whole," the Ancients recommended the payment of the utmost attention in any given case to the achievement of a good start; and what is commonly regarded as an exaggerated statement on their part really errs, in my opinion, by falling short of the truth. It may be asserted with confidence that the starting point is not "half the whole" but that it extends right to the end. It is quite impossible to make a good start in anything without, in anticipation, mentally embracing the completion of the project or realizing in what sphere and to what purpose and for what reason the action is projected. It is equally impossible adequately to summarize any given course of events without, in the process, referring to the starting point and showing whence and how and why that point has led up to the actual transactions of that moment. Starting points must accordingly be regarded as extending not merely to the middle but to the end, and the utmost attention ought, in consequence, to be paid to starting points by both writers and readers of Universal History.

I am not, of course, unaware that a considerable number of other historical writers have delivered themselves in the same tone as myself, and have professed, as writers of Universal History, to have attempted work upon a greater scale than any of their predecessors. Personally, I shall crave the indulgence of Ephorus (the first and only historian who has genuinely attempted to write on the universal scale), but shall firmly refuse to pursue the subject or to mention any of the other claimants by name, and shall confine myself to noting the fact that certain contemporary writers, on the strength of having described the Romano-Carthaginian War in three or four columns, lay claim to the title of universal historians. Now no one is so ignorant as to be unaware that in that period a vast number of transactions of the utmost importance occurred in Spain and North Africa as well as in Sicily and Italy; that the Hannibalic War is the most celebrated and the most protracted that there has ever been, except for the War of Sicily;[1] and that the vastness of its dimensions compelled us all to focus our attention upon it. In spite of this, there are writers whose references are even more brief than the entries of those official records that are inscribed in public places in chronological order and tabular form, and who yet assert that they have included in their survey all the transactions of the Hellenic and the non-Hellenic world. The reason is that it is perfectly easy to lay verbal claim to the most imposing accomplishments, but not so easy in practice to achieve any of the things worth achievement. Pretentiousness is an article of common property which is virtually at the disposal of everybody possessed of the mere audacity to assume it, while practical attainment is exceedingly rare and attends few individuals in actual life. I have been provoked into making these observations by the imposture of writers who magnify themselves and their own productions, but I will now return to the starting point of the events which I propose here to record.

THE UNITY OF HISTORY

(POLYBIUS: Book VIII. chapter 2)

I FLATTER myself that the actual record of the facts has now confirmed the truth of a principle which I have repeatedly emphasized at the beginning of my work—the principle that it is impossible to obtain from the monographs of historical specialists a comprehensive view of the morphology of Universal History. By reading a bald and isolated narrative of the transactions in Sicily and Spain, it is obviously impossible to realize and understand either the magnitude or the unity of the events in question, by which I mean the methods and institutions of which Fortune has availed herself in order to accomplish what has been her most extraordinary achievement in our generation. This achievement is nothing less than the reduction of the entire known world under the dominion of a

[1] *I.e.* the First Punic War. [ED.]

single empire—a phenomenon of which there is no previous example in recorded history. A limited knowledge of the processes by which Rome captured Syracuse and conquered Spain is, no doubt, obtainable from the specialists' monographs; but without the study of Universal History it is difficult to comprehend how she attained to universal supremacy, by what local and particular events she was impeded in the execution of her general projects, and what, again, were the events and the conjunctures that contributed to her success. For the same reasons, it is by no means easy to apprehend the magnitude of Rome's efforts or the potency of her institutions. That Rome should contest the possession of Spain or again of Sicily, and that she should conduct campaigns on both elements, would not appear remarkable if considered in isolation. It is only when we consider the fact that the same government and commonwealth was producing results in a variety of other spheres simultaneously with the conduct of these operations, and when we include in the same survey the internal crises and struggles which hampered those responsible for all the above-mentioned activities abroad, that the remarkable character of the events comes out clearly and obtains the attention that it deserves. This is my reply to those who imagine that the work of specialists will initiate them into Universal and General History.

SECTION IV.—LAW AND CAUSATION

DETERMINISM

(HERODOTUS: *passim*)

1. EVIL had to befall Candaules, and so, not long afterwards ... (Book I. chapter 8).

2. Evil had, however, to befall Scyles, and it accordingly availed itself of the following opportunity . . . (Book IV. chapter 79).

3. Naxos was not to be destroyed by this expedition, and therefore the following incident occurred . . . (Book V. chapter 33).

4. Corinth had to reap a harvest of evil from the seed of Eetion, for . . . (Book V. chapter 92δ).

5. This story had, apparently, to come to light in order to deprive Damaratus of his throne . . . (Book VI. chapter 64).

6. The priestess of Delphi would not permit the punishment of Timo and declared that she was not responsible, but that Miltiades had to come to a bad end, and that it had fallen to Timo to guide his feet into the paths of destruction . . . (Book VI. chapter 135).

7. *Xerxes to Artabanus:*

"It is impossible for either party to extricate themselves. The lists are set for victor and victim, in order that all our dominions may fall to the Hellenes or all theirs to the Persians. In this issue there can be no compromise . . ." (Book VII. chapter 11).

8. Artabanus . . . put on Xerxes' clothes, seated himself on the royal throne and afterwards went to bed, whereupon there duly appeared to him in his sleep that same dream that had been haunting Xerxes. The presence stood over Artabanus and said: "Are you the man who is discouraging Xerxes from undertaking the expedition against Hellas, out of professed regard for his interests? I warn you that you shall not with impunity attempt to avert what has to be, either immediately or hereafter. As for Xerxes, the penalty which he incurs by disobedience has been revealed to him in person." In execution of these verbal threats, the presence appeared to Artabanus to be in the act of searing his eyes with hot irons, when he started up with a scream . . . (Book VII. chapters 17-18).

9. At length, when they were at their wits' ends, the Orientals discovered a means of entry into the citadel, for the oracle had foretold that all the mainland of Attica had to fall into the power of the Persians (Book VIII. chapter 53).

10. Evil had to befall Artaynte and all her house, and accordingly she replied to Xerxes: . . . (Book IX. chapter 109).

PREMONITION

(HERODOTUS: Book VI. chapter 98)

DATIS then set sail with his expedition for his first objective, Eretria . . . and after his departure from Delos the island was shaken by an earthquake—the first and last occasion up to the present, as the inhabitants aver. This was presumably a portent revealed by God to Mankind as a premonition of coming disasters. In the three successive generations covered by the reigns of Darius son of Hystaspes, Xerxes son of Darius and Artaxerxes son of Xerxes, a greater number of disasters was suffered by Hellas than during all the twenty generations previous to Darius—some at the hands of the Persians and others at the hands of the leading Hellenic powers themselves in their struggles for supremacy. It was therefore nothing extraordinary that Delos should be shaken by an earthquake after a previously unbroken record of immunity.

THE OMNIPOTENCE OF LAW

(HERODOTUS: Book III. chapter 38)

ALL the circumstances make it evident to me that Cambyses had completely lost his reason. Otherwise he would never have attempted to pour ridicule upon customs religious or secular. If the whole human race were given a free field and were instructed to choose out the best laws from all the laws in existence, after due consideration they would each choose their own laws—so convinced are they respectively of the immeasurable superiority of their own. It is therefore scarcely credible that anyone who has not lost his reason should make fun of such institutions. My assertion that all Mankind cherishes this conviction in regard to laws may be verified by a number of proofs, from among which I offer the following. When Darius was on the throne, he summoned into his presence the Hellenes at his court and asked them for what price they would consent to devour their fathers when they died. The Hellenes replied that all the money in the world would not induce them to do such a thing, whereupon Darius summoned the Callatian Indians, who do eat their parents, and asked them (in the presence of the Hellenes, who were kept informed, through an interpreter, of the tenor of the conversation) for what price they would be willing to burn their fathers when they died. The Indians shrieked aloud and begged him not to pursue such an unmentionable subject—a story which illustrates the habitual attitude of Mankind toward this question, and which, in my opinion, justifies the poetic aphorism of Pindar that "Law is lord of all."

NATURAL LAW

(School of HIPPOCRATES OF COS (460/459–ca. 368 B.C.): Collected
Works, Teubner text, ed. by H. Kuehlewein: Vol. I. pp. 64–
66=*The Influences of Atmosphere, Water and Situation,*
chapter 22)

THE natives attribute the causation of this disease[1] to God,
and they revere and worship its victims, in fear of being
stricken by it themselves. I, too, take the view that these
phenomena come from God; but I take the same view in
regard to all phenomena and look upon no given phenomenon
as more divine or more human than any other. All, in my
view, are uniform and all are divine; but each phenomenon
obeys its own law, and Natural Law knows no exceptions. I
will now proceed to explain my theory of this disease. . . .

[A scientific analysis follows.]

The victims of this disease are not the lowest class among
the Nomads, but the members of the best families who possess
the strongest physical constitutions. They contract it by rid-
ing, and the poor are comparatively immune because they do
not ride. On the assumption, however, that this disease is in
some sense more divine than others, it ought not exclusively
to attack the best connected and the wealthiest Nomads, but
all classes alike, or, if there were discrimination, it ought to
tell against those with narrow means—that is, if the Gods
really take pleasure in being honored and admired by human
beings and requite such attentions with their favors. Presumably it is the wealthy, with the ample funds at their command, who make frequent sacrifices to the Gods and dedicate
votive offerings and pay honors, while the poor are less active
in the matter, partly through lack of means and in a secondary
degree through their resentment against the Gods for not endowing them with worldy goods. On this showing, those with
narrow means ought to incur the penalties for such lapses,
rather than the wealthy. In reality, however, as I have stated
already, this phenomenon is only divine in the same sense as
every other, and every phenomenon obeys Natural Law.

[1] The author is discussing a disease peculiar to the nomadic population of the
steppes to the north of the Black Sea. [ED.]

ENVIRONMENT AND CHARACTER

(HERODOTUS: Book IX. chapter 122)

THIS individual Artayctes, who was crucified as I have described, had a grandfather named Artembares, and it was he who first suggested to his Persian fellow countrymen the proposition which they adopted and laid before Cyrus, to the following effect:

"Now that Zeus has put down Astyages from his seat and has given the dominion to the Persians as a nation and to you, Sire, as an individual, why should we not emigrate from the confined and rocky territory which we at present possess, and occupy a better? There are many near at hand and many more at a distance, of which we have only to take our choice in order to make a greater impression on the world than we do as it is. This is a natural policy for an imperial people, and we shall never have a finer opportunity of realizing it than now, when our Empire is established over vast populations and the entire continent of Asia."

Cyrus, who had listened and had not been impressed, told his petitioners to do as they wished, but he qualified his advice by telling them in the same breath to prepare their minds for exchanging positions with their present subjects. Soft countries, he informed them, invariably breed soft men, and it is impossible for one and the same country to produce splendid crops and good soldiers. The Persians capitulated to the superior intelligence of Cyrus, confessed their error, abandoned their proposition, and elected to live as an imperial people in a rough country rather than to cultivate the lowlands as some other nation's slaves.

ENVIRONMENT AND POLITICS

(HIPPOCRATES: *Influences of Atmosphere, Water and Situation*, chapter 16)

WE have now discussed the organic and structural differences between the populations of Asia and Europe, but we have still to consider the problem why the Asiatics are of a less warlike and a more tame disposition than the Europeans. The deficiency of spirit and courage observable in the human inhabitants of Asia has for its principal cause the low margin of seasonal variability in the temperature of that continent, which is approximately stable throughout the year. Such a climate does not produce those mental shocks and violent bodily dislocations which would naturally render the temperament ferocious and introduce a stronger current of irrationality and passion than would be the case under stable conditions. It is invariably changes that stimulate the human mind and that prevent it from remaining passive. These, in my view, are the reasons why the Asiatic race is unmilitary, but I must not omit the factor of institutions. The greater part of Asia is under monarchical government; and wherever men are not their own masters and not free agents, but are under despotic rule, they are not concerned to make themselves militarily efficient but, on the contrary, to avoid being regarded as good military material—the reason being that they are not playing for equal stakes. It is theirs, presumably, to serve and struggle and die under compulsion from their masters and far from the sight of their wives and children and friends. Whenever they acquit themselves like men, it is their masters who are exalted and aggrandized by their achievements, while their own share of the profits is the risking and the losing of their lives. And not only this, but, in the case of people so circumstanced, it is also inevitable that the inactivity consequent upon the absence of war should have a taming effect upon the temperament, so that even a naturally courageous and spirited individual would be inhibited on the intellectual side by the prevailing institutions. A strong argument in favor of my contention is furnished by the fact that all the Hellenes and non-Hellenes in Asia who are not under despotic rule, but are free agents and struggle for their own benefit, are as warlike as any populations in the world—the reason being that they stake their lives in their own cause and reap the rewards of their own valor (and the penalties of their own cowardice, into the bargain). You will also find that the Asiatics differ among one another, some being finer and others poorer in quality, and these differences also have their cause in the seasonal climatic variations, as I have stated above.

ENVIRONMENT AND RACE

(HIPPOCRATES: *Influences of Atmosphere, Water and Situation,*
chapter 24)

OUR comparative survey of Europe and Asia is now complete in general outline. In Europe itself there are, however, a number of distinct stocks differentiated by physical structure and proportions and by moral qualities. The differentiating factors are the same as those described in previous connections, but I will explain them again with greater precision. Inhabitants of mountainous, rocky, well-watered country at a high altitude,[1] where the margin of seasonal climatic variation is wide, will tend to have large-built bodies constitutionally adapted for courage and endurance, and in such natures there will be a considerable element of ferocity and brutality. Inhabitants of sultry hollows covered with water meadows,[2] who are more commonly exposed to warm winds than to cold and who drink tepid water, will—in contrast—not be large-built or slim, but thickset, fleshy and dark-haired, with swarthy rather than fair complexions and with less phlegm than bile in their constitutions. Courage and endurance will not be innate in their characters to the same degree, but will be capable of being produced in them by the coefficient of institutions. If there are rivers in the country which drain it of the stagnant water and the rainfall, the population will be healthy and in good condition; while, if there are no rivers and their drinking water comes from stagnant lakes and marshes, their bodies will run to spleen and incline to be pot-bellied. Inhabitants of rolling, wind-swept, well-watered country at a high altitude[3] will be large-built and unindividualized, with a vein of cowardice and tameness in their characters. Inhabitants of thin-soiled, waterless country without vegetation, where the seasonal climatic variations are abrupt and violent,[4] will tend to have bony, muscular bodies, fair rather than swarthy complexions, and headstrong, self-willed characters and temperaments. Where seasonal changes are most frequent and show the widest margin of variability, there you will find the greatest differentiation in the human body, character and organism.

These are the most important varieties of organism, and then there is the effect of the country and the water which constitute the human environment. In the majority of cases, you will find that the human body and character vary in accordance with the nature of the country. Where the soil is rich and soft and well-watered, and where the water remains extremely near the surface, so that it is tepid in summer and chilly in winter, and where the climatic conditions are also favorable, the inhabitants will be fleshy, loose-jointed, flaccid, unenergetic and poor-spirited as a general rule. Laziness and

---

[1] *E.g.* Aetolia. [ED.]
[2] *E.g.* "Hollow Lacedaemon." [ED.]
[3] *E.g.* the interior of the Anatolian Peninsula. [ED.]
[4] *E.g.* the steppes of South Russia. [ED.]

sleepiness will be prominent among their characteristics, and they will be clumsy instead of being neat or quick at skilled occupations.[1] Where the country is rocky, waterless and without vegetation, and suffers from severe winters and from scorching suns,[2] you will find the inhabitants bony and without spare flesh, with well-articulated joints and muscular, shaggy bodies. Such constitutions are instinct with energy and alertness, and their possessors have headstrong, self-willed characters and temperaments, with a tendency towards ferocity instead of tameness, and with a superior quickness and intelligence in skilled occupations, and a superior aptitude for war. You will further find that the non-human fauna and flora of a given soil likewise vary according to the quality of that soil. I have now described the extreme contrasts of type and organism; and if you work out the rest for yourself on the analogy of these, you will not go wrong.

THE DENUDATION OF ATTICA

(PLATO: Collected Works, Oxford text, Vol. IV.: *Critias*, 111 A–D)

CONTEMPORARY Attica may accurately be described as a mere relic of the original country, as I shall proceed to explain. In configuration, Attica consists entirely of a long peninsula protruding from the mass of the continent into the sea, and the surrounding marine basin is known to shelve steeply round the whole coastline. In consequence of the successive violent deluges which have occurred within the past 9000 years,[3] there has been a constant movement of soil away from the high altitudes; and, owing to the shelving relief of the coast, this soil instead of laying down alluvium, as it does elsewhere, to any appreciable extent, has been perpetually deposited in the deep sea round the periphery of the country or, in other words, lost; so that Attica has undergone the process observable in small islands, and what remains of her substance is like the skeleton of a body emaciated by disease, as compared with her original relief. All the rich, soft soil has molted away, leaving a country of skin and bones. At the period, however, with which we are dealing, when Attica was still intact, what are now her mountains were lofty, soil-clad hills; her so-called shingle-

---

[1] *E.g.* the inhabitants of Colchis or Western Georgia, described in chapter 15 of this monograph. [ED.]

[2] *E.g.* Attica. [ED.]

[3] The interval that separates our own times from the period with which we are dealing. [AUTHOR.]

plains of the present day were full of rich soil; and her mountains were heavily forested—a fact of which there are still visible traces. There are mountains in Attica which can now keep nothing but bees, but which were clothed, not so very long ago, with fine trees producing timber suitable for roofing the largest buildings; and roofs hewn from this timber are still in existence. There were also many lofty cultivated trees, while the country produced boundless pasture for cattle. The annual supply of rainfall was not lost, as it is at present, through being allowed to flow over the denuded surface into the sea, but was received by the country, in all its abundance, into her bosom, where she stored it in her impervious potter's earth, and so was able to discharge the drainage of the heights into the hollows in the form of springs and rivers with an abundant volume and a wide territorial distribution. The shrines that survive to the present day on the sites of extinct water supplies are evidence for the correctness of my present hypothesis.

CAUSATION THE ESSENCE OF HISTORY

(POLYBIUS: Book XI, chapter 19[a])

WHAT does it profit the reader to wade through wars and battles and sieges of towns and enslavements of peoples, if he is not to penetrate to the knowledge of the causes which made one party succeed and the other fail in the respective situations? The results of transactions are merely entertaining to the reader, whereas research into the previous dispositions of the agents is profitable to the serious student. The analysis of a given event, in all the detail of its mechanism, is the best education of all for readers with the patience to follow the process.

ULTIMATE AND PROXIMATE CAUSES

(POLYBIUS: Book XXII. chapter 18)

THE beginning of the irremediable disasters which overtook the royal house of Macedon can be traced from this period. I am of course aware that several historians of the war between Rome and Perseus, in their attempts to explain the causes of the quarrel, have cited first the expulsion of Habrupolis from his own principality in reprisal for his raid upon the mining district of Pangaeum after Philip's death (when Perseus came to the rescue, utterly defeated the prince aforementioned, and expelled him from his own dominions). In succession to this, they cite Perseus' invasion of Dolopia and his visit to Delphi, as well as the plot hatched at Delphi against King Eumenes of Pergamum and the assassination of the Boeotian embassy—events from which, according to some writers, the war between Perseus and Rome arose. In my own opinion, nothing is so essential either for writers or for students of History as to understand the causes underlying the genesis and development of any given series of events; but the problem has been confused in the writings of most historians through a failure to grasp the difference between the occasion and the cause, and again between the beginning and the occasion of a war. At the present juncture, I find myself so distinctly prompted by the subject matter before me that I am compelled to return to the discussion of this question.

Of the events mentioned above, the first are occasions, while the subsequent group (including the plot against King Eumenes, the assassination of the embassy and other simultaneous occurrences of a similar character) unmistakably constitute the beginning of the war between Rome and Perseus and of the overthrow of the Macedonian Empire. Literally none of these events, however, is a true cause, as I shall now proceed to demonstrate. I have previously maintained that it was Philip son of Amyntas who conceived and proposed to carry out the project of the war against Persia, while Alexander was an agent who transacted the business in pursuance of his father's previous decisions. In precisely the same way I now maintain that it was Philip son of Demetrius who originally conceived the project of undertaking the final war against Rome, and who had prepared all the armaments in readiness for this enterprise, while Perseus was an agent who transacted the business when his father had made way for him. If this is correct, my contention is self-evident, for the causes of the war cannot be posterior in date to the death of the individual who decided and planned to make it. That, however, is the implication of the account given by other historians, for all the events cited in their works in this connection are posterior to the death of Philip.

THE CONSOLATIONS OF PHILOSOPHY

(MARCUS AURELIUS ANTONINUS THE EMPEROR: *Addresses to Himself*: Oxford text, ed. by I. H. Leopold: Book II. chapter 17[1])

HUMAN life! Its duration is momentary, its substance in perpetual flux, its senses dim, its physical organism perishable, its consciousness a vortex, its destiny dark, its repute uncertain —in fact, the material element is a rolling stream, the spiritual element dreams and vapor, life a war and a sojourning in a far country, fame oblivion. What can see us through? One thing and one only—Philosophy, and that means keeping the spirit within us unspoiled and undishonored, not giving way to pleasure or pain, never acting unthinkingly or deceitfully or insincerely, and never being dependent on the moral support of others. It also means taking what comes contentedly as all part of the process to which we owe our own being; and, above all, it means facing death calmly—taking it simply as a dissolution of the atoms of which every living organism is composed. Their perpetual transformation does not hurt the atoms, so why should one mind the whole organism being transformed and dissolved? It is a law of nature, and Natural Law can never be wrong.

SECTION V.—ARGUMENT
AND OBSERVATION

THE ORIGINS OF THE HELLENIC RACE

(HERODOTUS: Book I. chapters 56–8)

CROESUS made inquiries as to which were the greatest powers in Hellas, with a view to securing their friendly support, and, as a result of these inquiries, he found that the Lacedaemonians and the Athenians stood out among the peoples of Dorian and Ionian race respectively. Of these peoples that had thus made their mark, the latter was originally a Pelasgian and the former a Hellenic nationality, and, while the latter had never yet moved from its home, the former had been exceed-

---

[1] Written in camp at Carnuntum, on the Danube frontier. [ED.]

ingly migratory. In the time of King Deucalion, the former nationality had occupied the territory of Phthiotis, and in the time of Dorus son of Hellen the country called Histiaeotis at the foot of Mounts Ossa and Olympus. After being expelled from Histiaeotis by the Cadmeians, it had settled in Pindus and acquired the name of Macedni. From Pindus it made another move to Dryopis, and from Dryopis it eventually passed into the Peloponnese, where it came to be known as Dorian. As regards the language spoken by the Pelasgians, I have no exact information; but it is possible to argue by inference from the still existing Pelasgians[1] who occupy the city of Creston[2] in the hinterland of the Tyrrhenians; from the other Pelasgians[3] who have settled in Placia and Scylacè on the Hellespont; and from the various other communities of Pelasgian race which have changed their national name. If inferences may legitimately be drawn from this evidence, then the original Pelasgians were speakers of a non-Greek language, and the once Pelasgian Athenian nation must have learned a new language at the time when they changed from Pelasgians into Hellenes. At all events, the inhabitants of Creston and of Placia, who in neither case speak the same language as their present respective neighbors, do speak the same language as one another, and thereby demonstrate that they have preserved the specific language which they brought with them when they originally migrated to those two places. In contrast to this, the Hellenic race has employed an identical language continuously, ever since it came into existence.[4] After splitting off from the Pelasgian race, it found itself weak, but from these small beginnings it has increased until it now includes a number of nationalities, its principal recruits being Pelasgians, besides many other nationalities of non-Hellenic origin. It is my further opinion that the non-Hellenic origin of the Pelasgians accounts for the complete failure of even this nationality to grow to any considerable dimensions.

EGYPT THE CRADLE OF CIVILIZATION

(HERODOTUS: Book II. chapters 48–58)

EXCEPT for the choral element, the Egyptian ritual in the festival of Dionysus is practically identical in every detail

---

[1] Former neighbors of the people now called Dorians, at the period when they (the Pelasgians) occupied the district now called Thessaliotis. [AUTHOR.]

[2] In the region now called Eastern Macedonia. [ED.]

[3] Formerly domiciled in the same territory as the Athenians. [AUTHOR.]

[4] This is a point on which I, personally, entertain no doubts. [AUTHOR.]

with the Hellenic. . . . My own theory is that Melampus, who was a man of genius, not only invented a procedure of divination for himself but also sought information from Egypt, as a result of which he introduced the cult of Dionysus and many other innovations into Hellas, with slight alterations from their original form. I cannot admit that the resemblance between the Dionysiac rituals of Egypt and Hellas is accidental, for in that case the Hellenic ritual would have been homologous with other Hellenic rituals and would not have been a recent introduction. Nor can I admit that the Egyptians adopted either this institution or any other from the Hellenes. I imagine that Melampus' principal source of information in regard to Dionysus was Cadmus of Tyre and his fellow colonists from Phoenicia, who settled in the country now called Boeotia. The truth is that the names of almost all the Gods have come to Hellas from Egypt. The general fact of their non-Hellenic origin I have established by inquiry, and in my opinion their particular place of origin is most likely to be Egypt. I have already mentioned that, with the exception of Poseidon, the Dioscuri, Hera, Hestia, Themis, the Graces and the Nereids, the names of all the other Hellenic Gods are indigenous in Egypt;[1] and, in regard to the Gods with whose names the Egyptians do not claim to be acquainted, I imagine that they are derived from the Pelasgians.[2] There is nothing, however, in Egypt corresponding to a cult of the Saints.[3]

These institutions, as well as others which I shall proceed to describe, have been borrowed by the Hellenes from Egypt. The Hellenic representation of Hermes, on the other hand, has been copied not from the Egyptians but from the Pelasgians, from whom it was borrowed first by the Athenians and, through them, by the rest of the Hellenes.[4] My meaning will by understood by any individual who has been initiated into the sacraments of the Cabeiri as celebrated in Samothrace, whose inhabitants borrowed them from the Pelasgians.[5] Copying the Pelasgians, the Athenians were the first Hellenes to represent Hermes in the posture that I have indicated. The

[1] In this I am simply repeating the statements of the Egyptians themselves. [AUTHOR.]

[2] With the exception of Poseidon, of whom the Hellenes learned from the Berbers, among whom alone the name of Poseidon is indigenous, and who have always honored this divinity. [AUTHOR.]

[3] In Greek, "Heroes." [ED.]

[4] At that time the Athenians, who already counted as Hellenes, had a community of Pelasgians domiciled in their country, and this, incidentally, was how the Pelasgians came to be regarded as Hellenes. [AUTHOR.]

[5] Samothrace was formerly occupied by the particular Pelasgians who had been domiciled in Athenian territory, and it is from these Pelasgians that the Samothracians have borrowed the sacraments. [AUTHOR.]

Pelasgians have a doctrine on this subject, which is revealed in the sacraments at Samothrace. Formerly (as I know from personal inquiry at Dodona) the Pelasgians, in all their religious services, merely invoked "the Gods," without giving either name or title (of which they were still ignorant) to any of them. They called them "Gods" because it was they who had "got" into order and kept in order the Universe and all its subdivisions. Subsequently, after a long interval, they informed themselves from Egyptian sources of the names of all the Gods except Dionysus, and, after another long interval, of the name of Dionysus as well. After a time, the Pelasgians came to inquire at the Oracle of Dodona[1] as to whether they should adopt these names of foreign provenance. The Oracle commanded them to do so, and from that time onwards the Pelasgians invoked the Gods by name in their services, while the Hellenes subsequently took over the practice from the Pelasgians.

It would hardly be an exaggeration to say that, as recently as yesterday or the day before, the Hellenes remained in ignorance of the respective origins of the Gods, of their outward appearance, and of the question whether or not they had existed from eternity. Hesiod and Homer, whose date I should place not more than four centuries earlier than my own generation, were the authorities who first gave the Hellenes a genealogy of the Gods, provided the Gods with their titles, assigned them their honors and occupations, and visualized their outward appearance.[2] My sources for the first series of statements made above are the priestesses at Dodona, while for the remainder, which relate to Hesiod and Homer, I am responsible myself.

The problem of the relationship between the oracle in Hellas and the oracle in North Africa[3] is the subject of an Egyptian story which I will proceed to relate. The priests of Theban Zeus[4] state that two Theban priestesses were once transported from the country by Phoenicians, and that inquiry showed that one of them had been sold in North Africa and the other in Hellas. It was these women, they assert, who originally founded the oracles in the territory of the nations aforementioned. I asked them how they were in a position to speak with such precise knowledge, to which they replied that an active search for these women had been conducted by

---

[1] This oracle is considered to be the most ancient in Hellas, and was the only one in existence at the period in question. [AUTHOR.]

[2] The poets who are alleged to be anterior of these two are really posterior to them, in my opinion. [AUTHOR.]

[3] I.e. Zeus of Dodona in Epirus and Amen of Siwah in the Libyan Desert. [ED.]

[4] I.e. Amen of Thebes in Egypt. [ED.]

them, and that while they had not succeeded in discovering them, they had eventually obtained the information which they were now retailing to me. This was what I heard from the priests at Thebes, whereas the prophetesses at Dodona tell the following story: Two black doves flew from Egyptian Thebes to North Africa and to Dodona respectively. The latter perched upon a beech tree and proclaimed, with human voice, that an oracle of Zeus should be established on that spot. The Dodonaeans regarded the message as supernatural and accordingly carried it into effect. The dove which went to North Africa is said to have commanded the Berbers to establish the oracle of Amen, which is another oracle of Zeus. This was the story as told me by the priestesses at Dodona,[1] who were corroborated by the other local inhabitants connected with the shrine. My personal views on the subject are as follows. If the Phoenicians did in reality transport the holy women and sell one of them in North Africa and the other in Hellas, then, in my opinion, the particular district of the identical country, now called Hellas and formerly called Pelasgia, in which she was sold, must have been Thesprotia.[2] During her subsequent period of servitude there, she must have founded a shrine of Zeus under a wild oak, as indeed it was natural that the former ministrant of a temple of Zeus at Thebes should preserve the memory of it in her new place of residence. In due course, when she had mastered the Greek language, she instituted an oracle; and she must have mentioned that a sister of hers had been sold in North Africa by the same Phoenicians by whom she had been sold herself. The women must, in my opinion, have been called "doves" by the Dodonaeans for the reason that they were non-Hellenes and so appeared to the natives to twitter like birds. When they say that, after a time, the dove spoke with human voice, they mean: when the woman began to talk intelligibly to them; while, so long as she was speaking a foreign language, she appeared to them to be talking like a bird. How, after all, could a dove speak with human voice in the literal sense of the words? Again, when they say that the dove was black they indicate that the woman was an Egyptian. The methods of divination employed respectively at Egyptian Thebes and at Dodona are, in fact, almost identical, and the science of divination by entrails is likewise of Egyptian origin.

The Egyptians were also the first members of the human race to hold festivals, processions and services, all of which

[1] Their names were Promenea (the eldest), Timareta (the next eldest) and Nicandra (the youngest). [AUTHOR.]

[2] I.e. Southwestern Epirus. [ED.]

were copied by the Hellenes from them. I infer this from the fact that in Egypt these ceremonies appear to have been in use since a remote date, while in Hellas they are recent innovations.

ARE THE COLCHIANS EGYPTIANS?

(HERODOTUS: Book II. chapters 104–5)

THE Colchians[1] appear to be of Egyptian origin—a fact which I noticed for myself before I was informed of it by others. As soon as it had engaged my attention, I made inquiries among both nations and found that the Colchians had more recollection of the Egyptians than the latter had of them. The Egyptians advanced the theory that the Colchians were a relic of Sesostris'[2] army. I based my own conjecture upon the fact that the Colchians have dark complexions and woolly hair—characteristics inconclusive in themselves, as being common to other races—and more confidently upon the further fact that the Colchians, Egyptians and Sudanese are the only members of the human race who practice infantile circumcision. The Phoenicians and the Palestinian Syrians frankly admit that they have borrowed the custom from the Egyptians, while the Syrians on the rivers Thermodon and Parthenius[3] and their neighbors, the Macrones state that they have borrowed it only recently from the Colchians. This is an exhaustive list of the races that practice circumcision, and they all appear to be imitators of the Egyptians. As between the Egyptians themselves and the Sudanese, I cannot say which party were the borrowers, for the custom apparently dates from remote antiquity in both countries. For the theory that the others borrowed it by intercourse with the Egyptians I find strong confirmation in the following fact. Phoenicians who have intercourse with Hellas cease to imitate the Egyptians and omit to circumcise the next generation. Incidentally, let me mention another point in which the Colchians resemble the Egyptians. They and the Egyptians are the unique possessors of an identical method of working linen[4] besides

[1] Colchis occupied the western half of the present country of Georgia in Trans-Caucasia. [ED.]

[2] A legendary figure, in whom several of the great historical Egyptian conquerors were blended. [ED.]

[3] Two Anatolian rivers, now called Terme-Su and Bartin-Su, which flow into the Black Sea between Unie and Samsun and between Amasra and Zonguldaq respectively. [ED.]

[4] In Hellas, the trade name for Colchian linen is "Sardinian," while the linen which comes from Egypt is called "Egyptian." [AUTHOR.]

which, there are strong resemblances between the two nations in their social life and their languages.

CASTE

(HERODOTUS: Book II. chapters 164–8)

IN Egypt there are seven castes entitled respectively Priests, Fighting Men, Cowherds, Swineherds, Tradesmen, Dragomans, and Master Mariners. The number is seven and the names are occupational. The Fighting Men are called Calasiries and Hermotybies, and come respectively from the following departments.[1] To the Hermotybies belong the departments of . . . [names omitted] . . . and their strength, at its maximum, was 160,000. Not one of these individuals has been trained in any illiberal trade. They are all devoted to the profession of arms. To the Calasiriës belong the other departments of . . . [names omitted] . . . and their strength, at its maximum, was 200,000. They, too, are prohibited from practicing any ordinary art or craft, and practice nothing but the art of war by hereditary transmission. Whether this institution likewise has been borrowed from the Egyptians by the Hellenes I am unable precisely to determine, seeing that the Thracians, Nomads, Persians, Lydians[2] and almost all other non-Hellenic peoples treat persons apprenticed to the arts and crafts, and the issue of such persons, as lower in class than other members of the community, while persons unconnected with handicrafts are regarded as being of gentle birth, especially those who are devoted to the military career. In any case, this social custom has been adopted by all Hellenes and particularly by the Lacedaemonians—the Corinthians, by contrast, being the nation that shows least contempt for the manual worker. In Egypt, the military caste possessed the following special privileges, which were enjoyed by no other class of the population except the priests: First, a reservation of twelve select acres[3] of land per head tax-free, the income from each allotment passing in rotation from one individual to another and never remaining in perpetuity in the same hands; while, in the second place, a thousand Calasiriës and an equal contingent of Hermotybiës served annually as a royal bodyguard. In addition to their allotments, the individuals engaged in any given year upon this special service

[1] The whole territory of Egypt is divided up into departments. [AUTHOR.]
[2] Inhabitants of the modern Vilayet of Aidin in Western Anatolia. [ED.]
[3] The Egyptian acre is one hundred Egyptian cubits square, the Egyptian cubit coinciding in length with the Samian. [AUTHOR.]

received, as a bonus, a daily ration amounting per head to five minas of baker's bread, two minas of meat, and four ladles of wine.

THE TRANSMISSION OF THE ALPHABET

(HERODOTUS: Book V. chapters 58–9)

AMONG the many useful innovations introduced into Hellas by the Phoenicians who came with Cadmus and colonized the country now called Boeotia, was the Alphabet, which, in my opinion, was previously unknown in the Hellenic world. They originally introduced the script which is in universal use among the Phoenicians, but in process of time they changed the style of the letters simultaneously with their spoken language. During this period, their Hellenic neighbors on almost every frontier were of Ionian nationality; so the Ionians learned the art of writing from the Phoenicians, adopted their script with slight modifications, and recorded the obligation by calling this script "Phoenician"—as was only just, considering that the Phoenicians had originally introduced it into Hellas. The Ionians have also retained the ancient name of "leathers"[1] for "papers," because at one time the scarcity of papyrus compelled them to employ goatskins or sheepskins[2] as writing materials. I have seen the "Cadmean Script" with my own eyes in inscriptions[3] engraved upon three tripods in the shrine of Ismenian Apollo at Thebes in Boeotia.

DID THE ALCMAEONIDAE BETRAY ATHENS?

(HERODOTUS: Book VI. chapters 121–4)

To my mind, the supposition that the Alcmaeonidae would ever have displayed a shield[4] as a signal to the Persians, with

[1] In Greek "diphtherai," a word which was borrowed by the contemporary Oriental world and survives in modern Persian in the word "defter" (=ledger), whence it has been reintroduced through Turkish into Modern Greek! [ED.]

[2] In many non-Hellenic countries, similar skins are employed as writing materials down to the present day. [AUTHOR.]

[3] Herodotus proceeds to quote these inscriptions and to identify the persons mentioned in them. The internal evidence of style and language proves them to have been comparatively recent forgeries. [ED.]

[4] See Herodotus, Book VI. chapter 115. The shield was used for flashing heliographical messages, and when the Persian expedition had re-embarked after its defeat at Marathon, a signal was supposed to have been flashed to it, advising it to sail round Attica and land again on the opposite coast before the Athenian army could march back across country. [ED.]

the intention of bringing Athens under the yoke of the Orientals and of Hippias, is too incredible to be accepted. Everything goes to show that the Alcmaeonidae were at least as strong opponents of despotism as Callias,[1] who was the only man in Athens bold enough, when Peisistratus had been driven out of the country, to purchase his property at the treasury auction, and who never lost an opportunity of working against Peisistratus in the bitterest spirit of hostility. The Alcmaeonidae were at least as strong opponents of despotism as he, so that I reject as incredible the accusation that they displayed a shield on this occasion. The Alcmaeonidae had been kept in exile by the despots during the whole period of their rule, and it was through their machinations that this rule of the Peisistratidae was brought to an end—which means, in effect, and in my own judgment, that the Alcmaeonidae were the liberators of Athens in a far truer sense than Harmodius and Aristogeiton. By assassinating Hipparchus the latter merely exasperated the surviving members of the Peisistratid family, without contributing to the overthrow of their dominion, while the Alcmaeonidae patently liberated Athens, if it was really they who induced the priestess at Delphi to preface every response that she gave to the Lacedaemonians with an exhortation to liberate Athens, according to the story that I have explained above. If it is argued that they may have had some grievance against the commons of Athens which led them into this attempt to betray their country, it may be answered that, in the Athenian world, there was no other family that enjoyed a greater reputation or that had been invested with greater honors. It is therefore quite illogical to suppose that a shield would have been displayed by this particular family for such a reason. A shield undoubtedly was displayed; there is no getting over the fact; but I am unable to approach any nearer than I have here done towards an answer to the question: Who was the traitor who displayed it?

DID THE ARGIVES BETRAY HELLAS?

(HERODOTUS: Book VII. chapters 148[2]–152)

THE Argives give the following account of the part played by themselves [in the Great Persian War]. From the very outset, they had received information of the storm that was gathering against Hellas from the Oriental world, and, with this infor-

[1] Son of Phaenippus and father of Hipponicus. [AUTHOR.]

mation in their hands, they learned that the Hellenes intended to negotiate for their co-operation against the Persian. Accordingly, they sent *nuncii* to Delphi to ask the God what course of action would secure them the best results. Only recently, 6000 of their men had been killed in battle by the Lacedaemonians (Cleomenes son of Anaxandridas commanding), which (according to their account) was their reason for sending this mission. The priestess answered their inquiry in the following verses:

> By Heaven beloved, by neighbors sore oppressed,
> Draw back thy jutting pike and wait at rest:
> Guard thou the head; the head will save the rest.

The delivery of this response by the priestess of Delphi was previous to the arrival of the Confederate mission at Argos, where they were received in audience in the Chamber and presented their instructions. The House replied to their representations to the effect that Argos was prepared to accept their proposals on two conditions—a thirty years' peace with Lacedaemon and an equal share in the command over the entire Confederate forces. They added that in strict justice Argos was entitled to the exclusive command, but that she would be satisfied to share it on equal terms with one other power. This (according to the Argive version) was the Chamber's reply, in spite of the fact that the Oracle had placed a veto upon the alliance with the Hellenes. Their dread of the Oracle, however, was outweighed by their anxiety for a thirty years' peace, in order, as they represented, to enable their boys to grow to manhood in the interval. In the absence of such a peace, they apprehended that, in the event of their being overtaken by further disaster in the campaign against the Persian, upon the top of their previous misfortune, the cumulative result would be the permanent subjection of Argos to Sparta. The Spartan members of the Confederate mission answered the pronouncement of the Argive Chamber by declaring that they would refer the question of the treaty to their principals; but that, on the question of the command, they must be guided by their positive instructions, which were that there were two kings in Sparta and only one in Argos, and that it was impossible to remove either of the Spartan kings from his command, but that there was no objection to the Argive king being admitted to vote along with the two Spartan kings. According to the Argives' own account, this declaration put them out of patience with the aggressiveness of the Spartans and made them prefer to fall under the dominion of the Orientals rather than to yield an inch to the Lacedaemonians. Consequently, they warned the mission to be beyond the frontier before sunset, under pain of being treated as enemies. Thus far the Argives themselves, but there is a different story current in Hellas to the effect that Xerxes sent an envoy to Argos before he mobilized for his expedition against Hellas. Upon his arrival, this envoy is reported to have delivered the following *note verbale:*

"Argives, King Xerxes has a message for you. We believe our own progenitor to have been Perses, the son of Perseus[1] by Andromeda daughter of Cepheus. If so, we must be descended from your stock, and it would be equally unnatural on our part to make war upon our ancestors, and on yours to set yourselves in opposition to us in defense of a third party. Your best course is to stay at home and preserve your neutrality, and if I am successful, there is no country that I shall treat with greater honor than yours."

The Argives are reported to have been so greatly impressed by this message that they not only refrained at the moment from making any overtures to or demanding any concessions from the Hellenic Confederates, but, when the Hellenes attempted to obtain their co-operation, they deliberately demanded a share in the command, which they were aware that the Lacedaemonians would not concede, in order that they might have a pretext for maintaining neutrality. For confirmation of this version, some Hellenic authorities point to another story, relating to events of a very much later date. An Athenian mission, consisting of Callias son of Hipponicus and his suite, happened to find themselves on other business at Susa,[2] when an Argive mission, simultaneously dispatched, arrived to inquire from Artaxerxes son of Xerxes whether the *entente* which Argos had cemented with Xerxes still held good, or whether she was regarded by his government as a hostile power—to which King Artaxerxes is reported to have replied that the *entente* most certainly held good and that there was no state which he regarded as a more friendly power than Argos.

Whether Xerxes really sent an envoy to Argos with the aforementioned instructions, and whether an Argive mission really visited Susa in order to make inquiries from Artaxerxes regarding the *entente,* I am unable to say for certain, and I express no opinion on the subject beyond that which is stated by the Argives themselves. I only know this much, that if all the members of the human race were to bring their individual burdens into common stock with a view to exchanging with

[1] Son of Danae. [AUTHOR.]
[2] The city of Memnon. [AUTHOR.]

their neighbors, the closer inspection of their neighbors' burdens would make them delighted to carry home again the respective contributions which they had brought themselves. On this showing, the Argives are not the worst sinners in History. My personal duty is to reproduce what is related, but I am under no obligation whatever to believe it—a principle which applies, incidentally, to all my work. *A propos* of this, there is a further story to the effect that it was the Argives who called in the Persian against Hellas, because they had done badly in war against the Lacedaemonians and felt anything to be preferable to their present humiliation.

HOW ATHENS SAVED HELLAS

(HERODOTUS: Book VII. chapter 139)

AT this point, no alternative is open to me but to record a judgment which will be ill received by the generality of public opinion, but in which I cannot refrain from following up what appears to me to be the truth. Supposing that the Athenians had been so demoralized by the oncoming danger as to emigrate from their country, or supposing that—short of emigrating—they had stayed and submitted to Xerxes, in that event nobody would have attempted to put up a resistance to the King on sea, and, if no one had opposed Xerxes on sea, then the sequence of events on land would have been as follows. However many layers of prepared positions had been drawn across the Isthmus of Corinth by the Peloponnesians, the Lacedaemonians would have been deserted by their allies —not deliberately but under *force majeure*, as they succumbed, individually, to the naval forces of the Oriental—and would have been reduced to isolation. In their hour of isolation the Lacedaemonians would have performed magnificent exploits and died a glorious death—unless they had detected that the other Hellenes were going over to the Persian side in time to come to terms with Xerxes themselves—but in either alternative Hellas would have fallen under the Persian yoke. As regards the positions drawn across the Isthmus, I am at a loss to discover what their military value would have been had the King commanded the sea. In the actual circumstances, it would be the strict truth to say that the Athenians were the saviors of Hellas. The balance was bound to incline in favor of whichever cause the Athenians espoused; and it was the Athenians, and the Athenians alone, who willed that Hellas

should survive as a free society, who rallied all the rest of
the Hellenic world (in so far as it did not go over to the Persians), and who (next to the Gods) beat back the King's invasion. Not even the apprehension produced by the alarming
oracles that came in from Delphi could move them to emigrate from Hellas. They held their ground and did not flinch
from meeting in arms the invader of their country.

THE SOCIAL EFFECTS OF THE GREAT
PERSIAN WAR

(DIODORUS: Book XII. chapters 1–2[1])

ANYONE who directs his attention to the incongruous element
in human life may be excused for falling into perplexity. In
practice, none of the supposed blessings of life is ever granted
to human beings in its entirety, and none of the evils occurs
in an absolute form without an admixture of good. A demonstration of this can be obtained by directing the attention
to past events, especially to those of outstanding importance.
The vastness of the forces employed in the expedition of
Xerxes King of Persia against Hellas cast the shadow of a
terrible danger over Hellenic society. The stakes for which
the Hellenes were called upon to fight were slavery or freedom, while the fact that the Hellenic communities in Asia
had already been enslaved created a presumption in every
mind that the communities in Hellas itself would experience
the same fate. When, however, the war resulted, contrary to
expectation, in its amazing issue, the inhabitants of Hellas
found themselves not only relieved from the dangers which
had threatened them but possessed, in addition, of honor and
glory, while every Hellenic community was filled with such
affluence that the whole world was astonished at the com-
pleteness with which the situation had been reversed.

During the half century that followed this epoch, Hellas
made vast strides in prosperity. During this period the effects
of the new affluence showed themselves in the progress of
the arts, and artists as great as any recorded in History, including the sculptor Phidias, flourished at the time. There was
an equally signal advance in the intellectual field, in which
philosophy and public speaking were singled out for special
honor throughout the Hellenic world and particularly at
Athens. In philosophy there was the school of Socrates, Plato
and Aristotle; in public speaking there were such figures as

Pericles, Isocrates and Isocrates' pupils; and these were balanced by men of action with great military reputations, like Miltiades, Themistocles, Aristides, Cimon, Myronides and a long array of other names too numerous to mention. In the forefront of all, Athens achieved such triumphs of glory and prowess that her name won almost worldwide renown. She increased her ascendency to such a point that, with her own resources, unsupported by the Lacedaemonians and Peloponnesians, she broke the resistance of powerful Persian forces on land and sea and so humbled the pride of the famous Persian Empire that she compelled it to liberate by treaty all the Hellenic communities in Asia.

THE INFLUENCE OF SEA POWER ON HISTORY

(Anonymous[1] (*floruit ca.* 460–410 B.C.): *Athenian Institutions:* Teubner edition, ed. by E. Kalinka, 1913: chapter 2, §§ 2–8 and 11–16)

FORTUNE has also endowed the Athenians with an advantage which may be stated in the following terms: The subject populations of a continental empire are in a position to combine the resources of a number of small communities and to co-operate in a war of liberation, while the subjects of a maritime empire, in so far as they are islanders, are not in a position to consolidate the resources of the individual communities. The sea divides them, and it is commanded by the dominant power. Even if the islanders succeeded in concentrating their forces in a single island without being intercepted, they would only starve; and so far as the continental communities under Athenian domination are concerned, the larger of them are ruled by fear and the smaller by their necessities. There is not a single community that can live without imports and exports, and these will be denied to any community that does not show itself submissive to the masters of the sea. Again, the masters of the sea are in a position (as is only occasionally the case with land powers) to devastate the territory of a stronger power. They can coast along to a point where no enemy forces, or only weak forces, are stationed, and can re-embark and sail away at the approach of reinforcements. The naval power can employ this strategy with less embarrassment than the power which attempts to effect the same object by land. Again,

---

[1] Preserved among the minor works of Xenophon, who is proved by internal evidence not to be the real author. [ED.]

the masters of the sea are in a position to operate with their fleet at as great a distance as you please from their base, while land powers cannot move many days' march from their home territory. In land operations the movements are slow and it is impossible to carry rations sufficient for a prolonged campaign. Further, an army operating on land must either move across friendly territory or fight for a passage, whereas a naval force can make a landing wherever it possesses a superiority, and, so far from being compelled to land at any point where the superiority lies with the other side, it can always coast along until it finds itself off friendly territory or off the shores of a weaker power.

Again, bad harvests due to atmospheric conditions fall with crushing weight upon even the strongest land powers, while sea powers surmount them easily. Bad harvests are never of worldwide incidence, and therefore the masters of the sea are always able to draw upon regions in which the harvest has been abundant. If I may venture to descend to minor details, I may add that the command of the sea has enabled the Athenians, in the first place, to discover refinements of luxury through their extensive foreign relations. Every delicacy of Sicily, Italy, Cyprus, Egypt, Lydia,[1] the Black Sea, the Peloponnese or any other country has been accumulated on a single spot in virtue of the command of the sea. Their familiarity, again, with every language spoken under the sun has enabled the Athenians to select this expression from that language and this from the other, with the result that—in contrast to other Hellenes, who, as a general rule, preserve their local dialect, life and costume—the Athenians rejoice in a cosmopolitan civilization for which the entire Hellenic and non-Hellenic worlds have been laid under contribution. . . .

Moreover, the Athenians are the only nation, Hellenic or non-Hellenic, that is in a position to accumulate wealth. If a country happens to be rich in ship-timber, what market is there for it, if it fails to conciliate the masters of the sea? Similarly, if a country happens to be rich in iron, copper or flax, what market is there for it, if it fails to find favor in the same quarter? But these are precisely the raw materials out of which I construct my ships—timber coming from one source, iron from a second, copper from a third, hemp from a fourth, flax from a fifth. In addition, they will refuse to license the export of these commodities to other markets or—those who choose to oppose our wishes shall be excluded from the sea! Thus I, who produce not one of these commodities in my home territory, possess them all by way of the sea, while no

[1] The modern Vilayet of Aidin, in Western Anatolia. [Ed.]

other country possesses any two of them simultaneously. The same country never produces both timber and flax, the soil being bare and untimbered wherever flax is abundant. Nor are copper and iron produced in the same country, nor any other two or three materials in a single country, but always one here and the other there.

In addition to this, again, every continental coastline possesses some projecting headland or inshore island or narrow passage which offers the masters of the sea a point of vantage at which they can lie to and inflict damage upon the continental population.

There is one thing, however, that is lacking to them. Supposing that the Athenians' command of the sea were exercised from an insular base, they would have been enabled to inflict as much damage as they chose without suffering any in retaliation (in the way of seeing their own territory devastated or expecting a hostile invasion), so long as they retained command of the sea. In the actual circumstances, however, the landed and propertied interests at Athens are more inclined to cringe to the enemy, while the proletariat, which is well aware that no property of its own is going to be burned or devastated, lives in security and refuses to cringe to them. In addition, they would have been exempt, had they been inhabitants of an island, from another anxiety. They would never have had to fear the betrayal of the city by a minority or the treacherous opening of the gates or the surprise attack of an enemy (contingencies which, in an insular country, would have been ruled out of account) or any internal trouble with the proletariat (which would have been equally inconceivable in an island state). In the actual situation, if internal disorders were to break out, it would be expectations of support from the enemy, whose forces they would attempt to introduce by land, that would bring the malcontents to the point of rebellion. In an island state, they would not have had to reckon with this contingency. However, they do not happen originally to have chosen an island for their home, and they therefore take the following precautions. They deposit their property in the islands with complete confidence in their naval ascendency, and show themselves indifferent to the devastation of their territory in Attica, realizing, as they do, that they can only show consideration for Attica at the price of sacrificing interests of greater importance.

THE PLAGUE AT ATHENS (430 B.C.)

(THUCYDIDES: Book II. chapters 47–53)

EARLY in the next summer, the Peloponnesians and their allies invaded Attica with two-thirds of their forces under the command of Archidamus son of Zeuxidamus, king of the Lacedaemonians, as they had done the year before, and settled down to devastate the country. They had not been many days in Attica before the Athenians began to be attacked by the plague. This malady is supposed to have broken out before at Lemnos and in many other places, but an epidemic on so great a scale and so destructive of life had never been heard of anywhere. The doctors were at first quite unable to cope with it, owing to their ignorance of its character, and the mortality was actually heaviest among them, because they exposed themselves most to infection. Neither medicine nor any other worldly science availed the sufferers; and prayers of intercession, the consultation of oracles and all the resorts of religion proved equally ineffective, until at last they were so completely overwhelmed by their sufferings that they sank into apathy.

The epidemic is supposed to have started in the Egyptian Sudan, and from there to have traveled to Egypt, North Africa and over the greater part of the Persian dominions. Its onslaught took Athens unawares. The first cases occurred in the Peiraeus, which gave rise to a story that the Peloponnesians had poisoned the reservoirs (the present wells were not yet in existence). Later, it made its way from the port to the city, and the mortality became far heavier. I shall leave it to other writers, professional or amateur, to make their own speculations regarding the origin of the malady and its causes (if causes can be suggested of sufficient potency to account for so great a disturbance in the order of nature), and shall confine my account to an objective description, particularly of the symptoms which would assist those instructed in them to diagnose the plague correctly if it were to break out again. I can do so authoritatively, since I was attacked myself and saw how other victims were affected.

It was an admitted fact that the year in question was exceptionally free from disease of other kinds, and any previous indispositions all determined in this. Persons in normal health sickened quite unaccountably and with no warning whatever. The first symptoms which declared themselves were violent fever in the head and inflammation of the eyes, followed immediately inside the mouth by a bloodshot discoloration of the throat and tongue and an abnormally offensive odor in the breath. The next symptoms were sneezing and hoarseness, and the affection rapidly descended to the chest, where it showed itself in a violent cough. In cases in which it settled in the stomach, it deranged it completely, and discharges of bile of every species classified by medicine ensued, all accompanied by acute distress. Most patients were attacked by an ineffectual retching producing violent convulsions, which in some cases passed off but in others remained very persistent. Externally, the body was not much above the normal temperature nor jaundiced in appearance, but was reddish, livid and covered with a rash of small pustules and ulcers. The internal temperature, however, was so agonizingly high that the patient could not bear the contact of the lightest material, even linen, on the naked flesh, and longed to plunge into icy water. Many who were neglected did so in the reservoirs, consumed by an unquenchable thirst—though it made no difference whether they drank much or little. From beginning to end, there was no relief from the horrors of insomnia and inability to rest. So long as the attack was at its height, the body did not waste away but revealed unexpected powers of resistance. Consequently, the patient either succumbed (as usually happened) to the internal fever on the ninth or the seventh day without having entirely lost his physical vitality, or, if he survived this stage, the malady descended to the intestines, which it threw into a state of violent inflammation accompanied by attacks of acute diarrhea. In this second stage, those who had survived the first usually succumbed to exhaustion. After effecting its first lodgment in the head, the disease thus worked its way downward through the entire body, and when a patient survived its passage through the vital parts, it left its mark on him by its aftereffects on the extremities. It attacked the fingers, the toes and the privy parts, and many escaped with the loss of those members, and some with that of their sight. Others were affected during convalescence with a temporary failure of memory which was so complete that they could not recognize their friends and forgot their own identity. Indeed, the horror of the disease defies description. It was a scourge beyond human endurance, and it is significant of its abnormal character that the birds and animals which feed on human carrion either refused in this case to touch the quantities of unburied bodies or else died of them. The fact is established by the unquestionable disappearance of carrion-birds at the time. They were not seen feeding nor indeed seen at all; but the phenomenon was more easily observable in the case of a domestic animal like the dog.

I have described the general character of the disease without going into the innumerable details of its peculiarities and variations in individual cases. During its prevalence, there was an immunity from the ordinary complaints, or if any of them appeared it determined in this. Some deaths were due to neglect, but other patients died in spite of the best nursing. No remedy was discovered which could be used as a specific, for what succeeded in one case proved injurious in another. No constitution, strong or weak, was fortified against attack. The disease devoured whatever it met and baffled every treatment. The two most appalling features were the despondency which descended upon anyone when he felt himself sickening (a kind of instantaneous despair which sapped the victims' resistance and left them a much easier prey to the disease) and the infection of nurse by patient, which made them die like sheep and was responsible for the heaviest mortality. Where the healthy refused to approach the sick for fear of infection, the sick died untended, and entire households were carried off down to the last inmate because no one could be found to nurse them. On the other hand, where they came to their assistance they were carried off themselves, and people with any standard of behavior suffered most in this respect, since their better feelings impelled them to sacrifice themselves by going to nurse their friends, while the horror was so overwhelming that the actual relatives of the dying were often worn out by their moans and abandoned their posts. The chief sympathizers with the sick and dying were the convalescents, who realized what they were suffering and had nothing more to fear for themselves, since the same person was never attacked a second time fatally. They were congratulated by everybody, and the elation of the moment inspired them with vain hopes of being for ever immune from death by any disease.

The suffering was aggravated by the concentration of the rural population in the city, especially in the case of the refugees themselves. There being no houses to receive them, they were lodged in this summer weather in stifling huts, and there were no bounds to the mortality. The bodies of the dying were heaped one upon another, while half-dead wretches writhed in the streets and swarmed round all the fountains in their desperate longing for water. Even the places of worship in which they had bivouacked were full of the bodies of sufferers who had died in the precincts, for the horror was so overpowering that people did not know how to face it and lost all regard for commandments sacred or profane. The customary funeral observances were entirely upset; they buried their dead as best they could; and many lost all sense of decency in the matter owing to the straits to which they had been reduced by the number of previous deaths in their households. The builders of a pyre would find themselves forestalled by others, who would lay their own dead upon it and set it alight; or the bearers would throw the body upon one already burning and hurry away.

Indeed, the plague gave an impulse to every anti-social tendency at Athens. The subterfuges and restraints with which certain kinds of behavior had formerly been hedged about were relaxed by the spectacle of the rapid transitions of fortune. The well-to-do were cut off in the twinkling of an eye and people hitherto penniless were suddenly endowed with their possessions. The inevitable moral was to spend quickly and to spend on pleasure, if life and wealth were things of a day. The will to persevere in the recognized paths of honor disappeared in the uncertainty whether death would not intervene before the goal were attained, and the place of honor and welfare was usurped by the pleasure of the moment and everything that contributed to it. The fear of God and the ordinance of Man ceased to exercise their inhibitions. Since death descended alike upon the just and the unjust, there seemed nothing to choose between piety and irreligion; and criminals no longer expected to live to be convicted and sentenced, or, rather they felt that the extreme penalty was already suspended over their heads and that life should be made to yield some enjoyment before the blow descended.

PART THREE
The Art of History

SECTION I.—TECHNIQUE

HERACLES AS A CHRONOLOGICAL PROBLEM

(HERODOTUS: Book II. chapters 43–5)

IN regard to Heracles, I heard it stated in Egypt that he was one of the Twelve Gods; but I never succeeded in finding a trace in Egypt of the other Heracles with whom Hellenes are familiar. Certainly the name was not borrowed from the Hellenes by the Egyptians but (if at all) from the Egyptians by the Hellenes, and this by the particular Hellenes who gave the name of Heracles to the son of Amphitryon. One of the many pieces of evidence that I find convincing on this point is the fact that the parents of Heracles, Amphitryon and Alcmena, were of Egyptian extraction, and the further fact that the Egyptians deny all knowledge of the names of Poseidon and the Dioscuri. These latter Gods have not been admitted into the Egyptian Pantheon, while, if they had borrowed the name of any divinity at all from Hellas, these three would have made a particularly strong and not a particularly faint impression upon their memories. It is my personal belief and considered judgment that the Egyptians had at that epoch already taken to the sea and that there was also by then a seafaring element in Hellas—conditions which would have made the names of these Gods more familiar to the Egyptians than the name of Heracles.[1] The Egyptians have, however, an ancient God of their own called Heracles, whom they include among their Twelve Gods; and the date at which they place the procreation of these Twelve Gods by the Eight is seventeen thousand years before the reign of Amasis.[2]

[1] Poseidon and the Dioscuri were the Hellenic patron saints of navigation. [ED.]

[2] 569–525 B.C. [ED.]

169

Wishing to obtain precise information on these points from those qualified to give it, I sailed to Tyre in Phoenicia, where I heard that there was a shrine consecrated to Heracles. I found it sumptuously ornamented with a vast number of votive offerings, including two columns, one of refined gold and the other of emerald (the latter of which remained brilliantly luminous in the dark). I entered into conversation with the priests of this God and asked them the date at which the shrine had been founded, whereupon I learned that they, no less than the Egyptians, were in disagreement with the Hellenes. They told me that the foundation of the shrine was coeval with the foundation of Tyre itself, the date of which event was 2300 years ago.

At Tyre I saw a second shrine of a Heracles entitled "Heracles of Thasos," and in Thasos itself (which I have also visited) I discovered a shrine of Heracles originally founded by Phoenicians who had colonized the island in the course of a voyage in search of Europa [1]—an event anterior by five generations to the birth in Hellas of the Heracles whose father was Amphitryon. The results of my researches demonstrate clearly that Heracles was an ancient God; and, in my opinion, the most correct procedure is that followed by those Hellenes who have founded and maintained duplicate shrines of Heracles, in which they honor the respective bearers of the name with two distinct rituals—one as an immortal included among the Olympians, and the other as a saint.[2] The Hellenes, who commit themselves to a number of ill-considered statements, recite a particularly childish legend relating to Heracles. Once upon a time Heracles visited Egypt, when the Egyptians begarlanded him like a sacrificial victim and led him forth in solemn procession to be sacrificed to Zeus. Up to this point the hero made no resistance, but when they were proceeding to immolate him at the altar, he fought for his life and slew them to the last man. In my opinion this story betrays the utter ignorance of the Hellenes regarding Egyptian character and institutions. Among the Egyptians, even animal sacrifices are *tabu,* with the sole exception of sheep, bulls and bull-calves. That they should make human sacrifices is therefore inconceivable. Again, on the Hellenic assumption that there was only one Heracles, and that this single individual was a human being, the idea that he should have slain his tens of thousands is irreconcilable with the course of Nature. That

---

[1] According to the Hellenic legend, Europa was a Phoenician princess who was kidnapped by the God Zeus in the form of a bull and carried away by him to Crete. [ED.]

[2] In Greek, "Hero." [ED.]

concludes my observations on the subject—for which I devoutly trust that neither Gods nor Saints will bear me ill will.

CHRONOLOGY EGYPTIAN AND HELLENIC

(HERODOTUS: Book II. chapters 142–6)

UP to this point in my narrative, my sources have been the Egyptians and their priests, who reckoned the period from the first king down to the priest of Hephaestus, whose reign concludes the series, at 341 generations, filled by exactly that number of high priests and kings respectively. Now 300 generations are equivalent to 10,000 years,[1] while the remaining 41 generations, additional to the 300, make 1340 years. In other words, the Egyptians were asserting that, for the last 11,340 years, there had been no God incarnate in human form—a character which, for that matter, is not ascribed to any of the remaining kings of Egypt, whether anterior or posterior to this period. In the course of the period in question, they asserted that on four occasions the Sun had risen away from his previous quarter—there being two cycles during which he had risen where he now sets and set where he now rises.[2] They added that these astronomical revolutions had produced no variation in the environmental conditions of Egypt, such as the properties of the soil and of the river, the state of public health and the death rate.

Before my time Hecataeus the chronicler[3] visited Thebes and proceeded to recite his own genealogy, in which he linked his ancestry to a God in the sixteenth generation, whereupon the priests of Zeus did to him what they afterwards did to me, though I refrained from following his example. They took him into the great inner hall of the shrine and counted up in his presence a series of wooden statues amounting to the number that I have mentioned—it being the custom for each high priest to set up a likeness of himself in that building during his own lifetime. The priests counted them over, in my presence, again, and claimed an unbroken descent from father to son, their procedure being to start from the statue of the priest most recently deceased and to work back through the

[1] Three generations=one hundred years. [AUTHOR.]

[2] A confused allusion to the astronomical cycle of the Egyptian calendar, in which the first month was intended to begin on the day of the heliacal rising of the star Sothis—a date with which it actually coincided only once in every fourteen hundred and sixty astronomical years. [ED.]

[3] An earlier chronicler and genealogist from the Hellenic city of Miletus (*floruit* in the sixth century B.C.). [ED.]

entire series until they had identified them all. On the occasion, however, on which Hecataeus recited his genealogy and linked himself to a God in the sixteenth generation, they were not content with counting the statues but cited their own genealogies against him, to show their scepticism regarding his assertion that a man had been begotten by a God. Their method of counter-citing their genealogies was to declare that each of the statues was "a *piromis* begotten by a *piromis*," [1] until they had identified all the 341 statues, and they refused to link them to God or saint. They were, of course, claiming that the whole series of individuals represented by the statues were human beings, altogether remote from Gods. They admitted, however, that, before the time of these men, the rulers of Egypt were Gods dwelling among Mankind, some one among whom had been successively sovereign. According to them, the last God-King of Egypt had been Horus son of Osiris,[2] whom the Hellenes call Apollo.

In Hellas the youngest of the Gods are supposed to be Heracles, Dionysus and Pan, while in Egypt Pan is the most ancient of the first group of Gods ("The Eight"); Heracles of the second group ("The Twelve"); and Dionysus of the third group descended from "The Twelve." The date at which the Egyptians place Heracles with reference to the reign of Amasis has already been explained. Pan is dated even earlier and Dionysus the latest of the three, though the interval that separates even Dionysus from the reign of Amasis is calculated at 15,000 years. The Egyptians declare that they know these facts for certain through an unbroken series of calculations and chronological records. In contrast to this, the Dionysus who is said to have been the son of Semele daughter of Cadmus lived approximately 1000 years before my day, Heracles son of Alcmena 900, and Pan son of Penelope[3] approximately 800, or not so long ago as the Trojan War. The reader must adopt whichever of these rival chronologies he finds the more convincing. My personal conclusions on the subject have been explained already. If the other two, by which I mean Dionysus son of Semele and Pan son of Penelope, had made their mark and lived to the end of their days in Hellas, like Heracles son of Amphitryon, it might have been arguable that the Hellenic bearers of these names had likewise been men who had acquired the names of their predecessors and namesakes the two Egyptian Gods. The Hel-

[1] *Piromis* is the Egyptian equivalent for the Greek word "Gentleman." [AUTHOR.]

[2] Horus, the last king in this series, mounted the throne of Egypt after overthrowing Typhos. The Greek for "Osiris" is "Dionysus." [AUTHOR.]

[3] According to the Hellenic tradition, Pan's mother was Penelope and his father Hermes. [AUTHOR.]

lenes, however, assert that Dionysus, immediately after birth, was sewn up by Zeus in his own thigh and transported to Nysa in the southern hinterland of Egypt, while they are unable to tell you what Pan did with himself when once he had been born. It is therefore plain to me that the Hellenes learned the names of these two Gods at a later date than those of the others, and that, in reckoning their genealogies, they date their birth from the period at which they themselves first heard of them.

DOCUMENTARY EVIDENCE

(POLYBIUS: Book III. chapters 26 [1-5] and 33 [17-18]; Book XII. chapter 11 [1-4])

I HAVE now described the features of these treaties,[1] the texts of which are preserved on bronze *plaques*[2] in the shrine of Zeus on the Capitol[3] in the muniment-room of the Aediles.[4] In the light of this, anyone has a right to be astonished at the historian Philinus,[5] not for being ignorant of the facts,[6] but for the incredible audacity of committing himself to the contrary assertion, to the effect that treaties between Rome and Carthage were in existence which prohibited the Romans from access to any part of Sicily and the Carthaginians to any part of Italy—an assumption from which he deduces that the Romans violated their solemn treaty-engagements when they made their first landing in Sicily.[7] Although no such written engagement whatever either was or ever had been in existence, this is the explicit assertion of Philinus in his second volume. I have referred to the point in the introduction to my own work, but have postponed dealing with it until the present occasion—on which I have now done so in detail, in view of the fact that many students of history have been led into

---

[1] The early treaties between Rome and Carthage. [ED.]

[2] Many fragments of Hellenic and Roman documents (legal and religious) engraved on bronze *plaques* have survived from antiquity, though the text here mentioned are not among the number. [ED.]

[3] *I.e.* Jupiter Capitolinus. [ED.]

[4] A college of annually elected officers at Rome whose functions were mainly economic. [ED.]

[5] A Hellenic historian of the First Punic War (265–242 B.C.), of which he was apparently a contemporary. [ED.]

[6] There is nothing astonishing in that, considering that even in our own day, these texts were unknown to the most apparently earnest students of public affairs, including those whose age endowed them with the longest span of memory. [AUTHOR.]

[7] In 264 B.C., the first campaign of the First Punic War. [ED.]

error in this connection owing to their reliance upon the work of Philinus. . . .

My readers must not be astonished at the minuteness of these returns,[1] even though I may have discussed the transactions of Hannibal in Spain in almost greater detail than a firsthand authority would venture to give of the current affairs that had passed through his own hands; nor must they condemn me unheard if I have acted suspiciously like mendacious historians when they wish to create an impression of veracity. This list is a discovery of my own at the shrine of Lacinium,[2] where it was placed on record on a bronze *plaque* by Hannibal, during the period of his Italian campaigns. I feel so confident of the trustworthiness of this document, at any rate on such points as those which I have cited, that I have decided to take it as my guide. . . .

If our friend Timaeus[3] had been able to lay hands upon any public archives or commemorative monuments in support of his contention, are we to suppose that he would have failed to mention them? Timaeus is the historian who collates the list of the annual Directory at Lacedaemon with the list of the Kings (right back to the earliest times); who arranges the annual officers of Athens and the priestesses at Argos in parallel columns with the victors at the Olympian Games; who exposes the errors of Governments in their official records of these data, in which he proves a three month margin of inaccuracy. It is Timaeus, again, who has discovered the records inscribed on the wrong side of public buildings and the lists of foreign consuls on the door-jambs of shrines.

THE PLACE OF GEOGRAPHY IN HISTORY

(POLYBIUS: Book III. chapters 57–9)

Now that I have conducted my own narrative and the commanders of the opposing forces and the war itself [4] to the threshold of Italy, I wish, before embarking upon the military operations, to discuss briefly certain points which are not irrelevant to my work. Possibly some readers may be curious to know how it is that, after enlarging upon the geography of

---

[1] The returns of the force with which Hannibal invaded Italy. [ED.]

[2] A famous shrine of the Goddness Hera in the territory of Croton, a Hellenic city-state in the Toe of Italy. [ED.]

[3] Timaeus of Tauromenium *ca.* 346–250 B.C., a famous Hellenic historian whose works are lost, and regarding whom our chief information is derived from Polybius' detailed and violent attacks upon him. [ED.]

[4] The Hannibalic or "Second Punic" War between Rome and Carthage. [ED.]

Northwest Africa and Spain, I have not specially dilated upon the Straits of Gibraltar, the Atlantic Ocean and its peculiar phenomena, the British Isles and the tin industry, or the silver mines and gold mines in Spain itself—subjects to which previous historians have devoted many pages of controversy. My reason for leaving aside this branch of History has not been any idea that it is irrelevant, but an unwillingness, in the first place, to be perpetually interrupting the narrative and diverting the attention of the serious reader from my transactional subject matter, and, in the second place, a positive decision not to deal with this material in a disjointed or incidental manner, but to assign to this branch a special place and time of its own and then to give as accurate an account of it as may lie in my power. My readers must therefore not be astonished if in the following chapters, when I come to other regions of special geographical interest, I leave aside this branch of inquiry—my reasons for doing so having now been explained. If any reader insists upon receiving this information piecemeal, region by region, he may possibly be unaware that he is behaving very like the glutton at the dinner table. The glutton who tastes every dish does not genuinely enjoy any of the viands at the moment of eating and does not obtain any permanent benefit from them in the way of digestion and nourishment, but precisely the contrary. Similarly, the gluttonous reader defeats himself, whether his aim be momentary amusement or permanent instruction.

The actual need of close thinking and of reform (in the direction of greater accuracy) under which this branch of History at present labors more than any other, is made manifest by many considerations, of which I will mention the most cogent. Almost all writers of History, or at any rate the vast majority, have attempted to describe the situation and the peculiarities of countries on the borderline of our known habitable world, and in doing so the majority have fallen into innumerable errors. There is therefore no excuse for leaving this subject aside, but, at the same time, whatever has to be said in answer to our predecessors must be said with the full attention of the mind and not in an incidental and disjointed manner. Nor, again, must it be said in a spirit of censure or in a tone of castigation. It is fairer to praise their efforts while correcting their ignorance, in recognition of the fact that, had these writers been able to avail themselves of the opportunities of the present day, they would have effected corrections and rearrangements in much of their own published work. In the past, it would be impossible to point to more than an insignificant number of Hellenes who have attempted to investigate the borderlands—the deterrent being the impracticability of the enterprise. At that time the dangers of sea travel were almost literally innumerable, though they were only a fraction of the dangers by land. Even, moreover, if a traveler succeeded, by choice or necessity, in reaching the ends of the Earth, he was still apt to be frustrated in the accomplishment of his object. Any extensive firsthand observation was rendered difficult by the fact that some regions had become decivilized and others were uninhabited, while the differentiation of human speech made it still more difficult to obtain information by inquiry regarding the objects that met the eye. Even, however, when the information was obtained, the most difficult achievement of all from the observer's point of view was to exercise sufficient self-restraint to resist the temptations of sensationalism and marvel-mongering, to give his own first allegiance to the truth and to report to us the whole truth and nothing but the truth. In consequence, accurate historical research into the subjects aforementioned was not so much difficult as impossible in times past; and, so far from deserving censure for their errors and omissions, the writers of the day may justly claim our approbation and admiration for such facts as they ascertained and for the degree to which they advanced the knowledge of the subject under adverse conditions. In modern times, however, the empire of Alexander in Asia and the supremacy of Rome elsewhere have opened up almost the entire world to maritime or overland travel, while men of action have found their ambitions diverted from military and political careers and have been presented by the new conditions with many important facilities for investigation and research into the subjects aforesaid, so that it is incumbent upon us to acquire better and more accurate knowledge in previously uncharted fields. I shall attempt to make my own contribution to this task when I arrive at a suitable point in my work for this branch of inquiry, and I shall hope to initiate serious students into the subject in a comprehensive way. Indeed, my principal object in exposing myself to the dangers which I have encountered in my travels in Africa and Spain, and also in Gaul and on the Ocean which washes the further shores of these countries, has been to correct the ignorance of our predecessors in this branch of knowledge and to make this part of the world as familiar to the Hellenic public as the remainder.

THE METHOD OF ALTERNATE CHAPTERS

(POLYBIUS: Book XXXVIII. chapters 5–6)

I AM not unaware that some readers will criticize my work on the ground that I have given an incomplete and disjointed narrative of events—that, for example, in proceeding to relate the siege of Carthage, I have suddenly abandoned it in the middle, interrupted my train of thought and passed in succession to the transactions of Hellas, Macedonia, Syria or other areas. Serious students, I shall be told, demand continuity and desire to follow a subject out to its conclusion—the method which procures the maximum amount of gratification and instruction to the attentive reader. For my own part, I not only dissent from this view but cherish the opposite, in support of which I am prepared to call the evidence of Nature herself. Nature does not like, in the exercise of any single sense, to dwell continuously upon an identical object. She is the faithful patroness of change, and, if she must attend to identical objects, she prefers to do so at intervals and from different angles. My proposition may be illustrated from the sense of hearing, which does not like to dwell continuously upon identical passages, whether sung or recited, but is stimulated by variations and, in a general way, by anything discursive or characterized by violent and rapid modulations. Similarly, the sense of taste will be found to be incapable of keeping, without a change, to even the richest dishes. It cloys so readily that it delights in variety and often welcomes plain food more heartily than rich food for novelty's sake. The same phenomenon will be noticed in the case of the sight. The sight is practically incapable of focusing continuously upon one object, but is stimulated by diversity and change in the field of vision. The most signal example of the law, however, is afforded by the intellect. Laborious intellectual workers find an equivalent of recreation in the transference of the mental focus and attention from one object to another. In fact, I believe that the most brilliant ancient historians consciously adopted this means of recreation, some by introducing digressions in the form of legend or anecdote, others by so far diversifying their historical narrative as not to confine their transitions to different parts of Hellas, but to embrace the outer world. I am thinking of such cases as a historian who, in the middle of narrating the history of Thessaly and the transactions of Alexander of Pherae, breaks off in order to describe the enterprises of the Lacedaemonians in the Peloponnese, or possibly the enterprises of the Thebans, or, again, events in Macedon or Illyria, and who then proceeds to linger over the expedition of Iphicrates to Egypt or the outrages of Clearchus in the Black Sea. The upshot is that all historical writers will be found to have employed this method of treatment, but to have done so unsystematically, whereas I have been systematic. For example, my predecessors, after recording how the Illyrian king Bardyllis or the Thracian king Cersobleptes obtained their thrones, not only break off without giving the next chapter in the story but also omit to recur to the sequel after an interval, instead of which they revert to their original subject and treat the other as a mere insertion. My own method has been to keep distinct from one another all the most important regions of the world and the transactions of which they have been respectively the theaters; to adhere, in surveying them, to a fixed order of sequence; and to narrate, within the limits of each successive year, the contemporaneous events that occurred in it. In this way I make it impossible for serious students to mistake the points at which I pick up continuity with events previously narrated or interrupt my narrative of events in any given case, so as to leave none of the subdivisions aforementioned incomplete or defective from the point of view of the serious reader.

THE FIRST PERSON IN NARRATIVE

(Polybius: Book XXXVI. chapter 12)

My readers must not be surprised if I sometimes refer to myself by my proper name and sometimes by such general expressions as "When I said this" or "When I concurred in this." The fact that I am deeply involved, in the personal sense, in the transactions which I have to narrate from this point onwards, makes it essential for me to vary my references to myself. I have to avoid giving offense by a monotonous repetition of my name, and I have equally to be on my guard against drifting into vulgarity by using the words "me" and "on my account" on every occasion. I shall therefore avail myself of all these formulas, selecting the variant most suitable to any given occasion, as my best chance of being acquitted by my readers of the extremely tiresome vice of self-advertisement— a trick of style which arouses an instinctive repulsion, although it is often unavoidable when there is no alternative method of presenting subject matter. Happily Fortune has assisted me to solve this problem by the fact that, to the best of my knowledge, no other individual before my time has possessed the proper name "Polybius."

SPEECHES: THEIR USE AND ABUSE

(POLYBIUS: Book XXXVI. chapter 1, and Book XII. chapter 25[a-b])

POSSIBLY some of my readers may be curious to know how it is that I have not attempted to shine by reproducing the speeches delivered by the various parties, when I have found myself in possession of so grand a theme and so vast a canvas. Why have I not followed the example of the majority of historians, who marshal the speeches proper to the occasion on either side? The fact that I personally do not reject this branch of historical writing has been made sufficiently clear in several passages of my work, in which I have frequently reported the speeches and compositions of public men; but it will now become evident that I am not determined to follow this practice in season and out of season, considering that it would not be easy to find a more magnificent theme than the present[1] or more abundant material to serve up to my readers. I may add that nothing would be simpler for me than to produce a literary effort of the kind, were I not convinced that the same rule applies to the historian as to the politician. The politician's duty is not to speechify or to enlarge upon every detail of any subject that comes up for discussion, but to adapt his words to the given occasion; and similarly the historian's duty is not to practise upon his readers or to show off his literary ability at their expense, but to do his best to investigate and elucidate the words actually spoken, confining himself throughout to the most vital and effective passages. . . .

It is proverbial that one drop from the largest jar is enough to identify the whole tincture which it contains, and the moral of this is applicable to the subject in hand. When once one or two misstatements have been detected in a historical work, and these misstatements have been made deliberately, it is evident that no further reliance or confidence can be reposed in any of the assertions of such a writer. In the hope of convincing even the ardent champions of Timaeus, I propose to say something concerning his policy and practice in regard to speeches and pleadings, diplomatic *notes verbales* and, in short, the whole genus of orations, which may almost be regarded as summaries of events and as the unifying element of historical writing. The fact that Timaeus has falsified, and intentionally falsified, the speeches included in his works, can hardly have escaped his readers. Instead of reproducing the words spoken in their actual form, he determines what ought to be said and

---

[1] The outbreak of the third and last war between Rome and Carthage (150/149 B.C.). [ED.]

then proceeds to detail what purport to be the speeches and the other corollaries of the given series of events, precisely as though he were a student who had been set a theme as an exercise and was endeavoring to make it an occasion for the display of his abilities, instead of reporting the words actually spoken.

It is the function of History in the first place to ascertain the exact words actually spoken, whatever they may be, and in the second place to inquire into the cause which crowned the action taken or the words spoken with success or failure. The bare statement of the facts themselves is merely entertaining without being in the least instructive, whereas the additional explanation of the cause makes the study of History a fruitful employment. The analogies that can be drawn from similar situations to our own offer materials and presumptions for forecasting the future, in regard to which they sometimes act as a warning, while at other times they encourage us to strike out boldly into the oncoming tide of events in virtue of a historical parallel. A historian, however, who suppresses both the words spoken and their cause and replaces them by fictitious expositions and verbosities, destroys, in so doing, the characteristic quality of History; and this is precisely the offense of which Timaeus is guilty. The fact that every volume of his works is full of such spurious matter is common knowledge.

SPEECH AND NARRATIVE IN HISTORY

(DIODORUS: Book XX. chapters 1–2 [2])

WRITERS who insert long-winded set speeches in historical works, or who introduce perpetual declamations, are deserving of censure. They not only break the continuity of their narrative by the irrelevance of these intrusive orations, but they interrupt the play of intellectual curiosity in the minds of even the most enthusiastic seekers after historical knowledge. After all, it is open to anyone who may be desirous of displaying his literary ability to compose set speeches, diplomatic *notes verbales*, encomiums, invectives and so on as independent works. By paying due regard to literary form and by working out his themes separately in the two branches of writing, he might reasonably hope to obtain distinction in both spheres. Actually, however, some writers have carried the insertion of declamatory passages to such lengths that they have made their whole history a mere appendage to the speeches—

oblivious of the fact that taste is offended not only by bad writing, but by writing which in another context would be considered relevant and felicitous, when it happens to have strayed out of its proper place. Consequently the readers of such works either skip the declamations, however masterly they may be considered to be, or else their spirit is so utterly broken by the writer's prolixity and irrelevance that they abandon the attempt to read him altogether. For this they cannot be blamed, since History, as a branch of literature, is simple and homogeneous, and bears a general resemblance to a living organism, whose *disjecta membra* are bereft of the grace of vitality, while, so long as it retains its essential co-ordination, it is preserved in its happiest form and renders the reader's task agreeable and easy on account of the homogeneity of its structure throughout.

At the same time, I do not go so far as to condemn declamatory passages without qualification and to eject them altogether from my historical work. Requiring, as she does, the ornament of variety, History is unable to dispense with such passages here and there (a touch which I myself should be reluctant to forego in its proper place). Accordingly, whenever the situation demands a diplomatic *note verbale,* a parliamentary oration, and so on, the historian who has not the courage to descend into the oratorical arena is equally open to criticism. There are, indeed, a considerable number of occasions which will be found to render a resort to declamation essential. Full, able and pointed speeches may have been delivered as a historical fact, in which case it would be a mistake to discount and pass over memorable passages which might be not devoid of instruction from the historical point of view. Or, again, the subject matter may possess such importance and such brilliance that the words spoken cannot be allowed to appear inadequate to the actions performed. Sometimes, again, a *dénouement* may be so surprising that we may find ourselves compelled to employ speeches in consonance with the subject in order to offer the solution of the puzzle.

WHAT MAKES A GOOD HISTORICAL
SUBJECT?

(DIODORUS: Book XVI. chapter 1)

IN all historical works, the writers should aim at embracing in their respective volumes transactions, whether of states or sovereigns, which are self-contained from beginning to end. This is the method which is found, on examination, to present History to the reader in the clearest and most easily remembered form. Incomplete transactions, with no continuity between the end and the beginning, interrupt the play of intellectual curiosity in the serious reader; while transactions embracing a continuity of action right down to the conclusion supply a narrative which constitutes a whole in itself. When, however, the genius of the events themselves co-operates with the writer's endeavor, then no excuse whatever is left him for not attempting to realize this ideal. Accordingly, I shall do my best, for my own part, now that I have arrived at the transactions of Philip, son of Amyntas, to embrace the career of that sovereign in the present volume. During the twenty-four years of his reign as King of Macedonia, in which he started with the slenderest resources, Philip built his own kingdom up into the greatest power in Europe. Having found Macedonia under the yoke of the Illyrians, he made her mistress of many great nations and states; and, by force of personal character, he established his ascendency over the entire Hellenic world, whose component states offered him their voluntary submission. He subdued the criminals who had plundered the shrine at Delphia, and was recompensed for his championship of the Oracle by being admitted to the Council of the Amphictyons,[1] in which he was assigned the votes of the conquered Phocians as a reward for his zeal on behalf of Religion. After subduing the Illyrians, Paeonians, Thracians, Nomads and all the surrounding nations, he projected the overthrow of the Persian Empire, landed forces in Asia and was in the act of liberating the Hellenic communities when he was interrupted by Fate— in spite of which, he bequeathed a military establishment of such size and quality that his son Alexander was enabled to overthrow the Persian Empire without requiring the assistance of allies. These achievements were not the work of Fortune but of his own force of character, for this king stands out above all others for his military acumen, personal courage and intellectual brilliance.

[1] An international organization which administered the shrines at Delphi and Thermopylae, and which represented a greater proportion of the Hellenic world than any other formally organized body. [ED.]

SECTION II.—CRITICISM

POLYBIUS ON ZENO OF RHODES

(*Floruit* in the first half of the second century B.C.)

(POLYBIUS: Book XVI. chapters 14, 17 [8]–18 [1] and 20)

THE period within which these events[1] in Messenia, as well as the aforementioned naval operations, occurred, happens to have been treated by several historical specialists, concerning whom I propose to say a few words. Since I cannot deal with them all, I shall confine myself to those who in my opinion will repay discussion and examination, whom I take to be Zeno and Antisthenes of Rhodes. I have several reasons for selecting these two writers. Both are contemporaries; both have had practical experience of politics; and in general it may be said that both have produced their works from motives of ambition and other considerations entirely honorable to politicians, and not from motives of self-interest. The fact that they deal with the same events as I do forbids me to pass them over, under penalty of seeing serious students follow their authority in preference to my own on the occasional points of disagreement between us, owing to the reputation of their country and the presumption that naval operations must be the special province of Rhodian writers.

The first fault that I have to find with Zeno and Antisthenes is that they both represent the engagement off Lade as having been more and not less violent and hotly contested than that off Chios,[2] both in the details of the action and in its general result, in regard to which, they claim in general terms that the victory rested with the Rhodians. I will go so far as to admit that historians may legitimately incline the scales in favor of their own countries, but not that they may commit themselves, for their countries' sake, to assertions contradicted by the facts. The errors of ignorance to which writers are exposed by human fallibility are sufficiently serious; but if we historians deliberately falsify the facts for the benefit of friends or country, we shall be descending, surely, to the level of those who devote themselves to the same malpractice as a remunerative profession. Such characters bring their works into discredit by taking their own material interests as their standard

---

[1] 202-1 B.C. [ED.]

[2] Both engagements were fought in 202-1 B.C.—that off Chios between Philip V. of Macedon and the combined naval forces of Rhodes and Pergamum, that off Lade between the Macedonian and the Rhodian fleets alone. [ED.]

of composition, and, in a similar way, politicians frequently involve themselves in the same consequences by yielding to the pressure of their sympathies and antipathies. This is a factor for which the reader must be sedulously on the watch and the writer equally sedulously on his guard. My point is driven home by the facts themselves. . . .

[A series of illustrations follows.]

All the illustrations that I have so far given appear to me in the light of oversights which admit of explanation and condonation—most of them being errors of ignorance, while the version given of the naval engagement is an error of patriotism. On what point, then, is Zeno fairly open to serious criticism? Surely, on account of the fact that he has devoted most of his attention not to research or composition but to style, in regard to which Zeno, like a number of other celebrated historians, not unfrequently betrays his self-conceit. My own view is that of course thought ought to be given and attention paid to a worthy presentation of the subject matter,[1] but that sober judges ought not to give to style the position of primacy and predominance. So far from that being right, there will be found to be other factors in historical writings of a higher order, success in which would more nearly justify self-conceit in the mind of a politician. I can explain my meaning most clearly by an example. . . .

[An illustration follows.]

In my opinion, these and other similar lapses involve a historian in serious disgrace; and while our ideal (and it is a noble ideal) should be to master all the factors in historical writing, the second-best alternative is to concentrate attention upon those which are most important and most truly essential. I have been induced to offer these remarks by the similarity of the spectacle presented nowadays by History and by the other arts and professions. In every case, truth and utility are depreciated, while charlatanism and pretentiousness are commended and admired as something imposing and wonderful, though in reality they are more facile to achieve and less exacting in their standards—not only in History but in other branches of literature.

As regards Zeno's ignorance of the topography of Laconia, his margin of error was here so great that I did not hesitate to

---

[1] It is obvious that this is not only an element, but an element of the first importance, in all successful historical writing. [AUTHOR.]

write to the author himself. The principle upon which I acted, in taking this step, was not to regard my neighbor's mistakes as so many points gained to me, which is the vicious habit of some writers, but to do my best to improve and correct the works of my contemporaries is if they were my own, for the sake of the general advancement of knowledge. When Zeno received my letter, he was profoundly mortified to realize that it was impossible to make any changes in his work owing to the fact that it had already been published; but although he found himself impotent in regard to the material point, he was good enough to take my action in the most friendly spirit. I shall seize this opportunity to make a personal request to my readers in my own and future generations. If I am detected deliberately introducing falsehoods or deliberately ignoring the truth at any point in my work, let them censure me without mercy; but where I am convicted of *bona fide* ignorance, I crave indulgence—and particularly in my special case, considering the scale of my composition and the universal range of my subject matter.

DIONYSIUS OF HALICARNASSUS ON HERODOTUS, THUCYDIDES AND THEOPOMPUS

(Dionysius of Halicarnassus: *The Three Literary Letters*, ed. by W. Rhys Roberts, Cambridge, 1901, University Press: *Letter to Pompeius*, chapters 3 and 6)

You also ask for my views regarding Herodotus and Xenophon and suggest my writing on the subject. This I have done already in my *Notes to Demetrius on Imitation*. The first of these essays deals with the problem of Imitation; the second with the best models for Imitation in the four branches of Poetry, Philosophy, Historiography and Public Speaking; while the third, on Method, remains unfinished. I will quote you what I say in the second regarding Herodotus, Thucydides, Xenophon, Philistus and Theopompus, whom I select as the most suitable models:

"Here are my ideas regarding Herodotus and Thucydides, if I am to include them in my survey. The first and really essential business of a historian, no matter what his vein may be, is to choose a good subject which will give pleasure to his readers. To my mind, Herodotus has been more successful in this than Thucydides. The older writer has produced a general history of the Hellenic and Oriental worlds, 'with the object of saving the past of Mankind from oblivion and ensuring that the extraordinary achievements' and so on—to quote his own preface, of which the book, from cover to cover, is simply an expansion. Thucydides writes the history of a single war, which was neither glorious nor beneficial and would have been better unfought or (failing that) should have been deliberately consigned to oblivion and concealed from posterity. The badness of his subject is betrayed by his own preface, in which he remarks that in this war a number of Hellenic countries were devastated, some by non-Hellenes and others by fellow Hellenes; and that the expatriation of populations and destruction of life were on an unparalleled scale, as well as the earthquakes, bad harvests, epidemics and other disasters. Thus the reader, who has no desire to hear of all these misfortunes happening to Hellas, is repelled by the author's subject by the time that he has finished his preface. The story of the extraordinary achievements of the Hellenic and the Oriental worlds is superior to that of cruel disasters experienced by Hellenes alone, and this means that Herodotus has shown greater judgment in his choice of subject than Thucydides. It cannot even fairly be said that Thucydides had no alternative but to write what he did if he was to avoid covering the same ground as his predecessors, although he may have recognized the inferiority of his own subject. On the contrary, he depreciates the past in his preface and claims that his own generation had lived through the greatest experience in History, which shows that his choice of subject was deliberate. This is quite unlike Herodotus, who was not deterred by the fact that earlier writers like Hellanicus and Charon had published works on the same subject, but trusted, not unwarrantably, in his own ability to produce something better.

"The second business of the historian is to settle where to begin and where to leave off; and, here again, Herodotus' judgment is obviously better than Thucydides'. Herodotus begins with the cause of the first aggression of Orientals upon Hellenes, and stops when he has carried his narrative down to the punishment inflicted upon the Orientals in retribution. Thucydides begins at the point at which the Hellenic world began to decline, which was wrong on the part of a Hellene and an Athenian (especially considering that he was not one of the despised and rejected, but a prominent public man who had been carried by the suffrages of his countrymen to high command and office). He is also so malicious as to saddle his own country with the ostensible responsibility for the war, when he might have traced it to many other origins. Instead of beginning his narrative with Corcyra, he might have begun with the magnificent achievements of his own country immediately after the Persian War, which he does mention later in the wrong place and in a perfunctory and cursory way. After doing patriotic justice to these, he might then have brought the Lacedaemonians on to the scene, explained their growing fear and envy of Athens, and shown how they introduced pretexts of another kind for precipitating the war. He need not have mentioned Corcyra and the *Megarians Act* and the rest of it apart from these preliminaries. The conclusion of his work is still more faulty. After stating that he witnessed the whole war and promising a complete exposition of it, he stops at the naval battle between the Athenians and Peloponnesians off Cynossema,[1] which occurred in the twenty-second year of hostilities. He would have done better to tell the whole story and to conclude his work with the magnificent re-entry of the exiles from Phyle, which inaugurates the restoration of Athenian liberties, thus ending on a note that would have thoroughly pleased his readers.

"The third business of the historian is to consider what to include and what to omit; and in this, again, I feel Thucydides inferior. Herodotus realized that a narrative of any considerable length must be varied by pauses if it is to have an agreeable effect on the reader's mind, and that it cannot keep on in one identical rut (however able the workmanship) without creating a painful sense of monotony. He accordingly aimed at giving variety to his writing, like his hero and example Homer; and the reader who has picked up his works finds himself spellbound down to the last syllable and always hungry for more. Thucydides embarks on one particular war, pulls himself together, and goes through with it in a single breath. Battle crowds upon battle, armament upon armament, page upon page, until the unfortunate reader's attention flags and faints by the wayside. Pindar could have told him that 'Honey can cloy and Love's sweet flowers,' and at intervals he does realize the saving virtue of change and variety for the historian. There are one or two places in which he has condescended to them, such as his digressions on the rise of the Odrysian Empire and on the states in Sicily.

"Another business of the historian is to group and arrange his material. Let us see how our two authors perform these operations respectively. Thucydides keeps to the chronological order, while Herodotus follows the grand divisions of his subject. This makes Thucydides obscure and hard to follow, for in a given summer and winter there are naturally many events in different localities, and he has to break off one series

---

[1] Presumably because death overtook him. His work bears obvious marks of being unfinished. [Ed.]

in order to take up another. Equally naturally, we lose the thread and have hard work to puzzle out the sequence of his exposition. Herodotus starts with the Kingdom of Lydia, carries it down to the reign of Croesus, passes straight on to Croesus' conqueror Cyrus, and then takes up the tale of Egypt, the Steppe-Countries and Northwest Africa. There is sometimes a show of logical sequence; material is worked in to round things off; and episodes are introduced to make the story more entertaining. Proceeding, he narrates the history of the Hellenes and Orientals over a total period of two hundred and twenty years and a field embracing all three continents, and finishes off with the flight of Xerxes, without ever breaking continuity. What it comes to is that the writer who has taken a single subject has succeeded in breaking a unity into fragments, while the writer who has preferred a miscellaneous plurality of subjects has created a harmonious unity out of the congeries.

"I will touch upon one feature in the treatment of subject matter which, in any historical work, claims our attention at least as much as the points already considered. What is the writer's own attitude towards his subject? Herodotus' attitude is invariably rightminded. He rejoices in good and hates evil. Thucydides' attitude is uncompromising and bitter, and he can never forgive his country for having sent him into exile. He is merciless in detailing anything that goes wrong, but when something comes right, he either ignores it altogether or only vouchsafes it a grudging mention. . . .

"Theopompus of Chios,[1] the most celebrated pupil of Isocrates, is the author of a quantity of speeches (complimentary and political), of the *Chian Letters*, and of some important treatises. As a professional historian he has many virtues. His subjects—*The End of the Peloponnesian War* and *The Life of Philip*—are both good; the arrangement in either case is clear and easy to follow; but his strongest point is his literary conscientiousness and industry. Internal evidence, apart from his explicit statements, would have revealed the laboriousness of his preparatory work, the cost entailed in the collection of his material, the number of events of which he was an eye witness, and the number of prominent contemporary soldiers, politicians and thinkers with whom he put himself in touch. Evidently he was always thinking of his work. Some people make History their hobby; Theopompus gave up his life to it. The wide range of his interests will give some idea of his colossal labors. He records the genesis of races and the foundation of states, paints the private lives and characters of mon-

[1] *Ca.* 380–310 B.C. [ED.]

archs, and incorporates in his work any remarkable or prob-
lematical phenomenon on land or sea. It would be a mistake to
suppose that this is merely attractive. On the contrary, it is
instructive to a degree. I will content myself with the universally admitted fact that the higher literary education demands a knowledge of sociology,[1] law, political science and
biography. On all these subjects Theopompus is a mine of
information, and this information is not artificially divorced
from its historical context. These are some of the admirable
qualities of our author. In addition, his whole work abounds
in fine religious teaching and moral philosophy; and his crowning and most characteristic achievement has never been approached in exactitude or ability by any writer before or after
him. I refer to his capacity not merely for seeing and stating
the obvious aspects of any given event, but for exploring the
hidden causes and motives and the psychological concomitants, which ordinary people find it difficult to interpret, and
for revealing all the mysteries of assumed virtue and undetect-
ed vice. Possibly the legendary examination of souls released
from the body at the judgment-seat of the other world may be
as searching a test as those applied by Theopompus the historian; and this has given him the reputation of maliciously
embroidering relevant strictures upon distinguished personalities with irrelevant details. In reality, he is a surgeon who
carries his cauterizations and incisions as deep as the diseased
tissue which he is removing extends, without attacking the
normally healthy organs.

"This is substantially the character of Theopompus as revealed in his treatment of his subject matter as distinct from
his syle . . . but he is not immaculate, especially in the matter of digressions. They are sometimes superfluous, inoppor-
tune and extremely childish. Think of the apparition of the
Silenus in Macedonia or the fight between the sea serpent and
the warship—and these are not unfair examples of his stories.
. . ."

IS HERODOTUS MALICIOUS?

(PLUTARCH'S *Moralia*: Teubner text, Collected Works, Vol. V., ed.
by G. N. Bernadakis: chapters 1, 11, 15, 28, 29)[2]

MANY readers of Herodotus are taken in by his plain, un-
labored, flowing style, and still more by his character. If Plato

[1] Non-Hellenic as well as Hellenic. [AUTHOR.]
[2] This essay, entitled *Malice in Herodotus,* has been handed down among Plutarch's works, but some critics believe it to be apocryphal. [ED.]

is right in saying that the last refinement of immorality is the false appearance of probity, it is equally true that the consummate achievement of malice is the assumption of such good nature and simplicity as to defy detection. The malice of Herodotus is mostly directed (though he spares nobody) against the Boeotians and Corinthians, and I therefore feel called upon to defend truth and my ancestors in the same breath by exposing this part of his work in particular. If a critic were to deal with all his falsehoods and fictions, he might fill many volumes. However, to quote Sophocles, "Persuasion hath a cunning countenance," and especially when she resides in writings so full of charm and so masterly in concealing not merely this or that eccentricity but the whole character of the author. When the Hellenes revolted from Philip V. and joined Titus Flamininus, the king remarked that the collar into which they had put their necks was smoother but thicker. Now the malice of Herodotus is certainly smoother and softer than that of Theopompus, but it is also more penetrating and more wounding, just as draughts blowing slily through a crack are more injurious than the winds of heaven. . . .

Take his treatment of Io the daughter of Inachus at the very outset of his story. It is the general opinion in Hellas that this famous heroine has received divine honors from the Orientals and has bequeathed her name to many seas and to the principal straits of the world, and that she is the ancestress of the most distinguished royal houses. But what does our chivalrous historian say of her? That she threw herself at the heads of some Phoenician merchant seamen, because she had been seduced (though not against her will) by the captain and was afraid that her pregnancy would be detected. This pretty story he libelously attributes to the Phoenicians; cites Persian historians as evidence that the Phoenicians had kidnapped Io and other women; and proceeds to enunciate the opinion that the Trojan War—the greatest and most splendid achievement of Hellas—was fought out of stupidity for the sake of a worthless woman. "It is evident," he remarks, "that they would not have been kidnapped if they had not been willing victims." In that case, we must call the Gods stupid for visiting the violation of the daughters of Leuctrus upon the Lacedaemonians or for punishing Ajax for outraging Cassandra. According to Herodotus, at any rate, it is clear that they would not have been outraged if they had not been willing victims. Yet Herodotus himself states that Cleomenes was taken alive by the Lacedaemonians, and the same fate afterwards befell the Achaean general Philopoemen, while

Regulus the Roman consul was captured by the Carthaginians. We would like to hear of braver fighters or better soldiers than these were. But there is nothing extraordinary in their experiences, considering that leopards and tigers are taken alive by human beings. All the same, Herodotus denounces women who have been violated and whitewashes the men who have raped them. . . .

When he comes to the Seven Sages (he calls them "uplifters"), he traces the family of Thales to a Phoenician, or in other words to a non-Hellenic origin; and he impersonates Solon in order to insult the Gods as follows: "Sire, I know for a fact that the Godhead is invariably envious and destructive, and then you question me regarding human life!" This is his own opinion about the Gods, and in palming it off upon Solon he adds malice to blasphemy. . . .

Now let us examine his account of the sequel to the battle [of Marathon]. "The Orientals," he writes, "pushed off in their remaining ships, picked up the slaves from Eretria at the island on which they had left them, and started to sail round Sunium, intending to reach the city [of Athens] before the Athenians themselves. At Athens it was alleged that this stratagem had been suggested to them by the Alcmaeonidae, who were supposed to have displayed a shield[1] as a signal to them after they were once more on board. So the Persians started to sail round Sunium." A reader might pass over his reference to the Eretrians as slaves, although they had shown as gallant a spirit as any other Hellenes and had suffered a fate unworthy of their character. Nor does it so much matter that he has slandered the house of the Alcmaeonidae, with all the great families and distinguished individuals belonging to it. But it is unpardonable to have spoiled the greatness of the victory and to have made the world-famous achievement of Marathon end in nothing. Obviously there can have been no battle or action of any consequence, but only a brief "scrap" with an enemy landing party (as detractors and belittlers maintain), if after the battle, instead of their cutting their cables, taking to flight and abandoning themselves to whatever breeze would carry them furthest from Attica, they received a treacherous signal by the display of a shield, bent their sails for Athens in the hope of capturing the city, rounded Sunium at their ease and lay to off Phalerum, while the most prominent and distinguished Athenians were betraying Athens in despair of her salvation. Later, he does acquit the Alcmaeonidae, but only to attribute the treachery to others.

[1] Used as a heliograph. [Ed.]

"A shield undoubtedly was displayed," writes our eye witness,[1] "and there is no getting over the fact." What an extraordinary occurrence, when the Athenians had just won a smashing victory! But even if it had occurred, it would not have been observed by the enemy, who were being driven headlong into their ships under close pressure with heavy casualties, and were leaving the field as fast as each individual soldier could manage. Again, in affecting to defend the Alcmaeonidae against charges which he was the first to bring against them, he writes: "To my mind, the supposition that the Alcmaeonidae would ever have displayed a shield as a signal to the Persians, with the intention of bringing Athens under the yoke of Hippias, is too incredible to be accepted." But this merely reminds me of the nursery rhyme:

> Stay where you are, Mr. Crab.
> When I've caught you, I'll soon let you go.

Why so eager to catch him, if you are going to let him go again? And so you, sir, first accuse and then defend. You indict slanders against famous men and then erase them. We must infer that you distrust your own evidence, for you heard from nobody but yourself that the Alcmaeonidae displayed a shield to the enemy when they were defeated and in flight.

. . .

Then there are the Argives. Everybody knows that they did not refuse to help the other Hellenes, but only insisted that they should not be under the permanent command of the Lacedaemonians, their bitterest enemies. These being the facts, he insinuates a most malicious accusation, writing that, when the Hellenes asked the Argives to join them, the latter knew that the Lacedaemonians would not share the command with them and therefore laid down this condition, in order to have an excuse for remaining neutral. He adds that Artaxerxes, when subsequently reminded of this incident by Argive ambassadors who had made the journey to Susa, declared that there was no state which he regarded as a more friendly power than Argos. Then, characteristically, our author takes refuge in innuendoes, declaring that he has no exact information on this point but that he knows very well that nobody is immaculate and that the Argives are not the worst sinners in History. "My personal duty," he comments, "is to reproduce what is related, but I am under no obligation whatever to believe it—a principle which applies, incidentally, to all my work. *A propos* of

---

[1] When Marathon was fought, Herodotus was probably not yet born. The author is, of course, writing ironically. [ED.]

this, there is a further story to the effect that it was the Argives who called in the Persian against Hellas, because they had done badly in war against the Lacedaemonians and felt anything to be preferable to their present humiliation." The reader is reminded of Herodotus' own story in which he records the Aethiopian's dictum regarding the scents and dyed-stuffs: "The ointments and the clothes of the Persians are equally deceitful!" What a motto for our author! "The phrases and artifices of Herodotus are equally deceitful!"—"They twist and turn, all roundabout, and naught's straightforward." Painters throw their lights into relief by their shadows. Herodotus intensifies his slanders by his denials of them, and heightens the effect of his insinuations by equivocation. Of course it is undeniable that the Argives did decline to join the Hellenes and that they left the palm of valor to the Lacedaemonians owing to their objection to leaving them the command. To that extent, they disgraced the noble lineage of Heracles; for it would have been better to fight for the freedom of Hellas under the command of Siphnians or Cythnians than to lose their share in those great and glorious struggles by disputing the command with the Lacedaemonians. But if it was they who invited the Persian into Hellas because they had done badly in war against the Lacedaemonians, why did they not openly take sides with him when he arrived? Short of joining forces with the King, they might have stayed behind and devastated Laconia, made a fresh attempt on Thyrea, or embarrassed the Lacedaemonians by some ot' er form of intervention. By preventing them from sending so large an expeditionary force to Plataea, they could have dealt a great blow to the Hellenic cause.

But at least he has magnified the Athenians in this part of his work and has proclaimed them the saviors of Hellas? Very right and proper, if his praises were not interspersed with so much vituperation. These are his words: "The Lacedaemonians would have been deserted by the other Hellenes and would have died a glorious death after performing magnificent exploits in their hour of isolation—unless they had detected that the other Hellenes were going over to the Persian side in time to come to terms with Xerxes themselves." In this passage his real object is obviously not to praise the Athenians. On the contrary, he only praises them in order to abuse the others. The reader can hardly any longer resent the torrents of bitter insults which he discharges upon the Thebans and Phocians, when he convicts those who risked their lives for Hellas of treachery which did *not* occur in fact though it might have occurred in his opinion under hypothetical conditions. He even casts an incidental aspersion upon the Lacedaemonians by making it an open question whether they would have died on the field of honor or have capitulated, the account of themselves which they had given at Thermopylae being doubtless too insignificant to impress him! . . .

Having to describe four battles against the Orientals, what does he do? From Artemisium he makes the Hellenes run away, at Thermopylae, when their king and commander was risking his life for them, he makes them stay at home and think of nothing except the celebration of the Olympian and Carnean festivals; when he comes to Salamis, he devotes more space to Queen Artemisia than to the whole battle; and finally, at Plataea, he declares that the Hellenes stayed in camp and were unaware of the engagement until it was over. Presumably those who went into action agreed to fight in silence in order not to attract the others' attention, like the scene in the burlesque epic of *The Battle of Frogs and Mice*, written as a joke by Artemisia's son Pigres. He also makes out that the Lacedaemonians were no braver than the Orientals and only defeated them because of the disparity in equipment. Remember that when Xerxes himself had been present at Thermopylae, they had had to be driven forward with whips before they would advance against the Hellenes; and now, apparently, at Plataea, they had become reformed characters and "were not inferior in *moral* or physical strength. Their weak point was their equipment, which included no body armor, so that they had to fight exposed against troops under cover." It effectively disposes of any glory attaching to the Hellenes on account of these battles, if the Lacedaemonians were fighting unarmed men, if the rest were unaware that a battle was taking place in their vicinity, if the cemeteries of the Glorious Dead contain no corpses, if the inscriptions with which the war memorials are covered are lies, and if nobody knows the truth except Herodotus, while every other human being who has taken an interest in Hellas and believes that her achievements in the Persian War were superhuman, has been taken in by a legend. Is it not more likely that our author, with his picturesque and entrancing style, his charm and wit and grace, has been telling us "old wives' tales, with all the poet's skill," and not merely with the poet's polish and sweetness? No doubt everybody finds him attractive and enchanting, but evil-speaking and slander lurk among his smooth, pretty phrases like stinging flies among roses. Be on your guard, or he will poison your minds with grotesquely false ideas of the noblest and greatest countries and men of Hellas!

LUCIAN OF SAMOSATA (*ca.* A.D. 125–200) ON HIS CONTEMPORARIES

(LUCIAN: Collected Works: Teubner text, ed. by C. Jacobitz: Vol. II., *How to Write History*, chapters 14–16, 41, 43)

I WILL quote you some historians of this war [1] from what I can remember of their recitations, some of which I was privileged to hear in Ionia not long ago and others in Achaea on an earlier occasion. I will stake my literary reputation on the truth of what I am going to say. Indeed, I should be prepared to give sworn evidence, if it were good taste to turn an essay into a deposition. One of them began straight away with the Muses by issuing an invitation to these ladies to take a hand in his work. You will note how admirably in tune this exordium was, how nicely it fitted a historical work and how appropriate it was to this branch of literature. A little lower down he compared our commander to Achilles and the Shah to Thersites, without realizing that his Achilles would have been the better for defeating not Thersites but Hector, in which case a mighty man of war would have "fled before" and "a better than he" would have "followed after." Then he introduced a eulogy of himself, to prove that his pen was not unworthy of his glorious subject. Further on, there was another encomium, this time of his native town Miletus, with a note to point out what an improvement this was upon Homer, who had passed his native town over in silence. Finally, at the close of his preface, he promised outright, in so many words, to magnify our achievements and to "do his bit" in beating down the enemy. This is how he actually began his narrative, in which he plunged into a discussion of the origins of the war: "The war was made by that unspeakable and unpardonable criminal Shah Wologesus. His ambitions were"—and so on.

So much for one author. Another of them was an out-and-out admirer of Thucydides, and modeled himself so faithfully on his pattern that he opened with the same words, just substituting his own name. When I quote it, I think you will taste the fine flavor of the Attic spirit and will agree that it is the most felicitous opening that you have ever heard: "Crepereius Calpurnianus of Pompeyville has written the history of the war between the Parthians and the Romans. He began to write as soon as war broke out." After an exordium like that, it is superfluous to mention how he transplanted the Corcyraean speaker to Armenia when he wanted to make an oration

[1] The Partho-Roman War of A.D. 161–5. [ED.]

there; or how, when he inflicted a plague upon Nisibis for taking the wrong side, he lifted it bodily out of Thucydides.[1] I left him still burying the poor Athenians at Nisibis and departed with an accurate knowledge of every word that he was going to recite after I had gone. It really is a fairly common fallacy nowadays for an author to imagine that he is writing like Thucydides if he repeats his words with a few variations. Yes, and there was another point in the same author which I have almost forgotten to tell you. He used the Roman words for a number of weapons and apparatuses, and even for "trench," "bridge" and so on. Imagine how loftily Thucydidean it looked to see these Italian words embedded in the Attic sentences, setting off the purple like jewels and showing up to such good advantage and harmonizing so excellently with their background.

There was another who had composed a bare memorandum of events in the most commonplace prosaic style, such as you would expect to find in the diary of a soldier or of an artisan or tradesman attached to the army. This amateur historian was comparatively unpretentious. You could size him up in a moment as a hewer of wood and drawer of water for someone with a better literary and historical endowment than his own. I only quarreled with his title, which was more high-falutin than anything in the world of letters has a right to be. "*Parthian Chronicles*, Book I., Book II., and so on, by Dr. Callimorphus of the Sixth Lancers." Incidentally, he had perpetrated an excruciatingly affected preface, on the theme that historical composition came within the sphere of Medicine, because Aesculapius was the son of Apollo and Apollo was the Conductor of the Muses and the general patron of culture. Also, he started, I cannot imagine why, by writing in Ionic and then went off at once into common or garden Greek, with a few Ionic words sprinkled here and there like plums in a cake, but otherwise the ordinary vocabulary, and that, if anything, too colloquial. . . .

My own ideal historian is fearless, incorruptible, highminded and a frank exponent of the truth. He will satisfy the requirements of the proverb by calling figs figs and a spade a spade. The impartiality of his judgment will not be affected by sympathy or antipathy, good feeling or sentiment, shame or shyness. He will do his best for all his characters so far as he can do it without favoring one at the expense of another. He will

---

[1] The only things that he omitted were the Pelasgicum and the Long Walls, in which the Athenian victims of the plague were domiciled; but he appropriated everything else, including the Sudan, whence his plague duly spread to Egypt and over the greater part of the Persian dominions, though on this occasion it was obliging enough not to travel farther. [AUTHOR.]

be a stranger and a sojourner in the land of books, a law unto himself and acknowledging no allegiances. He will not stop to consider what A or B will think, but will state the facts.

I admire the ruling of Thucydides and his criterion of good and bad writing. (He was thinking of the reputation enjoyed by Herodotus, which was so great that his volumes were called after the Muses.) Thucydides claims to be producing a permanent contribution to knowledge rather than an ephemeral *tour de force*, and takes credit for resisting the temptation to embroider and for leaving to posterity a record of the facts as they actually occurred. He also introduces the idea of utility and of what is obviously the rational object of History, which is, as he explains, to enable Mankind to cope successfully with current problems in the light of records of the past, in the event of circumstances repeating themselves.

This is the spirit which I want to find in my historian; and, as regards delivery and expression, I do not want him, when he begins to write, to have acquired the cutting edge of the expert stylist with his exaggerated nippiness, neatness and fluency. I want something less aggressive—the thought consecutive and concentrated, the language clear and practical, the exposition distinctive.

PART FOUR
Epilogues

XENOPHON

(*A History of Hellenic Affairs:* Book VII. chapter 5 [26-27])

THE result of the battle[1] was the exact opposite of that which everybody had expected. Almost the whole of Hellas had mobilized upon one side or the other, and it was taken for granted that, if it came to an action, the victors would be masters while the vanquished would be at their mercy; but God so disposed it that both sides erected monuments in token of victory while neither attempted to prevent the other from doing so; both sides restored the enemy dead under flag of truce in token of victory while both received their own dead back under flag of truce in admission of defeat; and either side claimed the victory although neither could show the slightest gain in territory, allies, or empire beyond what they had possessed before the battle. On the contrary, there was more unsettlement and disorder in Hellas after the battle than before it—but I do not propose to carry my narrative further and will leave the sequel to any other historian who cares to record it.

POLYBIUS

(Book XXXVIII. chapters 1–4, and Book XXXIX. chapter 8)

HELLAS, in her time, has suffered frequent falls, of general as well as local extension; yet there is not one of her previous reverses that can be characterized so justly by the name of "disaster," with all the connotation of that word, as the events of our own generation.[2] The Hellenes are not simply to be

---

[1] The Battle of Mantinea, fought in 362 B.C. between the Thebans and the Lacedaemonians with their respective allies, in which the author lost his son. [ED.]

[2] The last rising of Macedonia in 149–8 B.C. and the war between the Achaean Confederacy and Rome in 146 B.C. [ED.]

pitied on account of their sufferings upon this occasion. In the light of the facts as seen in detail, they must be held responsible for a disaster on account of their deliberate actions. Even the supreme tragedy of Carthage is not too great to be compared with this tragedy of Hellas, which in some respects actually exceeds it in dimensions. The Carthaginians have at least bequeathed to future generations materials for justifying their memory to the uttermost degree, whereas the Hellenes have presented no reasonable basis whatsoever to would-be apologists for their sins. The Carthaginians, moreover, were happy in being annihilated in the moment of catastrophe and so released from all future consciousness of their mishaps, whereas the Hellenes have become spectators of their own disasters in order to bequeath their misfortune to their children's children. It is a commonplace that sufferers lingering on in tribulation are more to be pitied than those who escape from life in the hour of affliction; and, on this analogy, the disasters of Hellas are more to be pitied than the fate of Carthage—unless, in delivering judgment, we ignore decency and honor and pay exclusive regard to material considerations. The truth of my present proposition will be realized by any reader who recalls the historic calamities of Hellas in order to compare them with this *finale*.

One historic occasion on which Fortune suspended her terrors over the heads of Hellas was Xerxes' invasion of Europe. At that moment all Hellas was in jeopardy, yet remarkably few of her children suffered a fall—an observation which is especially true of the Athenians, who were sufficiently provident to evacuate their country in good time with their women and children. The Athenians did not, of course, escape unscathed from the crisis, for the Orientals occupied their capital and destroyed it in a spirit of revenge; but at the same time the victims, so far from incurring shame or disgrace, won worldwide glory and renown because they had deliberately sacrificed their all in order to share the fortunes of their fellow Hellenes. In consequence, their noble resolution was rewarded, not only by the prompt recovery of their country and their national territory, but by a development which enabled them before long to dispute with Lacedaemon the supremacy over all Hellas. At a later date, again, when their military power had been broken by the Spartans, they were reduced to such a pass that they were compelled to demolish the fortifications of their home city; yet here, again, the odium falls not upon Athens herself but upon Lacedaemon, inasmuch as Lacedaemon exploited too harshly the power which Fortune had bestowed upon her. The Spartans, in their turn, were defeated by the Thebans, lost their supremacy in Hellas, and, after renouncing their empire abroad, were eventually confined within the limits of Laconia. Yet, after all, what dishonor was there in that? In competing for the highest prizes of honor, they had simply so far fallen as to be compelled to beat a retreat within the bounds of their ancestral domain. Thus the events which I have mentioned may legitimately be called "mishaps," but cannot possibly be described as "disasters." The Mantineans (to continue) were forced to leave their homes, when their town was broken up by the Lacedaemonians, and to settle in scattered villages; but all the odium for this piece of folly fell upon Lacedaemon and not upon Mantinea. The Thebans, at a somewhat later date, saw their home razed to the ground when Alexander, who was contemplating the invasion of Asia, calculated that the terror inspired by the punishment of Thebes would serve to hold Hellas in check while he was preoccupied with his own ambitions. Yet, once again, everybody pitied Thebes as the victim of a cruel injustice, while nobody attempted to justify this action of Alexander's. Consequently, it was not long before the Thebans obtained support which enabled them to reoccupy their homes in security. The fact is that the sympathy of third parties is an important asset to the undeserving victims of misfortune, in view of the common phenomenon that Fortune herself veers round in sympathy with the tendencies of public opinion, until the very victors repent and repair with their own hands the catastrophes which they had so indefensibly inflicted. Again, Chalcis and Corinth and several other countries were condemned by their strategic value to a period of subjection under the Crown of Macedonia, during which they were occupied by Macedonian garrisons; yet the enslaved communities had the consolation that everybody was eager to do anything in his power to liberate them, while the destroyers of their liberty were regarded with utter and universal hatred and hostility. In short, whenever Hellenes suffered a fall or came to grief in previous epochs, it was generally particular communities only that were affected, and the occasions of stumbling were either competitions for political power or else acts of treachery on the part of autocrats and sovereigns. For these reasons, the instances are rare indeed in which odium attached to the victims or in which the word "disaster" became permanently associated with their misfortunes. "Misfortune" is the proper name for undeserved calamities in public as well as in private life; whereas the name of "disaster" should be reserved exclusively for acts of folly which bring odium upon their authors.

At the period in question, however, "disasters" simultaneously overtook the Peloponnesians, Boeotians, Phocians, . . .,[1] Locrians and several of the Hellenic communities on the Adriatic coast, as well as the Macedonians,[2] so that the calamity on this occasion was greater both quantitatively and qualitatively than any that had preceded it. In fact, on this occasion Hellas suffered what was not a "misfortune" at all, but a "disaster" of the most odious and dishonorable kind conceivable.[2] She displayed a combination of disloyalty and cowardice, and committed acts so monstrous[3] as to disgrace her name.[3] Therefore, she forfeited everything that had ennobled her existence, and in this fateful hour her sons—with their backs to the wall, if not in mere cowardly passivity—voluntarily admitted the Rods and Axes into their countries. They were overcome with terror at the enormity of their individual sins—if it is fair to call them "individual." Personally, I should say that the majority had strayed from the true path in ignorance, and that the sin lies with the politicians by whom an ignorance of such profundity had been fostered.

On this topic, I shall make no apology for breaking the conventions of historical narrative and giving what may seem a more controversial and personal tone to my presentation. Possibly I shall be criticized in some quarters for writing acrimoniously, when my duty first and foremost was to draw a veil over the sins of the Hellenes. Personally, I differ. Right-thinking people, I take it, would never regard as a genuine friend the coward who shirked the duty of plain speaking; and, in just the same way, they would never regard as a good citizen that other coward who deserted the truth for fear of the momentary offense which it was bound to cause to certain people. When it comes to the historian of public affairs, the profession should be closed altogether to the writer who values anything more highly than the truth. A historical record reaches a far wider public over a far longer period of time than any ephemeral observations; and that gives the measure of the value which the author ought to place upon the truth and which his readers ought to place upon an exalted standard of truth in the author. At the moment of crisis, it is the duty of every Hellene to help Hellas by every means in his power—to fight in her defense, to draw a veil over her sins, to plead with the victors to have mercy upon her—and this, in the hour of need, I have done in all sincerity. It is equally, however, the

---

[1] A name has been lost in the manuscript. [ED.]

[2] In this passage, where the Greek text has been badly mutilated, I have followed the conjectural restoration made by Friedrich Hultsch. [ED.]

[3] Conjectural restoration by Theodor Heyse. [ED.]

duty of a Hellene, when he is bequeathing to future generations a historical record of past events, to bequeath it altogether uncontaminated by falsehood. The purpose of History is not the reader's enjoyment at the moment of perusal, but the reformation of the reader's soul, to save him from stumbling at the same stumbling block many times over.

•   •   •

After accomplishing my mission,[1] I left Rome in order to return to my country. I could feel that I had achieved some, at least, of those political objects for which I had labored all my life, and that I had been generously rewarded for my friendliness toward Rome. And now I will offer up a prayer to all the Gods that I may spend the rest of my days in the same activities and under the same conditions. I have watched the workings of Fortune; I know her genius for envious dealing with Mankind; and I also know that her empire is most absolute over just those oases in human life in which the victim fancies his sojourn to be most delectable and most secure.

[1] Polybius had been attached as an expert adviser to the Roman Board of Commissioners which had been sent to liquidate the Achaean Confederacy after the Romano-Achaean War of 146 B.C. After obtaining every possible mitigation of their lot for his fellow countrymen, Polybius had been left in charge by the Commissioners in order to wind up their business after their departure, until he eventually followed them to Rome himself in order to present his report. [ED.]

FINIS

INDEX

Aaron, xvii
Abraham, Heights of, 103n
Abydos, 99
Acarnanians, 33
Achaea, 195
Achaean Confederacy, x, 199n, 203n
Achaeans, 44, 136
Achaemenids, xii
Achillas, 113 ff.
Achilles, 32, 195
Acusilaus of Argos, 64, 65
Adalia, Gulf of, 55n
Adiabene, 61
Adriatic, 44, 54, 75n, 202
Aeaces, 119
Aediles, 173
Aegina, 38, 103
Aeginetans, 38, 124
Aegospotami, 124n
Aelii, 58
Aeschylus, xxiii, 123
Aesculapius, 196
Aetolia, 145n
Aetolians, 33, 44
Africa, 44, 45, 54, 72, 74, 90, 110n,
    136, 138, 152, 153, 165, 175, 176,
    188
Agamemnon, 35, 123
Agathias of Myrrhina, ixff., 87, 90,
    93
Agrippa, 69
Agyrium, xiv, 52
Ajax, 190
Albano, 115
Alcaeus, 42n
Alcestis, 95
Alcinous, 96
Alcmaeonidae, 156, 157, 191, 192
Alcmena, 169, 172
Alexander, son of Priam, 30
Alexander, the Great, xi, 50, 52, 54,
    57, 70, 72, 73, 109, 148, 176,
    182, 201
Alexander, father of Dionysius, 59
Alexander of Pherae, 177
Alexandria, xiv, 68
Am Tor von Asien, 85n
Amasis 120 ff., 133n, 169, 172
Amasra, 154n
Ameinocles, 37
Amen, 152n, 153
America, xxin
Amphictyons, 182
Amphipolis, 43
Amphitryon, 169, 170, 172
Amyntas, 72, 73, 148, 182
Anatolia, 155n, 103n
Anatolian Peninsula, 145n
Anatolians, xin
Anaxandridas, 158
Anaximenes, 53
Ancient Greek Historians, xin
Andromeda, 159
Antigone, 128
Antigonus, 57
Antiochus, the Great, King of Syria,
    44, 136, 137
Antiochus Epiphanes, 67n
Antiochus, philosopher, 65

Antisthenes of Rhodes, 183
Antium, 58
Antonius, 75
Anytus, 94
Apion, 63
Apollo, 37, 156, 172, 196
Apollodorus of Athens, 52
Appian of Alexandria, xiv, 70, 76,
    110n
Arabia, 61n, 72
Aramaic, xxii, 60n, 61n
Aratus of Sicyon,, 44
Arcadia, xii, 32
Arcadians, 35, 65
Archidamus, 165
Archipelago, 33
Ares, 127
Argives, 105, 157 ff., 192, 193
Argos, 29, 31, 35, 157 ff., 174, 192
Aristides, 162
Aristippus, 94n
Aristobulus, 70
Aristogeiton, 40, 157
Ariston, 89
Aristotle, 161
Armenia, 195
Arne, 37
Arrian of Nicomedia, xiv, 70
Artabanus, 100, 117, 140
Artaxerxes, 67, 141, 159, 192
Artayctes, 143
Artaynte, 140
Artembares, 143
Artemisia, 194
Artemisium, 194
Asia, 30, 34, 44, 45, 51, 54, 70, 72,
    90, 143, 144, 161, 162, 176, 182,
    201
Asia Minor, 115
Asiatics, 144
Assinarus, 106
Assyria, 62
Assyrian Empire, 54, 111
Assyrians, 72
Astyages, 143
Ate, 117
Athena, 133
Athenians, 31, 33, 34, 35, 38, 39,
    41, 42, 100 ff., 149 ff., 160, 162
    ff., 186, 191 192, 193, 196, 200
Athens, ix, x, xi, 31, 32, 35, 37, 39,
    40, 41, 42, 52, 55, 59, 65, 72,
    101 ff., 109n, 124, 156, 157, 160,
    161, 162, 164, 165, 168, 174, 187,
    191, 192, 200
Athens, Constitution of, xi
Atlantic Ocean, 55, 175
Atreus, 35
Attica, 32, 35, 94, 140, 146, 147,
    156n, 164, 165, 191
Augustus, 58, 73n, 75, 77
Aurelian Gate, 111, 112

Babylon, 67n
Babylonia, 66
Balaustion's Adventure, xxiii
Balkan hinterland, 33n
Balkans, 88n
Bardyllis, 178

203

Bartin Su, 154n
Battle of Frogs and Mice, 194
Becker, I., ixn, 77
Belisarius, 84, 87
Berbers, 116 151n, 153
Bernadakis, G. N., 189,
Black Sea, 54, 142n, 154n, 163, 178
Boeotia, 32, 37, 92, 151, 156
Boeotians, 37, 104, 190, 202
Boor, C. de, 94, 96
Britain, 72
British Isles, 175
Browning, xxiii
Burnet, J.,
Bury, J. B., xin
Buttner-Wobst, W., 28, 43, 46
Byzantine Civilization, ix, xii
Byzantines, xi
Byzantium, 93, 125

Cabeiri, 151
Cadmeians, 150
Cadmus, 64, 127, 151, 156, 172
Caesarea, 91
Calasaries, 155
Callatian Indians, 141
Callias, historian, 65
Callias, son of Hipponicus, 159
Callias, son of Phaenippus, 157
Callimachus, 94n
Callimorphus, 196
Calliphon, 122
Calpurnii, 58
Cambyses, 37, 38, 122, 141
Candaules, 139
Capitol, 173
Cardia, 57
Caria, xiii, xxiin
Carians, 34
Carnean festivals, 194
Carnuntum, 149n
Carpathians, 88n
Carthage, xxin, 55, 74, 75, 110, 136, 173, 175n, 177, 179n, 200
Carthaginians, 38, 44, 45, 173, 191, 200
Cassandra, 190
Caucasus, 72
Celtic War, 52
Celto-Roman War, 52
Celts, 75
Centaur, 94
Cepheus, 159
Cersobleptes, 178
Chadwick, xixn
Chaeronea, 112
Chalcis, 38, 201
Chalcocondyles, Laonicus, xii
Chaldaea, 64
Chaldaeans, 64, 66
Chaones, xxin
Charon, 186
Chian Letters, 188
Chios, 39, 113, 183, 188
Chosroes, 92
Christian Fathers, xin
Christians, 125
Chrysippus, 35
Cimon, 162
Civilization and Character, xin, xiin, xivn
Claudius Nero, 55
Claudius II, 79
Clearchus, 178
Cleomenes I, 158, 190
Cleomenes III, 136
Cnossus, 121n

Colchians, 154
Colchis, 30, 146n, 154
Colophon, ix
Commodus, 76
Constantinople, 93n, 95n
Corcyra, 186, 187
Corcyraeans, 37, 38, 105
Corfu, 101, 103
Corinth, 37, 42, 136, 140, 160, 201
Corinthians, 37, 107, 155, 190
Cornelia, 114, 115
Cornford, F. M., x, 126n
Corpus Scriptorum Historiae Byzantinae, ixn
Cos, 142
Crepereius, Calpurnianus, 195
Creston, 150
Cretans, 30n
Crete, xiiin, 170n
Critias, 133, 146
Croesus, 31n, 38, 118, 119, 149, 188
Cronus, 126, 127, 130
Croton, 122, 174n
Cyclops, 94
Cynossema, 187
Cyprus, 72, 112, 115, 163
Cyrene, 94
Cyrus, 37, 143, 188
Cythnians, 193

Dacians, 88n
Damaratus, 140
Danae, 159n
Danube, 44, 88n, 149n
Daphniaca, 89
Dardanelles, xxiiin, 99, 124n
Darius, 38, 72, 141
Datis, 140
Delivery of the Sceptre, 35
Delos, 34, 37, 140, 141
Delphi, 89, 140, 148, 157, 158, 161, 182
Delta, 133
Demetrius II, of Macedon, 44, 148
Demetrius of Phalerum, x, 108, 109
Demetrius of Philippi, 125
Demosthenes, 104, 106n, 107
Deucalion, xii, 133, 150
Dexippus, 78, ff.
Diaeus, x
Dindorf, L., 78, 81, 87, 92, 93
Dio Cassius Cocceianus of Nicaea, xiv, 76
Diodorus of Agyrium, xiv, 48, 161, 180, 181
Dionysius of Halicarnassus, xi, xiv, xvii, xviii, 53, 59, 185
Dionysus, 150, 151, 152, 172, 173
Dioscuri, 151, 169
Divina Commedia, xxn
Dodona, 152 ff.
Dodonaeans, 153
Dolopia, 148
Dorians, 37, 149
Dorus, 150
Dracon, 65
Dryopis, 150

Eetion, 140
Egypt, xxiin, 29, 31, 54, 64, 72, 73, 112, 115, 120, 121, 134, 150 ff., 155, 163, 165, 169, 170 ff., 177, 188, 196n
Egyptian civilization, xxiv
Egyptians, 64, 114, 150 ff., 153, 154, 169, 170 ff.
Eleatic Gulf, 90

End of the Peloponnesian War, 188
Epaphroditus, 63
Ephesus, x, 125
Ephorus, 47, 65
Euphratas, 93
Euphrates, 60, 61
Epic and Romance, xixn
Epidaurian War, 42
Epidauros, 102
Epirus, 57, 152n, 153n
Erechtheus, xii
Eretria, 191
Eretrians, 191
Ethiopians, 72
Etruria, xxin
Etruscan language, xxi
Euboea, 41
Eumenes, 148
Eunapius of Sardis, xiv, 78
Eurasian Steppe, 88
Europa, 170
Europe, 30, 44, 51, 54, 72, 90, 143, 144, 182
European War, xvii
Euryelus, 104
Eurymedon, 104
Eurystheus, 35
Eurytanes, xxiin
Eutychianus, 89

Fabius Maximus, 58
Far Eastern civilization, xxiv
Faust, xxn
Federal War, 44
Florii, 90

Galilaeans, 68
Gallipoli Peninsula, 36n
Gaul, 176
Gaza, ixn, 82, 83
Gelii, 58
George of Pisidia, ix
Georgia, 146n, 154n
Getae, 88
Gibbon, xiin
Gibraltar, 175
Goths, 111, 112
Graces, 92, 151
Greece, *passim*
Greeks, *passim*
Gyges, 121
Gylippus, 104 ff.

Habrupolis, 147
Hadrian, 112
Hagia Sofia, Church of, vi
Hagnon, 102
Halicarnassus, xi, 29, 59, 185
Halys, 38
Hamlet, xxn
Hannibal, 75, 136, 174
Hannibalic War, 44, 135, 136, 174n
Harmodius, 40, 157
Haury, J., 84, 86
Hecataeus, 172
Helen (wife of Menelaus), 30, 34, 127
Hellanicus, 65, 186
Hellas, *passim*
Hellen, son of Deucalion, 32, 150
Hellenes, *passim*
Hellenism, Introduction *passim*
Hellespont, xxiiin, 150
Hephaestus, 132
Hera, 122n, 151, 174n
Heracleidae, 35, 37, 52
"Heracleidae," 94

Heracles, 49, 95, 169 ff., 172
Heraclius, ix, 95n
Hermes, 151, 172
Hermotybies, 155
Herodes, 52, 69
Herodian the Syrian, xiv, 77
Herodotus of Halicarnassus, x ff., xvii ff., xxiii, 29, 65, 99, 117, 118, 119, 139 ff., 149, 150, 154 ff., 160, 169, 171, 185 ff., 189 ff., 197
Herodotus, brother of Menander the Guardsman, 93
Heroic Age, xixn
Herzfeld, E., 85n
Hesiod of Ascra, xix, 65, 126, 152
Hestia, 151
Heyse, T., 202n
Hieronymus, 57, 58
Hipparchus, 40, 157
Hippias, 40, 157, 192
Hippocratean School, xiii
Hippocrates, 142, 143, 144
Hipponicus, 157n
Histiaeans, 124
Histiaeotis, 150
Historici Graeci Minores, 78, 81, 87, 92, 93
Holy Scriptures, 69
Homer, ix, xix, 32, 35, 36, 64, 85, 96, 99, 152, 187, 195
Hort, F. J. A., 59
Horus, 172
Hude, C., 29
Hultsch, F., 202n
Hybris, 117
Hypatius, x, 125
Hystaspes, 141

Iliad, 99
Ilion, 111
Illyria, 177
Illyrians, 182
Inachus, 29, 190
India, 61n
Indian civilization, xxiv
Indians, 141
Io, 29 ff., 190
Ionia, 32, 33, 37, 120, 121n
Ionian Gulf, 75
Ionians, 37, 38, 156
Ionic, 196
Iphicrates, 177
Iranis, 61n
Iraqis, 61n
Isocrates, 162, 188
Israel, Children of, xvii
Isthmus of Corinth, 37, 136, 160
Italians, 116
Italy, xii, xvi, 37, 44, 45, 55, 58, 71, 75, 136, 138, 163, 173, 174
Ithaca, 95

Jacobitz, C., 195
Jacoby, C., 53
Jebb, R. C., 128
Jerusalem, 61, 67, 68
Jesus Christ, 83
Jewish war, 60
Jews, 49, 51, 60 ff.
Josephus, Flavius, of Jerusalem, xi, xiii, 60
Judaea, 64, 67
Judaeo-Roman War, 60
Julian, 81, 82
Julius Caesar, Gaius, 52, 75, 113, 115

Juppiter Capitolinus, 173n
Justin the Younger, 91
Justinian, x, 84, 86, 87, 91, 92

Kadmeis, 37
Kalinka, E., 162
Ker, W. P., xixn
Khosru II, 85n
Kuehlewein, H., 142

Lacedaemon, 39, 40, 42, 72, 145, 158, 174, 200
Lacedaemonians, 34, 35, 39, 41, 42, 44, 55, 107, 124, 149, 155, 157 ff., 162, 165, 187, 190, 192 ff., 199, 201
Lacinium, 174
Laconia, 184, 193, 201
Lade, 183
Laertes, 96
Lagus, x, 70
Langhorne, xvi
Laonicus. See Chalcocondyles.
Latin language, xxii, xxiii, 52, 58, 113
Latium, xxiii
Lemnos, 165
Leocoreum, 40
Leopold, I. H., 149
Lesbians, 120
Lesbos, 39
Les Misérables, xxn
Leuctrus, 190
Levant, 73n
Libyan Desert, 152n
Licinius Macer, 58
Life of Philip, 188
Locrians, 33, 202
Long Walls, 42, 124, 196n
Lucian of Samosata, 195
Lucius Cincius, 57
Lucius Lentulus, 115
Luke, S., 59
Lycia, xxin
Lycian language, xxi
Lycurgus, 80
Lydia, 31n, 90, 163, 188
Lydian language, xxi
Lydians, 155
Lyly, xxn

Macedni, 150
Macedon, 75, 108, 109, 147, 183n
Macedonia, 54, 55, 74, 125, 177, 182, 189, 200, 201
Macedonian Dominion, 54
Macedonian Dynasty, 73n
Macedonian Empire, 54, 73, 74, 111, 148
Macedonian Epoch, 50
Macedonian Kingdom, 109
Macedonian Powers, 56, 73
Macedonians, 44, 72, 109, 202
Macrones, 154
Maeandrius, 122
Magnesia-on-Maeander, 121, 122
Malice in Herodotus, xviiin, 189n
Mantinea, 199n, 201
Mantineans, 201
Mantinean War, 42
Marathon, 39, 156n, 191
Marchant, E. C., 124
Marcus Aurelius, xvi, 77, 149
Marcus Brutus, 115
Marcus Diaconus, ixn, xiv, 82
Marius, 75
Marseilles, 38

Mathias, 60
Maurice, 93
Medea, 30
Medes, 54, 72
Media, 62
Median Empire, 54, 110
Mediterranean, 29, 45, 55, 60n, 72, 75n
Megalopolis, xii
Megarians Act, 187
Melampus, 151
Melians, 124
Melos, x
Memnon, 159n
Memnonius, 90
Menander the Guardsman, xiv, 93
Menander (Athenian general), 104
Mendelssohn, L., 70
Mesopotamia, xxiin
Mesopotamian civilization, xxiv
Messenia, 183
Middle East, 61n
Middle Eastern civilization, xxivn
Miletus, 120, 171n, 195
Military History of Rome, 86
Miltiades, 140, 162
Milton, xx
Mimnermus, 29
Minoan civilization, xiii, xv, xixn, xxiv
Minos, 33, 34, 121n
Moralia of Plutarch, 189
Moses, xvii, 67
Mosul Vilayet, 61n
Murray, Gilbert, xixn, 99, 124, 129
Muses, 92, 195, 196
Mycenae, 35
Mycenaeans, 35
Myronides, 162
Myrrhina (in Asia), 90
Myrrhina (in Thrace), 90
Myrsus, 120

Naber, S. A., 60, 63
Naxos, 139
Neith, 133
Nereids, 151
Nero, 60, 87
New Testament, xviiin, 59
Nicandra, 153n
Nicias, 100 ff.
Nile, 115, 133, 134
Niobe, 133
Nisibis, 196

Ocean, 73, 127, 175, 176
Odrysian Empire, 187
Odysseus, xiv, 96
Oedipus, 127
Olympia, 88
Olympian Games, 34, 44n, 174
Olympians, 170
Olympus, 126, 127
Olympus, Mount, 150
Oribasius, 82
Orientals, 30, 62, 66, 140, 157, 158, 186, 188, 190, 191, 200
Oroetes, 121 ff.
Osiris, 172
Ossa, 150
Ottoman Empire, xii

Paeonians, 182
Pamphylian Gulf, 72
Pamphylian Sea, 55
Pan, 172, 173
Panathenaic procession, 40

Pangaeum, xiii, 148
Pantagnotus, 119
Paralus, 124
Parthenius, 154
Parthians, 61, 195
Paulus, 29
Pax Romana, xiv
Peiraeus, 42, 101, 124, 165
Peisistratidae, 157
Peisistratus, 40, 65, 157
Pelasgians, 32, 149 *ff*.
Pelasgicum, 196n
Pelopidae, 35
Peloponnese, 32, 34, 35, 37, 42, 55, 75n, 163, 177
Peloponnesians, 31, 41, 106, 124, 165, 187, 202
Peloponnesian War, xviiin, 31, 42, 188
Pelops, 34
Pelusium, 112
Penelope, 172
Pergamum, 82, 148
Pericles, x, xvi, 102, 162
Perseidae, 35
Perses, 159
Perseus, son of Danae, 159
Perseus, King of Macedon, 44, 109, 136, 147, 148
Persia, xii, 37, 39, 67, 85, 92, 109, 148, 161
Persian Empire, 44, 109, 111, 182
Persian Gulf, 72
Persian Monarchy, 38
Persians, 29, 30, 31, 44, 54, 72, 116, 140, 143, 155, 156, 161, 191, 192, 193
Persian War, xviiin, 38, 39, 41, 157, 161, 187, 194
Peter the Apostle, 112
Phaeacians, 96
Phaenippus, 157n
Phaethon, 133
Phalerum, 108, 191
Phasis, 30
Pherae, 177
Pherecydes, 64
Phidias, 161
Philinus, 173, 174
Philip II, of Macedon, 50, 70, 72, 73, 148, 182, 188
Philip V, of Macedon, 44, 136, 148, 183n, 190
Philip, freedom of Pompey, 114 *ff*.
Philippi, 125
Philistus, 65, 185
Philoctetes, 36
Philopoemen, 190
Phocaeans, 37
Phocas, 94n
Phocians, 193, 202
Phoenicia, 30, 64, 151, 170
Phoenicians, 29, 30, 31, 34, 64, 66, 99, 116, 152, 154, 156, 170, 190
Phoroneus, 133
Phrygian language, xxii
Phthiotis, 32, 150
Phthonos, 117
Phyle, 187
Pigres, 194
Pindar, 141
Pindus, 150
Pisidia, ix
Piso Calpurnius, 55
Pitane, Battalion, 40
Placia, 150
Plataea, 193, 194

Plato, xiii, 129, 133, 146, 161
Pleistolas, 42n
Plutarch, xvi, *ff*., 112, 189
Polis, xxii, xxiii
Politicus, 129
Polybius of Megalopolis, x, xii, *ff*., 43, 44n, 57, 58, 108, 109, 110, 111n, 116, 124, 135, 137, 138, 147, 173, 174, 177, 178, 179, 183, 198, 202n
Polycrates, 37, 119 *ff*.
Pompeius Magnus, 112 *ff*.
Porcius, Cato, 58
Porphyrius of Gaza, ixn, 82 *ff*.
Poseidon, 151, 169
Pothinus, 113, 115
Potidaea, 102
Priam, 30, 111
Priscus, xiv
Procopius of Caesarea, x, xiv, 84, 91, 92, 110, 125
Promenea, 153n
Prometheus, 132
Protestant peoples, xviiin
Ptolemies, 73n
Ptolemy I., son of Lagus, x, 70, 137
Ptolemy IV., Philopator, 44
Ptolemy XII., 112, 114
Punic Wars, 56, 57, 59, 138, 173n
Pylos, 107
Pyrrha, 133
Pyrrhus, 57, 136
Pythagoras, 64
Pythicus, 90

Quebec, 103n
Quintilius Varus, 67n
Quintus Fabius, 57
Qyzyl Yrmaq, 38n

"Rams," 116
Ranke, xiv
Regulus, 191
Renaissance, xxn
Review of the Fleet, 36
Rhodes, 183
Rhodians, 183
Rhys Roberts, W., 185
Rise of the Greek Epic, xixn
Roman Dominion, 62, 71
Roman Empire, 54, 61, 71, 77, 78
Roman Studies, 75, 110n
Romans, 44 *ff*., 60 *ff*., 68, 70 *ff*., 84, 115, 124, 136, 173
Romano-Achaean War, 203n
Romano-Carthaginian War, 138
Rome, 43, 44, 54, 55 *ff*., 68, 70, 71, 74 *ff*., 109, 111, 116, 124, 125, 147, 148, 173, 174, 176, 179n, 199n, 203
Roos, A. G., 70
Russia, 145n
Rzach, A., 126

Sais, 133
Saites, 133
Salaminia, 124n
Salamis, 80, 194
Salvius, 113, 114
Samians, 37
Samnites, 75
Samos, 37, 119 *ff*.
Samothrace, 151, 152
Samothracians, 151
Samsun, 154n
Sardanapallus, 87
Sardinia, 44

Scandinavian literature, xixn
Scionians, 124
Scipio, 111
Scylace, 150
Scyles, 139
Scythes, 114
Semele, 172
Septimius, 113, 114
Sergius, x
Sesostris, 154
Seven sages, 191
Severus, 76
Sicilian history, 65
Sicilian War, 136
Sicily, 37, 38, 39, 44, 52, 57, 72, 74 ff., 100, 101, 136, 138, 139, 163, 173, 187
Sicyon, 44
Sidgwick, A., 123
Sidon, 98
Silenus (writer), 57
Silenus in Macedonia, 189
Siphnians, 193
Socrates, 129 ff., 161
Solon, 118, 119, 133, 191
Sophocles, 128, 190
Sothis, 171n
Spain, 74, 137, 138, 139, 174, 175, 176
Sparta, 35, 39, 42, 52, 107, 158
Spartans, 158, 200
Sphacteria, 107
Stuart-Jones, H., 31
Sudan, 165, 196n
Sudanese, 154
Sulla, 75
Sunium, 191
Susa, 159
Syloson, 119
Syracusans, 104 ff.
Syracuse, 104, 123n, 139
Syria, xxin, 44, 177
Syrians, xin, 154
Syro-Iranian civilization, xii, xxiv
Syros, 64

Taq-i-Bustan, 85n
Tauromenium, 174n
Taurus, xiin
Telecles, 120
Temple, 61
Ten Years' War, 42
Terme-Su, 154n
Tethys, 96
Teutons, xixn
Thales, 64, 191
Thasos, 170
Thebans, 177, 193, 199n, 201
Thebes (Boeotia), 72, 127, 156, 201
Thebes (Egypt), 152, 153, 171
Themis, 151
Themistocles, 38, 79, 162
Theodora, 86
Theodore, 120

Theodotus, 113, 115
Theophanes, 113
Theophilus, 59
Theophylactus Simocatta, x, xiv, xxiii, 94
Theopompus, 53, 185, 188 ff.
Thermodon, 154
Thermopylae, 182n, 194
Thersites, 195
Thesproti, xxin
Thessalians, 37
Thessaliotis, 150n
Thessalus, 40
Thessaly, 32, 177
Thirty Years' Peace, 41
Thrace, xiii, 54, 90
Thracian littoral, 42
Thracians, 155, 182
Thucydides x, xi, ff., xvii, xxin, 31, 42, 65, 80, 89n, 100, 165, 185 ff., 195 ff.
Thyrea, 193
Timaeus, 57, 58, 65, 174, 179, 180
Timaeus, 133
Timareta, 153n
Timo, 140
Titans, xvii
Titus, Caesar, 61, 68
Titus Flamininus, 190
Toronians, 124
Tower of Hadrian, 112
Trans-Caucasia, 154n
Trojan War, 32, 36, 38, 52, 64, 172, 190
Trojans, 36
Troy, 29, 33, 34, 36, 37, 64, 127
Tyndareus, 34
Typhos, 172n
Tyre, 30, 151, 170
Tyrrhenians, 150

Unie, 154n

Valerius of Antium, 58
Vespasian, 68
Victorians, xvi
Vilayet of Aidin, 121 n, 155n, 163n
Vogel, F., 48

Wescott, B. F., 59
Western Civilization, xxiv
Wologesus, 195
Works and Days, xix, 126

Xenophon, xiii, xiv, 124, 162n, 185, 199
Xerxes, 67, 99, 100, 117, 140, 141, 159 ff., 188, 193, 194, 200

Zamolxis, 88
Zeno of Rhodes, 183 ff.
Zeus, x, 122, 123, 126 ff., 143, 152, 153, 170 ff., 173
Zeuxidamus, 165